ARIES

1999

TOTAL HOROSCOPE

♈ MAR 21 – APR 20 ♈

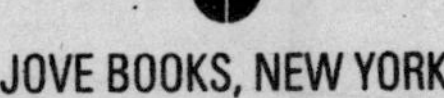

JOVE BOOKS, NEW YORK

The publishers regret that they cannot answer individual letters requesting personal horoscope information.

1999 TOTAL HOROSCOPE: ARIES

PRINTING HISTORY
Jove edition / July 1998

The Penguin Putnam Inc. World Wide Web site address is
http://www.penguinputnam.com

ISBN: 0-515-12304-8

A JOVE BOOK®
Jove Books are published by The Berkley Publishing Group,
a member of Penguin Putnam Inc.,
200 Madison Avenue, New York, New York 10016.
JOVE and the "J" design
are trademarks belonging to Jove Publications, Inc.

PRINTED IN THE UNITED STATES OF AMERICA

10   9   8   7   6   5   4   3   2   1

CONTENTS

MESSAGE TO ARIES

Dear Aries,

If there's a situation that requires positive action and healthy initiative, plunge right in. Don't worry about whether you should or shouldn't. Just do it and in the doing you will find yourself. Action will give you the courage to act. Initiative will add confidence to your character. Youthful zest will help put plans into swing and your approach will be positive, direct, energetic, and optimistic.

You're a strong-willed human being deep down and at your best you stand up for what you believe in—yourself. No matter how you may shrink from danger or confrontation you can be tough and fiery. You *can* be bold and daring and do whatever you must to attain your ends. You have strong impulses to do exactly as you please, take chances, try something new, get into new ventures, and be off on your own; yet external commitments often pose problems you just can't simply wipe out. You still have to deal with people.

You can't take life easy for too long. You're a positive, productive person when you can take healthy decisive action. But for that you need confidence. Without confidence you can be brash, crude, and hostile, and come on with a harsh air of noisy bravado that can turn people off.

To get the confidence you need, learn to recognize an opportunity and act on it. In this sense be practical. If you move too soon or too late you can spoil the timing. Develop your nose and learn to sniff out what's good for you. Move in when you can and then don't wreck your own chances.

You fear action because you either do not feel good about yourself or you jump in first and notice the crocodiles afterward. So you can flounder because of the holes in your own ego, or meet countless other crises through a thoughtless, impulsive manner. In a way, you are naive and immature, but that gives you a stubbornly youthful capacity for renewal. You can patch things up and start over, so even your serious blunders can be taken in stride.

Sitting around and waiting for miracles is unwholesome for you. You should be an active creator of your own fortune; a passive mystical approach to life has only limited value for you. Any mystical connection with the infinite is found in dynamism. Thus, your life is rarely easy because you need to build universes and make worlds. You are bored quickly and always need to cut through jungles and carve your way to a new life. You don't like to wait for the laggards at the back of the line and you despise yourself when you are trailing behind. You have the ambition to be a leader, but are often an unpopular one. If you are ever to get voted number one, you need to cultivate your sense of the other person. Confidence plus cooperation brings success with people.

Your vibrancy and competitive urge for immediate results can spur you on to action, action, and more action. Completing what you start isn't always important to you (though you may think and say it is), since you constantly crave newness and challenge. Your nose is at the front of civilization. You're at the head of the wagon train. You're perceptive, quick-witted, intelligent, inventive, creative, and gifted. As a human being you are noble and inspiring, fighting for the underdog in an unending battle for human rights. Often you are more involved with the fight for peace than the peace itself. You have many ideas with fresh approaches to many problems. Try to increase your natural decisiveness and clear a path for leadership and iniative.

Don't ever let conflicts or crises get you down. Learn to balance your arguments. When you are convinced you're right you refuse to listen to others. You detest domination or restrictions. You loathe having your impulses curtailed.

There are days when you feel dashingly beautiful, innocently happy, brave, inspired, helpful, loving, and deserving of all that is wonderful. Then there are days when you are cranky and hostile. You can be pushy and act tougher than you are. You may be conceited and obnoxious, selfish and cruel, and whack everyone down while speaking up for your own ends in the name of righteousness. Frank and candid when it suits you, you repress these traits in others. Up one minute, down the next. Yet through it all you pop up with an invincibility that is both exasperating and inspiring to others.

Leaving things unfinished is not always a solution, since you invariably run into the same problems over and over until they're completely worked out. Uniting your unbridled drive with method and responsibility is another way of improving your confidence and self-image. Obstacles can stimulate you and provide you with the sensitivity you need to conquer and win, which are your chief goals though you often deny it.

It's not always a question of being brave enough to take the plunge. Sometimes it's more an issue of learning to get in step with rhythms and cycles which are not entirely in your control. Maybe it's ultimately not your responsibility to take care of all the loose ends. Maybe when you get the urge to move on, or the forces of destiny call you, you simply must go and leave it all behind. You must do what you must do in this life. Although every action causes a reaction you must not fear action because of the possible consequences. Right conduct, even in its most noble form, will often make waves. Don't be afraid of the waves. Our lives are usually deeply wrapped up with those around us. Threads of interaction, webs of human relationships, are so intricately woven that everything we do produces a reaction in the lives of the people around us. But when something must be done in your life, sometimes you just have to do it.

It's not easy for your Aries nature to become diplomatic, for basically you are not. Although you cool off quickly and forgive easily, your angry acts of aggression can cause long-lasting hurt in others. You tend to press and insist just when patience, tact, and understanding are called for. Try not to resent criticism. Use objectivity and patience to develop your projects and relationships with nourishing temperate care. Resilience, self-reliance, and love of life should be combined with cooperation and consideration for others. The desire to be self-governing is an instinct you must never lose. Couple it with your awareness of the needs of other human beings. The outcome of human relationships depends on the blend of ego demands and concessions, self-reliance and diplomacy. Exciting figures come into your life, in addition to dangers, confrontations, and partnerships, all making demands for the transformation of your nature. You must stand up and face the challenge, see yourself more clearly than ever for what you really are, and define what matters most to you. Minimize the weaknesses and maximize the strengths. Your greatest enemy is inaction. Activity is your source of renewal.

You are truly an energetic person with many ideas, ambitions, and talents. When things start to bore, you tend to drop them. So direct yourself to an area where you will be constantly pitting yourself against new situations and challenges, new projects and problems. You'll be happiest when you have a strong measure of control over your own life. That will make you feel successful. You can be a warm, charming companion, and you add a streak of something alive and openly masterful to anyone's life. You can cajole, persuade, and argue, convince, win over, and seduce. You do have a strong capacity for decisive behavior in a crisis, and this is an asset in developing either salesmanship or artistry. You have the drive to win of a military general, but you often lack skill with people. Although you could really be weak in bedside manner despite your genuine feeling, you would still make a splendid doctor or professional person. You're often at home in any kind of business where aggressive behavior is most readily accepted.

Your bright, outgoing manner still attracts people. When you're not feeling argumentative or pugnacious, you have a winning way. You can defeat your opposition with a smile and go on without losing a moment. People like you and making friends is easy. Friendship can be fast and furious while it's new, but can soon exhaust itself and collapse, often through clashes and conflicts of interest. Your enthusiasm and quick shift of interest will frequently extend to people as well as work projects and ideas, for it is usually the newness you find fascinating and absorbing.

You probably feel you're not independent enough on some level, professional or personal. You are devoted to figuring out ways to assert yourself on one level or another. You want to be strong, positive, and aggressive, heading toward your first or your millionth love affair. You strive to be outgoing and friendly and often bury, quite successfully, any insecurities you may have beneath the bravado of a busy, independent life. When you're turned on, you are active, bold, and dynamic, often attracting a shy, dependent type. You face hardship and trouble with a courageous approach, willing everything to come out all right. You believe you are what you make of yourself and you want to hold destiny in your own hands. You prefer to live in candid idealism, wrestling with the devil himself if need be, and winning, of course. You live on because of your fantastic life resource: resilience.

Yours can be the story of success and renewal, different versions of the hero winning at everything: the rock star's first smash hit, the challenger becoming the champ, explorers discovering worlds. You are unimpeachably and creatively your own person. You are not your mother. You are not your father. You are you! And because you are so undeniably, uncontrollably, irrepressibly you, there is no pattern you have to repeat, nobody's rule you just have to follow. You possess a magic button that releases fuel, fire, and enough energy to light a thousand cities. Sexually, you are a potential dynamo. Each moment of your life is as new and magnificent as a sunrise, for you reflect the creative potential of a new day. You have your bad moments, of course: brief, dark depressions that are like quick blackouts against the backdrop of a long continuous stream of light. But ultimately you are bright and positive. Vote for yourself and take yourself for what you are. Don't dwell on limitations or ponder problems too seriously.

Some Aries are anything but aggressive and everything but independent. You are shy and introspective, with very little confidence. You think about doing more often than you do, and when you finally make a move you doubt all your actions and judgment. You are kind and thoughtful (which you don't mind admitting), gentle, considerate, helpful, and tender, putting yourself everywhere but first. You may be an Aries who is a quiet, timid, peaceful sort of person who doesn't really enjoy being on your own.

If you lack courage, confidence, and self-esteem, you have a problem to unravel. You may have to temper your self-oriented boldness with your respect for other human beings and channel your ego into useful or realistic action. You may thus be unable to allow yourself the freedom you think you deserve. You may be fighting an inward struggle with a desire to be free of all encumbrances, to eradicate or to destroy the very roots of your being. Whether you've been indifferent or indolent, inconsistent or fearful, now is the time to work consistently and systematically to build a new self-image. You can then fulfill your ambitions and force yourself to new heights of success.

In order to do this, you have to deal with the limitations that hamper you. Impatient with old conditions, social status, and personal restrictions, your resistance and rebelliousness point toward a whole new course of action. You must first make the transformation on a mental plane before you can change your everyday existence. You must think through the meaning of liberation, if it means freedom to break old ties, get away from family and friends, change personality, be someone else, or try something entirely new. Sexual breakthroughs and intellectual challenges are all part of the process of liberation. Whatever your choice of change, it must be the right one in order for you to lead a happy and satisfying life.

If you're in a personal relationship, don't bother to try to figure out who is the stronger one. It's often virtually impossible to tell. Sometimes the more outwardly bold and aggressive member of the pair is really the more dependent, deep down. If you are shy or unable to act out your feelings or urges, you need to find a direct way to rebuild your feeling of self-worth. Otherwise, you may act in unhealthy, ignoble ways or even turn the hostility inward upon yourself through physical weakness or disease. You cannot really let yourself be totally ruled or dominated by others. At some point you have to answer to yourself. It is often said that without a healthy self-image, it is hard to accomplish anything in this life, and that situation may be your special paradox.

Your desire for self-rule may be in conflict with a subtle lack of motivation or an inability to cooperate or work steadily and consistently toward the completion of tasks. Sometimes your reluctance to face the more complex sides of your personality is the very thing that holds you back. True, you're not very analytical as a rule, so your greatest successes depend more on your instantaneous response to challenge and crisis than your hashing over the past. What's done is done. Now you have to go on from here. But if you are not to go repeating mistake after mistake, you may need to grasp whatever it is that is eating at you, face it, and conquer it once and for all.

Whatever your paradox, the basic issue is the supremacy of the human will over all obstacles, limitations, threats, catastrophes, or conflicts. Aries represents the success of individuality over everything. Symbolized by the sunrise of a new day, it's a life not always based on facts, reason, or a realistic approach. It is the magic hunch, the action that brings amazing results. Of course, thoughtless impetuosity can cut a path of wide destruction, bitterness, and regret. The battle for ego supremacy can finish with a Pyrrhic victory where there is no real winner.

Yet is it impossible for one person to tell anyone else when it's time to move or act, declare war, or stand up for beliefs. That's the point of Aries: knowing when to seize an opportunity, take initiative and responsibility, and do something. The consciousness of action is generated from within and can most assuredly be cultivated and developed.

Your gift to the Zodiac is the spark of life that wipes away the past. It is rebirth of light out of the darkness, the beginning, creation, springtime. You must maintain that inextinguishable force of life, light, enthusiasm, and strength that comes from the energy of just being yourself, for better or worse, like it or not.

Michael Lutin

ARIES SNEAK PREVIEW OF THE 21st CENTURY

As the last decade of the twentieth century comes to a close, planetary aspects for its final years connect you with the future. Major changes completed in 1995 and 1996 form the bridge to the twenty-first century and new horizons. The years 1997 through 1999 and into the year 2000 reveal hidden paths and personal hints for achieving your potential, your message from the planets.

Aries individuals, ruled by fiery Mars, take heart in the dominance of fire signs in the late '90s. The taskmaster planet Saturn is transiting your sign from April 1996 through March 1999. With Saturn in Aries, your longing for independence is heightened. Your movements can be freed from everyday restrictions, allowing you to come and go more, to travel, to explore. Action takes the place of introspection, and you are set to blaze a new trail.

The great power of Pluto in Sagittarius, another fire sign, may already be starting its transformation of your character and lifestyle. Pluto in Sagittarius from late 1995 through the year 2007 creates a significant change in your idea pattern. As you move around more, the way you make a living may be fluctuating. As you explore through travel or education, your economic and material resources will be shifting. The strong idealistic aspects that Pluto in Sagittarius makes with your own Sun sign gives plenty of inspiration to fire your imagination.

As imagination is fired to take flight, the fuel and spark for the journey come from the good-luck planet Jupiter. With Jupiter in Capricorn and Aquarius, both

Saturn-ruled signs, responsibility is sharpened. The search for pleasure, freedom, and adventure becomes moderated. Jupiter in Capricorn all 1996 and into 1997 helps you monitor your actions for safe, successful performance. Jupiter in Aquarius from January 1997 to February 1998 stimulates original ideas that can lead to great good for society at large. Jupiter in Pisces from February 1998 to February 1999 hones and clarifies your vision, but also requires sacrifice and reasoned judgment. Then Jupiter in your own sign of Aries from February 1999 to March 2000 affords the opportunity for your pioneering spirit to take hold in public life.

With both Jupiter and Saturn in Aries during 1999 there can be heavy conflicts between love and work. There also is a danger of spreading yourself too thin, of starting and stopping, of abandoning a project before it has come to fruition. Significant crises can be turned into great successes or dismal failures depending on how you approach your goals. Finally, there is a possibility that, if you lose your idealism, ambition becomes narrow and self-centered, thinking becomes smug and traditional.

Never turn your back on the mysteries of life. Uranus and Neptune, both planets of enlightenment and renewed idealism, give you glimpses into the future, let you peek through the secret doorway. With Uranus in Aquarius early 1996 through the year 2003 a whole new consciousness of the environment is evolving. You can be in the forefront of change, your efforts can accelerate social reform. Neptune in Capricorn until November 1998 helps you build bridges into public life and community service, as the sober and maturing influence of Capricorn roots you to your goals. Neptune in Aquarius 1998 to the year 2011 gives full flower to your curiosity, your urge to explore and create, and your vision to help the people around you. A reminder to Aries as the century turns: as you seize responsibility, remember to share the glory.

THE CUSP-BORN ARIES

Are you *really* an Aries? If your birthday falls during the fourth week of March, at the beginning of Aries, will you still retain the traits of Pisces, the sign of the Zodiac before Aries? What if you were born late in April—are you more Taurus than Aries? Many people born at the edge, or cusp, of a sign have difficulty determining exactly what sign they are. If you are one of these people, here's how you can figure it out, once and for all.

Consult the table on page 17. Find the year of your birth, and then note the day. The table will tell you the precise days on which the Sun entered and left your sign for the year of your birth. If you were born at the beginning or end of Aries, yours is a lifetime reflecting a process of subtle transformation. Your life on Earth will symbolize a significant change in consciousness, for you are either about to enter a whole new way of living or are leaving one behind.

If your birthday falls at the end of March, you may want to read the horoscope book for Pisces as well as Aries, for Pisces holds the keys to many of your hidden uncertainties, past guilts, weaknesses, sorrows, unspoken wishes, and your cosmic unfoldment.

You are eager to start living, and possess, in a way, the secret of eternal youth. Obstacles enrage you but never beat you, for you usually feel you have sacrificed more than your share. In some way (after waiting) you will assert yourself and your right to make your own decisions.

However, though, you are often drawn back through

Pisces into a sense of responsibility, a duty to others, and a selfishness that at times eats away at your confidence and undermines your character. Honor and the vitality of life are your gifts.

If you were born late in April, you may want to read the horoscope book for Taurus as well as Aries. The investment could be revealing and profitable, for Taurus is often your means of putting your talents to practical use and turning your ideas into tangible rewards.

You are headstrong and determined; you have a sense of independence and fight that nothing can destroy. Sometimes you can vacillate and be worried and negative, but you never give up. You have the earthy sense of all your needs to meet responsibilities, do your duties, build, acquire, and collect. You are attracted to all you possess, and the more you possess, the more permanent your life. You are thus less able to simply pick up and go back to zero; what you start you must try to finish.

THE CUSPS OF ARIES

DATES SUN ENTERS ARIES
(LEAVES PISCES)

March 20 every year from 1900 to 2000,
except for the following:

March 21

1901	1911	1923	1938	1955
02	13	26	39	59
03	14	27	42	63
05	15	30	43	67
06	18	31	46	71
07	19	34	47	75
09	22	35	51	79
10				

DATES SUN LEAVES ARIES
(ENTERS TAURUS)

April 20 every year from 1900 to 2000,
except for the following:

April 19			April 21
1948	1972	1988	1903
52	76	89	07
56	80	92	11
60	81	93	19
64	84	96	
68	85	97	

ARIES RISING:
YOUR ASCENDANT

Could you be a "double" Aries? That is, could you have Aries as your Rising sign as well as your Sun sign? The tables on pages 20–21 will tell you Aries what your Rising sign happens to be. Just find the hour of your birth, then find the day of your birth, and you will see which sign of the Zodiac is your Ascendant, as the Rising sign is called. For a detailed discussion on how the Rising sign is determined, see pages 82–85.

Your Ascendant, or Rising sign, modifies your basic Sun sign personality, and it affects the way you act out the daily predictions for your Sun sign. If your Rising sign is indeed Aries, what follows is a description of its effects on your horoscope. If your Rising sign is some other sign of the Zodiac, you may wish to read the horoscope book for that sign as well.

With Aries Rising, look to planet Mars, the ruler of Aries. Mars gives you undaunted courage and strong recuperative powers. It makes you extraordinarily resistant to stress, strain, and sickness. You are especially lucky in that you probably will live a long life bent on success. The planet Pluto is often regarded as co-ruler of Aries. Pluto together with Mars can increase your chances of success. Pluto has a banishing effect on enemies and troubles. Just when you feel most hard pressed by personal loss or public enmity, Pluto negates the power of these harmful forces.

Aries Rising people stamp the environment with vitality. You have a great need for instant success, which imparts an urgency to all your undertakings. You are a picture of boundless energy, unlimited courage, untapped reserves. In love, in work, in study, you want rewards right away. As soon as the need is gratified, you may lose interest. At times you don't stay around to see things through. Some may say you lack foresight, but you do see a brighter horizon elsewhere. Your vision is as bold as your bid for self-actualization.

You are a loner, fiercely guarding your independence. You can be overconfident, sometimes boastful. You thrive on challenge. Reckless of danger, you often invite competition and combat. And you frequently gain by these means. You keenly feel oppression, being aware how rank, responsibility, and privilege confer power. If you cannot be at the head of things, you want at least a free hand. If you feel restricted, you may not participate. These traits make some of you poor team players, others of you notorious rebels.

Those of you with Aries Rising are blessed with the knack of invention. You know how to fix things. A good judge of character and situation, you swiftly size up a scene. You are handy and creative. You are eager to go ahead, to make daring new moves. Sometimes you are overeager, hasty, shortsighted. You scorn defeat, though, so no loss holds you back. Like the Ram, your zodiacal symbol, you butt your way through the obstacles.

Personal fulfillment is a driving force, and some people find you insensitive as you sweep forward. Your anger can be a blunt weapon at times leading to revenge, careless action, disorderly behavior. Combined with righteousness, anger can make you a formidable opponent of antiquated ideas, of a society rigid with restrictions. Aries Rising creates the character of the fearless pioneer.

The key words for Aries Rising are impulse and action. Self-fulfillment comes through a balance of these forces in order to meet the challenges of material success and inner growth.

RISING SIGNS FOR ARIES

Hour of Birth*	Day of Birth		
	March 20–25	March 26–30	March 31–April 4
Midnight	Sagittarius	Sagittarius	Sagittarius
1 AM	Sagittarius	Sagittarius; Capricorn 3/28	Capricorn
2 AM	Capricorn	Capricorn	Capricorn
3 AM	Capricorn	Capricorn; Aquarius 3/27	Aquarius
4 AM	Aquarius	Aquarius	Aquarius; Pisces 4/3
5 AM	Pisces	Pisces	Pisces
6 AM	Pisces; Aries 3/23	Aries	Aries
7 AM	Aries	Aries; Taurus 3/27	Taurus
8 AM	Taurus	Taurus	Taurus; Gemini 4/3
9 AM	Gemini	Gemini	Gemini
10 AM	Gemini	Gemini	Gemini; Cancer 4/2
11 AM	Cancer	Cancer	Cancer
Noon	Cancer	Cancer	Cancer
1 PM	Cancer; Leo 3/23	Leo	Leo
2 PM	Leo	Leo	Leo
3 PM	Leo	Leo	Virgo
4 PM	Virgo	Virgo	Virgo
5 PM	Virgo	Virgo	Virgo
6 PM	Virgo; Libra 3/24	Libra	Libra
7 PM	Libra	Libra	Libra
8 PM	Libra	Libra	Scorpio
9 PM	Scorpio	Scorpio	Scorpio
10 PM	Scorpio	Scorpio	Scorpio
11 PM	Scorpio; Sagittarius 3/22	Sagittarius	Sagittarius

*See footnote on facing page.

Hour of Birth*	Day of Birth		
	April 5–9	April 10–14	April 15–20
Midnight	Sagittarius	Sagittarius; Capricorn 4/12	Capricorn
1 AM	Capricorn	Capricorn	Capricorn
2 AM	Capricorn	Capricorn; Aquarius 4/11	Aquarius
3 AM	Aquarius	Aquarius	Aquarius; Pisces 4/18
4 AM	Pisces	Pisces	Pisces
5 AM	Pisces; Aries 4/7	Aries	Aries
6 AM	Aries	Aries; Taurus 4/11	Taurus
7 AM	Taurus	Taurus	Taurus; Gemini 4/18
8 AM	Gemini	Gemini	Gemini
9 AM	Gemini	Gemini	Gemini; Cancer 4/17
10 AM	Cancer	Cancer	Cancer
11 AM	Cancer	Cancer	Cancer
Noon	Cancer; Leo 4/8	Leo	Leo
1 PM	Leo	Leo	Leo
2 PM	Leo	Leo	Virgo
3 PM	Virgo	Virgo	Virgo
4 PM	Virgo	Virgo	Virgo
5 PM	Virgo; Libra 4/7	Libra	Libra
6 PM	Libra	Libra	Libra
7 PM	Libra	Libra; Scorpio 4/14	Scorpio
8 PM	Scorpio	Scorpio	Scorpio
9 PM	Scorpio	Scorpio	Scorpio
10 PM	Scorpio; Sagittarius 4/1	Sagittarius	Sagittarius
11 PM	Sagittarius	Sagittarius	Sagittarius

*Hour of birth given here is for Standard Time in any time zone. If your hour of birth was recorded in Daylight Saving Time, subtract one hour from it and consult that hour in the table above. For example, if you were born at 6 AM D.S.T., see 5 AM above.

LOVE AND RELATIONSHIPS

No matter who you are, what you do in life, or where your planets are positioned, you still need to be loved, and to feel love for other human beings. Human relationships are founded on many things: infatuation, passion, sex, guilt, friendship, and a variety of other complex motivations, frequently called love.

Relationships often start out full of hope and joy, the participants sure of themselves and sure of each other's love, and then end up more like a pair of gladiators than lovers. When we are disillusioned, bitter, and wounded, we tend to blame the other person for difficulties that were actually present long before we ever met. Without seeing clearly into our own natures we will be quite likely to repeat our mistakes the next time love comes our way.

Enter Astrology.

It is not always easy to accept, but knowledge of ourselves can improve our chances for personal happiness. It is not just by predicting when some loving person will walk into our lives, but by helping us come to grips with our failures and reinforce our successes.

Astrology won't solve all our problems. The escapist will ultimately have to come to terms with the real world around him. The hard-bitten materialist will eventually acknowledge the eternal rhythms of the infinite beyond which he can see or hear. Astrology does not merely explain away emotion. It helps us unify the head with the heart so that we can become whole individuals. It helps us define what it is we are searching for, so we can recognize it when we find it.

Major planetary cycles have been changing people's ideas about love and commitment, marriage, partnerships, and relationships. These cycles have affected virtually everyone in areas of personal involvement. Planetary forces point out upheavals and transformations occurring in all of society. The concept of marriage is being totally reexamined. Exactly what the changes will ultimately bring no one can tell. It is usually difficult to determine which direction society will take. One thing is certain: no man is an island. If the rituals and pomp of wedding ceremonies must be revised, then it will happen.

Social rules are being revised. Old outworn institutions are indeed crumbling. But relationships will not die. People are putting less stress on permanence and false feelings of security. The emphasis now shifts toward the union of two loving souls. Honesty, equality, and mutual cooperation are the goals in modern marriage. When these begin to break down, the marriage is in jeopardy. Surely there must be a balance between selfish separatism and prematurely giving up.

There is no doubt that astrology can establish the degree of compatibility between two human beings. Two people can share a common horizon in life but have quite different habits or basic interests. Two others might have many basic characteristics in common while needing to approach their goals from vastly dissimilar points of view. Astrology describes compatibility based on these assumptions.

It compares and contrasts through the fundamental characteristics that draw two people together. Although they could be at odds on many basic levels, two people could find themselves drawn together again and again. Sometimes it seems that we keep being attracted to the same type of individuals. We might ask ourselves if we have learned anything from our past mistakes. The answer is that there are qualities in people that we require and thus seek out time and time again. To solve that mystery in ourselves is to solve much of the dilemma of love, and so to help ourselves determine if we are approaching a wholesome situation or a potentially destructive one.

We are living in a very curious age with respect to marriage and relationships. We can easily observe the shifting social attitudes concerning the whole institution of marriage. People are seeking everywhere for answers to their own inner needs. In truth, all astrological combinations can achieve compatibility. But many relationships seem doomed before they get off the ground. Astrologically there can be too great a difference between the goals, aspirations, and personal outlook of the people involved. Analysis of both horoscopes must and will indicate enough major planetary factors to keep the two individuals together. Call it what you will: determination, patience, understanding, love—whatever it may be, two people have the capacity to achieve a state of fulfillment together. We all have different needs and desires. When it comes to choosing a mate, you really have to know yourself. If you know the truth about what you are really looking for, it will make it easier to find. Astrology is a useful, almost essential, tool to that end.

In the next chapter your basic compatibility with each of the twelve signs of the Zodiac is generalized. The planetary vibrations between you and an individual born under any given zodiacal sign suggest much about how you will relate to each other. Hints are provided about love and romance, sex and marriage so that you and your mate can get the most out of the relationship that occupies so important a role in your life.

ARIES:
YOU AND YOUR MATE

ARIES—ARIES

This is an exciting contest of wills. Assuming you ever agree on enough of each other's ideas to have any sort of union, yours is a relationship based on motivation and drive. You are a powerful case of like attracting like. You both share the spirit of adventure that flows through every Aries man and woman, and you engender excitement and energy in each other. You can fire each other up with enthusiasm, competition, and challenge, simply by the force and power of your own will.

On an emotional level, this is a mighty powerful collision. These days the key to successful relationships is equality but you'll both have to put up with a lot of jockeying for power, no matter who seems to be the weaker of the two. The battle for supremacy can end up in a total deadlock or in an explosive separation. If you don't grant each other freedom and the right to be, there will be no relationship.

You are both warm, amorous, and ambitious, but you are not the perfect example of the share-and-share-alike couple. You both need something to keep your interest in each other, and without the ingredient of constant stimulation, your mutual attraction could turn into repulsion. You both need outlets for your energy.

Hints for Your Aries Mate

If you treat your Aries partner just the way you would want to be treated, moment for moment, you will not be taken by surprise or disappointed by the reaction. After all, you both are children of the Ram, and the capacity for willfulness in the relationship doubles the norm. Don't jockey for position; alternate the dominating and subordinate roles in your relationship. Support and sacrifice, which both individuals of a couple need at different times, must be a function that each of you fulfills. It won't do to squelch your partner's outside interests. And you must be fair, yet tactful, to preserve your own. Otherwise one or both of you will see the intrusion as a choking of independence. On the other hand, don't let your own interests, or your mate's, foster a hostile competition between you. Rather, let people and activities come into your lives, separately as well as together, so you can keep up the sparkle in your partnership.

ARIES—TAURUS

Idealism meets practicality here. Taurus can be your greatest asset, for the sheer immovable force you will encounter every time you get restless or obnoxious will bring you down to Earth and make you think in simple terms of dollars and cents, and your earthly needs.

Sometimes the very qualities that attracted you to Taurus can be hard to cope with, for you are both growing at different rates and in different ways. What you may look upon as stubborn, unyielding obstinacy can be loyalty, endurance, and constancy—a strong stillness that is highly attractive and exciting. You can undermine Taurus when the chips are down, or you can provide encouragement and strength. Your unceasing energy and command over yourself (believe it or not) are the major components of your allure for Taurus.

It's not easy for Taurus to be pushed into action without careful consideration. As far as you're concerned, when you stand still for too long, you're all through. You are both pleasure lovers, but your orientation to life is usually different. It is speed versus certainty, trial-and-error versus order. This combination will tempt and control each of you in the extreme at the same time.

Hints for Your Taurus Mate

At all times, be friendly with your Taurus mate, whose sweet nature reflects the affection of Venus, their planetary ruler. Don't strive for glamour or heady emotion; that will only confuse Taurus into thinking a crisis is imminent, rather than just your own style of getting close asserting itself. Value your mate's need for comfort and good fun on a steady basis. Supply them without recklessness, and try very hard not to break appointments, be late, or switch plans. Your Taurus mate will be chagrined by challenges to his or her basic passivity, and will punish you by withdrawing. So don't push ideas or ambitions until you have spent a lot of time and discussion on them. Seeds need to be planted, and Taurus likes to germinate them until they are ready for harvest. Plant gently. Play down any dogmatism in your personality, and certainly do not be flippant romantically. Your relationship flowers the best in a deception-free environment.

ARIES—GEMINI

Your relationship is a dynamic one. That is, between you there is the ceaseless interchange of thought and energy, the urge to explore, travel around, experiment, and communicate. It could exhaust itself quickly, like a fast hot flame that burns out soon after ignition. But you are both positive, active creatures deep down, both gifted at bringing new elements, new surroundings, and general versatility into the relationship and thus keeping it vital, fluid, and alive. Sometimes those new elements will be a source of conflict, since each of you will feel threatened when it comes to your partner's tireless need for innovation and experimentation.

But you are pals, after all. Sometimes you can gab like teenage cousins. Such a relationship can have a friendship of a platonic quality that lacks strong emotions or depth on major levels. So from time to time you may both get restless. The frantic, hectic kind of liaison so possible for Aries and Gemini can be a mere puff of smoke, but don't sell it short. Remain friends. This blend can be a source of long-lasting companionship, as long as you part and come back together from time to time to swap stories and share successes.

Hints for Your Gemini Mate

As with any advice geared to a Twin, which your Gemini mate indeed is, there are double messages and they are contradictory. First, do exactly what you did when captivation hooked you both; keep it light and adventurous. Second, be totally different; you're a parent figure now. Go out a lot; nothing dispels gloom from the heart of an anxious Gemini than a treat on the town or a drive to a quaint place. Fun doesn't have to be exotic or expensive—just novel. Stay in a lot and talk; your Gemini mate needs to tell all, so be there to listen and ask questions. Don't force your view of life on your Gemini partner; pretend that your insights are spontaneous and gratuitous and that he or she need not accept them. Be a steadying influence; guide your Gemini mate into meaningful pursuits and out of foolish ones. Don't be a boss; share the responsibilities of your partnership. Be a manager; make decisions subtly so your Gemini feels liberated and at the same time the liberator.

ARIES—CANCER

If your relationship has survived the almost unbelievable amount of disruption and interference of the last decade, you can thank your own positive response to challenge and your Cancer's patient staying power. Many marriages will not have survived these forces, since they have been subjected to bombardment from unexpected reversals and social changes and the revision of all views on marriage and security, and on the way people behave in family situations. It's a question of personal independence, really.

If you have made it through together, you're both very changed. You can still get angry at the drop of a hat, and Cancer can still crawl under cover instantaneously. But now your better view of yourselves and each other will make you aware of the growing transformation taking place.

Changes that are slow in coming are usually the longest lasting. The success of your relationship depends on your appreciation of each other's integrity. Your Aries power of expansion and desire for new encounters will always be in conflict with Cancer's sense of family responsibility. That's healthy.

Hints for Your Cancer Mate

If you are in a long-standing relationship with a Moon Child, as your Cancer mate is affectionately called, you still may not truly know him or her, who is very hard to know. Honor that protective shell, which after all is your mate's defense against being hurt or unfairly influenced. That very same structure will be put to your service when you feel hedged and hounded by life's creditors; your Cancer mate can be a formidable ally on your behalf. So don't expose your mate to critiques of the psychological kind, and do not delve too deeply into the psychosexual fundaments of your relationship.

Rather, concentrate on your mate's career and business life; here's where you can give him or her the push that is needed. Be tough while at the same time you boost their confidence. Sexually and affectionally, you should be consistent in your attentions. A splurge-and-stint approach will bewilder your Cancer lover, closing that protective shell even tighter. Be totally open with your Cancer mate, for she or he will thrive on understanding and comforting you.

ARIES—LEO

A strong bond exists between you two. Once you have survived the wars waged by your egos, it will be hard to pry you apart emotionally. You are both idealistic, emotional creatures governed by the power of creation and the love of life. Love is your great source of energy, and you cannot be without it. When you are together and in love, your capacity to love each other (as well as yourselves) is limitless. Self-involved and demanding, you can have raging battles yet somehow remain loyal through it all. You can be adventurous and passionate, and can make a glamorous couple.

Ambitious and dynamic, you are both imbued with the fighting spirit and a joy of living that makes whatever you do radiant with the strength of your combined spirit. Whatever you dedicate yourselves to as a team will doubtless be a success, provided selfishness and ego don't expand faster than your mutual understanding. Leo may play the baby for a long, long time, but Aries will still be in love—tantrums, flirtations, and bossiness notwithstanding. Leo is grateful for that strong Aries influence, which can help make dreams come true, and can take new chances in life.

Hints for Your Leo Mate

Accent your alliance with all the loving gestures that make the proud Lion feel secure and wanted. Affectionately tease him or her; make a friendly fuss, not a bossy one, if you Aries want to keep your Leo mate happy. Never chastise Leo in a way that hurts the pride. A lot of backpatting will substitute for frank appraisals of what you feel is not being handled appropriately. You must respect Leo's need to keep a relatively private ego; unlike you, your Leo lover is not talkative or prone to use words to control a situation. Chances are Leo will welcome your passions as much as he or she expresses their own, so you do not have to repress your emotional nature. Nevertheless Leo expects you to be the idea person you are, and the route to compatibility is through the heart to the head. Stress the individuality of your lives with each other, for each of you is a leader. If you must divert Leo's demands upon you, talk about your needs and problems; nothing flatters your mate more than being asked to mother you.

ARIES—VIRGO

You two have very different perspectives, approaches, and philosophies. Yet you are probably curious about each other, feeling distant but still attracted in some strange way. It could be years before you ever really get to know each other, for you both require separateness to develop your individual beings. Neither of you is interested in relating constantly or revealing too much about yourselves, although you will often remain faithful in a personal relationship. But to make this work you both need to exert some sustained efforts at adjustment.

You will sometimes be the cause of separation and strife, since the assertion of independence is fundamental to your Aries personality. When your Virgo is hurt, you will see a retreat into coldness. That detached unreachability will frustrate and challenge you. Once inflamed, you can chase, court, win over. And the cycle begins again.

Virgo's shy approach is seductive, but Victorian attitudes can be a drag indeed. Your verve as an Aries is your inspiration, but impetuosity and aggressiveness repel a quiet Virgo nature. Success in this relationship depends upon the right blend of action and propriety. If you start out with mutual respect and trust, you will be giving yourselves the best insurance. Earthy practicality, discipline, and diligence can join with the daring zest of taking a chance on life and being successful.

Hints for Your Virgo Mate

Respect and interest will win the heart of your basically aloof Virgo mate. Be dutiful in small ways. Be grand in large ways. Conduct yourself with more aplomb than flamboyance, dressing for the occasion and affecting a casual demeanor, thereby pleasing your impeccable partner; let Virgo be the intense one. Introduce variety into your relationship by exciting plans for travel, work and community projects, education that can be shared. Skillfully guide your Virgo mate to assume and execute responsibilities. Sympathize with his or her problems. Listen patiently to the complaints and the analysis, agree with the value judgments, then gently nudge her or him back to whatever task seemed so onerous to begin with. When your Virgo partner criticizes you, accept it as constructive analysis. Do something tangible—don't just bolt. A small gesture proves its point but doesn't compromise your vision. Don't take your Virgo mate for granted; be attentive, but not sticky or silly.

ARIES—LIBRA

You have both been under heavy stress ever since the last decade. Unexpected reversals, changes, and removals have characterized your lives, and partnerships have taken unusual turns. It's a question of independence, really, and reflects basic questions about human commitments, the ability to form lasting unions, and the desire to cooperate with each other. Role playing in the sexual and emotional sides of the relationship has probably occurred.

Active or passive, aggressive or shy, independent or dependent, you have both learned how to cope with disruption, separation, and strange reversals. You now know how important it is to have a separate life in order to avoid exhausting the resources of the relationship. Each of you is still seeking to find your true self—who you are, defined by you, on your own terms. If you wrap yourself up totally in your partner, and plan all your life around one person, you may resent it and lose your self-esteem and confidence. Yet to destroy a good relationship can take away one of your major joys in living. Aim to blend self-fulfillment with the capacity to cooperate. Independence, equality, and awareness must characterize a long period of change and growth.

Hints for Your Libra Mate

You may sometimes be at a loss to understand your Libra mate, who revels in the moody and fluid side of their planetary ruler, Venus. Although words and talk are a large part of your sharing and good feeling, the actions that follow mutual disclosures seem to be incongruous, often contradictory. At such times, repress your need to confront, challenge, force change. Your Libra mate flees from conflict; the merest suggestion of a flawed performance pressures Libra to run. Go with your mate's moods, though never losing sight of your real goals. In the context of enlightened conversation, you can air all passions and grievances. As long as Libra feels the goal is mutual, your mate will work toward it. Be protective yet decisive; your Libra partner wants to participate in decision making, but may not be able to make quick and independent decisions, as you can. Parties and people are important to your Libra lover; generously supply both in your lives together. Allowing your Libra mate to take the lead in fashioning the social atmosphere will always earn you points and commitment.

ARIES—SCORPIO

This is an exciting (and dangerous) combination. You'll make Scorpio work for it, and your Scorpio will excite you deep down at the most primitive levels of your being. Instead of turning your energies against each other and developing a diabolical and constantly escalating war, try to work toward mutual inspiration on sexual, emotional, and creative levels.

You share the primary instincts for being: survival, life, death. When it comes to ambition, energy, and stamina, together you are unbeatable. You are both stubborn and strong-willed. You have conflicting views of openness and secrecy, freedom and control, but when you cooperate and don't get in each other's way, it's a dynamic combination.

You can be a couple of magicians, mystic sorcerers with a love for the mysterious. Together, your power of leadership, creativity, renewal, and regeneration can build a whole new world. Your collisions are explosive and exciting. The product of those eruptions could be enough light and energy to launch a thousand ships. At best, you are a deep and lasting alliance, resilient, indestructible, and powerful.

Hints for Your Scorpio Mate

You two Mars creatures certainly can give each other a run for the money. Both of you need to dominate, but your Scorpio's need is deep and abiding. Thwarted, it can turn to resentment or a malevolent form of retaliation. Fortunately you can give up the driver's seat and restrain your independent streak often enough to mollify your Scorpio lover. Play down your own flippancy, but don't let Scorpio's sarcasm rile you into attack. Harmless flirting or showing too much interest in other people will arouse wild jealousy. You must be a totally committed lover. And don't use words as a substitute for that strong, silent sexuality Scorpio wants to elicit from you. If you hope to preserve the relationship as well as your independent strengths, set up separate but equal domains. The best strategy when Scorpio retreats into that moody secretiveness is calm acceptance. Verbal confrontations or forcing your mate into action only engender strife. Setting a pace for relaxation and introspection will work wonders. Without being childish, allow your Scorpio mate to be protective of you.

ARIES—SAGITTARIUS

This is a strong love match. Sagittarius loves that Aries spirit, and you can light each other's fires with your passion for living life to the fullest. You can lift each other's hearts with a buoyancy and thrust that other less fiery types of people will envy and admire. You may have a time living with each other, since you can share a restlessness, blind idealism, or vain self-involvement that will irk each of you about your partner before long. You reflect each other's egotism royally.

Either one of you could fly off on a thousand tangents, never meeting, never really completing your connection. You could be terrible influences on each other, stimulating a lawlessness or thoughtlessness that can lead nowhere. Without practical discipline and methods your plans—in fact, your whole relationship—could never get off the drawing board.

You both share a fundamental joy, a love for adventure, and a hankering after new experiences. Your positive approach to life gives a healthy, lusty swing to everything you do, and together you are full of momentum, resilience, and energy. You are both freedom lovers and can raise each other to great heights of learning and travel and wisdom. Your turn Sagittarius on physically and as a creative inspired personality, blending energy and enthusiasm in the relationship.

Hints for Your Sagittarius Mate

Remember how exciting, spontaneous, and adventurous your courtship was? Keep up that happy acceptance of your Sagittarius mate and there never will be cause for your partnership to suffer. Don't try to pin your mate down to executing all the ideas she or he has shared with you. Great idealists, nevertheless your Sagittarius partner experiences some discomfort actually getting things done. Now you can't be too bossy in this regard, but you can be a controlling force without making Sagittarius feel their freedom is lost. Although your mate will pioneer ideas with you, you must be the one to initiate the action. You must also lay a gentle restraining hand on your mate, who can be even more reckless than you. Sagittarius loves arguments, so open a variety of topics to fire your mate's heart and mind. Share your partner's love of sports and the outdoors, a robust life of recreation and activity. You may wind up being more the homemaker and money manager than your mate, who will love you eternally for assuming these responsibilities.

ARIES—CAPRICORN

With your creativity, zest, and superconfidence and Capricorn's patience, method, and determination, your union has all the basics for success. You have the driving force and Capricorn has the way with people. Together you can accomplish the impossible. Of course, you will think it takes too long, and Capricorn will think it's a little harebrained or crazy, but when you put your heads together to confer or conspire, the result is the successful execution of any Herculean task.

Tension will be great in such a relationship, since the fire of your Aries spirit must submit to the cool, practical approach of Capricorn stability. Capricorn's need for control will be upset by your stubborn independence and refusal to knuckle under to facts. Without understanding and a mutual desire for growth, your relationship could come to a frustrating stalemate, a deadlock that even time cannot solve.

Despite the professional battles and crisis situations of the past few years, you can weather the storms for the purpose of sharing your goals. You both need sustenance and security. Any burdens or responsibilities that circumstances impose on your lives can help you grow closer and more determined to make the relationship succeed through loving each other.

Hints for Your Capricorn Mate

You, the Ram, and your Capricorn mate, the Goat, have a lot in common, so when you want to please him or her, do it the way you would please yourself. It's most important to support your mate's career and life goals; the ambitions of a Capricorn loom mightily. At the same time, show your partner how responsible you are to your own work and outside interests. In fact, let her or him in on your goals as well as your friendship circle. Your Capricorn mate will love you for the opportunity to give sound advice. As long as you are an admiring lover and a stable homemaker, your irascible moods won't bother your Capricorn partner. Of course, you cannot go dashing around starting things but not following through. And don't be sloppy or insensitive;

your mate abhors anything in bad taste. Sometimes you will have to push the Goat into action, to overcome your lover's shyness and fear of failure. Be bold and daring, and your Capricorn mate will have found the perfect partner.

ARIES—AQUARIUS

You may meet out of nowhere and strike up a full-blown friendship. You may develop a long-lasting spiritual relationship of support and mutual understanding, making valuable contributions to each other's lives. A successful partnership for you two might seem strange to the people around you, for it will probably be a volatile blend of independence and bohemianism. If you try to make your life simple, and free it from traditional jealousies and cloying attachments, you can make the relationship work. You need innovation, change, and excitement in your union. The element of surprise will keep fanning the flame of this zany match.

When the newness wears off, you could fall out of each other's lives as fast as you fell in. When jealousy and possessiveness replace spontaneity and respect for each other's way, sudden flare-ups and explosive confrontations can threaten your peace and even do irreparable damage to a growing and fruitful friendship. Involvements are getting more powerful now. New emotional and sexual scenes may be tipping the scales. Experimentalism and self-will can bring separations to this relationship—or they can bring greater growth through meeting an explosive and exciting time.

Hints for Your Aquarius Mate

Freedom and friendship are keys for a successful partnership. You can be as free as you like as long as you do not curtail the activities or censor the thoughts of your Aquarius mate. Even if you have passed the courtship stage, the emphasis should still be on the experimental and the radical. Don't stampede your lover's affections. A challenge to Aquarius unpredictability will make them even more moody and perverse than is the rule. And don't put stock in convention or routine; allow your Aquarius to be late, to miss appointments, to change plans. You can do this, too, and the more surprises you deliver to your Aquarius lover, the more loved you will be. Your recklessness with ideas and projects—not money—will appeal to your partner. Don't demand too much passion in your sexual relationship. The real delving in this partnership is in and of the mind. So focus your insight and vision on your Aquarius mate's intellectual capacities; stir her or him to express thoughts, feelings, and hopes.

ARIES—PISCES

This is a strange and mysterious combination. Yours is a fascinating challenge, since neither of you is terribly realistic and both of you have to learn about life through experience—often the hard way. Together you can know the meaning of a love that you may have thought impossible to achieve on Earth. You may be disillusioned and disappointed, having to start over again and again, forgiving and escaping, and forgiving again. You could find yourselves in a horribly perplexing situation. Together, you blend verve, enthusiasm, and sensitivity with guilty uncertainty. You can play on each other's guilt and sense of responsibility and can founder in deception and worry.

But your lives can be illuminated by gentle, devotional love, enhanced by poetry, music, and a spiritual understanding that can raise your mutual spirits out of the ordinary problems of personal relationships. Your passions are deep. Your desires for pleasure may excite the wildest parts of your lives together or can send you both fleeing in opposite directions. Being resilient takes you out of worry and confusion. Compassion and forgiveness awaken your sense of the other's needs and deepen the relationship between you.

Hints for Your Pisces Mate

You are almost complete opposites, but Pisces, the sign of the Fishes, has a double personality, so your relating to each other is even more complicated. Never be bewildered by your Pisces mate's emotional displays. Appreciate that need for drama, and be up to playing the antagonist in her or his movie. You can even play the villain—as long as you react! In real life matters, the situation is different, and you can be entirely yourself, doing what you do best: decide, direct, and drive, even if it feels like dragging your dreamy lover along. Don't criticize Pisces for inconsistency or laziness. Rather get him or her on a path and out of yours. Sometimes you should be more accepting of the dreamer that your Pisces partner is; tune in to the intuitive vibes, experience the melancholy and rapture for yourself. Encourage your lover's interest in the arts. Grace the relationship with Pisces by such thoughtful gestures as flowers, notes, surprise gifts.

ARIES:
YOUR PROGRESSED SUN

WHAT IS YOUR NEW SIGN?

Your birth sign, or Sun sign, is the central core of your whole personality. It symbolizes everything you try to do and be. It is your main streak, your major source of power, vitality, and life. But as you live you learn, and as you learn you progress. The element in your horoscope that measures your progress is called the Progressed Sun. It is the symbol of your growth on Earth, and represents new threads that run through your life. The Progressed Sun measures big changes, turning points, and major decisions. It will often describe the path you are making toward the development of your personality and the fulfillment of your desires.

Below you will find brief descriptions of the Progressed Sun in three signs. According to the table on page 43, find out about your Progressed Sun and see how and where you fit into the cosmic scheme. Each period lasts about 30 years, so watch and see how dramatic these changes turn out to be.

If Your Sun Is Progressing Into—

TAURUS, you begin to acquire possessions and wake up to your earthly needs. Money enters your life in a significant way. Though your fantasies grow richer, you need to develop your earthy sense of values. You want to earn your own way and be paid for your efforts.

GEMINI, you begin to move out, get around, and start contacting the people around you. You enter into a period of communication with everyone around you. Involvements with relatives and neighbors will occupy much of your time. Your curiosity will be ever whetted.

CANCER, you will now begin to feel a need to put down roots and seek the peace of your own private haven. You will tend to be a little withdrawn during this period of your life. Connections with the family will play a major role in all your activities, for good or ill, and you will find yourself more ready to accept attachments and dependencies than ever before.

HOW TO USE THE TABLE

Look for your birthday in the table on the facing page; then under the appropriate column, find out approximately when your Progressed Sun will lead you to a new sign. From that point on, for 30 years, the thread of your life will run through that sign. Read the definitions on the preceding pages and see exactly how that life thread will develop.

For example, if your birthday is March 24, your Progressed Sun will enter Taurus around your 27th birthday and will travel through Taurus until you are 57 years old. Your Progressed Sun will then move into Gemini. Reading the definitions of Taurus and Gemini will tell you much about your major involvements and interests during those years.

YOUR PROGRESSED SUN

If your birthday falls on:	start looking at TAURUS at age	start looking at GEMINI at age	start looking at CANCER at age
March 20–21	30	60	90
22	29	59	89
23	28	58	88
24	27	57	87
25	26	56	86
26	25	55	85
27	24	54	84
28	23	53	83
29	22	52	82
30	21	51	81
31	20	50	80
April 1	19	49	79
2	18	48	78
3	17	47	77
4	16	46	76
5	15	45	75
6	14	44	74
7	13	43	73
8	12	42	72
9	11	41	71
10	10	40	70
11	9	39	69
12	8	38	68
13	7	37	67
14	6	36	66
15	5	35	65
16	4	34	64
17	3	33	63
18	2	32	62
19	1	31	61

ARIES BIRTHDAYS

March 21	Otis Spann, Phyllis McGinley
March 22	Rosa Bonheur, Marcel Marceau
March 23	Dane Rudhyar, Joan Crawford
March 24	Wilhelm Reich, Clyde Barrow
March 25	Aretha Franklin, Gloria Steinem
March 26	Tennessee Williams, Diana Ross
March 27	Sarah Vaughan
March 28	Edmund Muskie
March 29	Pearl Bailey
March 30	Van Gogh, Warren Beatty
March 31	Descartes, Richard Chamberlain
April 1	Bach, Lon Chaney, Debbie Reynolds
April 2	Hans Christian Andersen, Casanova
April 3	Marlon Brando, Doris Day
April 4	Arthur Murray, Maya Angelou
April 5	Spencer Tracy, Bette Davis
April 6	Lowell Thomas, Baba Ram Dass
April 7	Walter Winchell
April 8	Billie Holiday
April 9	W. C. Fields, Paul Robeson
April 10	Omar Sharif, Clare Booth Luce
April 11	Charles Evans Hughes
April 12	David Cassidy, Ann Miller
April 13	Thomas Jefferson, Eudora Welty
April 14	Julie Christie
April 15	Leonardo Da Vinci, Bessie Smith
April 16	Wilbur Wright, Polly Adler
April 17	William Holden, J. P. Morgan
April 18	Leopold Stokowski, Hayley Mills
April 19	Hugh O'Brien, Jayne Mansfield
April 20	Miró, Nina Foch

CAN ASTROLOGY PREDICT THE FUTURE?

Can astrology really peer into the future? By studying the planets and the stars is it possible to look years ahead and make predictions for our lives? How can we draw the line between ignorant superstition and cosmic mystery? We live in a very civilized world, to be sure. We consider ourselves modern, enlightened individuals. Yet few of us can resist the temptation to take a peek at the future when we think it's possible. Why? What is the basis of such universal curiosity?

The answer is simple. Astrology works, and you don't have to be a magician to find that out. We certainly can't prove astrology simply by taking a look at the astonishing number of people who believe in it, but such figures do make us wonder what lies behind such widespread popularity. Everywhere in the world hundreds of thousands of serious, intelligent people are charting, studying, and interpreting the positions of the planets and stars every day. Every facet of the media dispenses daily astrological bulletins to millions of curious seekers. In Eastern countries, the source of many wisdoms handed down to us from antiquity, astrology still has a vital place. Why? Surrounded as we are by sophisticated scientific method, how does astrology, with all its bizarre symbolism and mysterious meaning, survive so magnificently? The answer remains the same. It works.

Nobody knows exactly where astrological knowledge came from. We have references to it dating back to the dawn of human history. Wherever there was a stirring of human consciousness, people began to observe the natural cycles and rhythms that sustained their life. The diversity of human behavior must have been evident even to the first students of consciousness. Yet the basic similarity between members of the human family must have led to the search for some common source, some greater point of origin somehow linked to the heavenly bodies ruling our sense of life and time. The ancient world of Mesopotamia, Chaldea, and Egypt was a highly developed center of astronomical observation and astrological interpretation of heavenly phenomena and their resultant effects on human life.

Amid the seeming chaos of a mysterious unknown universe, people from earliest times sought to classify, define, and organize the world around them. Order: that's what the human mind has always striven to maintain in an unceasing battle with its natural counterpart, chaos, or entropy. We build cities, countries, and empires, subjugating nature to a point of near defeat, and then . . . civilization collapses, empires fall, and cities crumble. Nature reclaims the wilderness. Shelly's poem *Ozymandias* is a hymn to the battle between order and chaos. The narrator tells us about a statue, broken, shattered, and half-sunk somewhere in the middle of a distant desert. The inscription reads: "Look on my works, ye mighty, and despair." And then we are told: "Nothing beside remains. Round the decay of that colossal wreck, boundless and bare, the lone and level sands stretch far away."

People always feared the entropy that seemed to lurk in nature. So we found permanence and constancy in the regular movements of the Sun, Moon, and planets and in the positions of the stars. Traditions sprang up from observations of the seasons and crops. Relationships were noted between phenomena in nature and the configurations of the heavenly bodies. This "synchronicity," as it was later called by Carl Jung, extended to thought, mood, and behavior, and as such developed the astrological archetypes handed down to us today.

Astrology, a regal science of the stars in the old days, was made available to the king, who was informed of impending events in the heavens, translated of course to their earthly meanings by trusted astrologers. True, astrological knowledge in its infant stages was rudimentary and beset with many superstitions and false premises. But those same dangers exist today in any investigation of occult or mystical subjects. In the East, reverence for astrology is part of religion. Astrologer-astronomers have held respected positions in government and have taken part in advisory councils on many momentous issues. The duties of the court astrologer, whose office was one of the most important in the land, were clearly defined, as early records show.

Here in our sleek Western world, astrology glimmers on, perhaps more brilliantly than ever. With all of our technological wonders and complex urbanized environments, we look to astrology even now to cut through artificiality, dehumanization, and all the materialism of contemporary life, while we gather precious information that helps us live in that material world. Astrology helps us restore balance and get in step with our own rhythms and the rhythms of nature.

Intelligent investigation of astrology (or the practical application of it) need not mean blind acceptance. We only need to see it working, see our own lives confirming its principles every day, in order to accept and understand it more. To understand ourselves is to know ourselves and to know all. This book can help you to do that—to understand yourself and through understanding develop your own resources and potentials as a rich human being.

YOUR PLACE AMONG THE STARS

Humanity finds itself at the center of a vast personal universe that extends infinitely outward in all directions. In that sense each is a kind of star radiating, as our Sun does, to all bodies everywhere. These vibrations, whether loving, helpful, or destructive, extend outward and generate a kind of "atmosphere" in which woman and man move. The way we relate to everything around us—our joy or our sorrow—becomes a living part of us. Our loved ones and our enemies become the objects of our projected radiations, for better or worse. Our bodies and faces reflect thoughts and emotions much the way light from the Sun reflects the massive reactions occurring deep within its interior. This energy and light reach all who enter its sphere of influence.

Our own personal radiations are just as potent in their own way, really. The reactions that go on deep within us profoundly affect our way of thinking and acting. Our feelings of joy or satisfaction, frustration or anger, must eventually find an outlet. Otherwise we experience the psychological or physiological repercussions of repression. If we can't have a good cry, tell someone our troubles, or express love, we soon feel very bad indeed.

As far as our physical selves are concerned, there is a direct relationship between our outer lives, inner reactions and actions, and the effects on our physical body. We all know the feeling of being startled by the sudden ring of a telephone, or the simple frustration of missing a bus. In fact, our minds and bodies are constantly reacting to outside forces. At the same time we, too, are generating actions that will cause a reaction in someone else. You may suddenly decide to phone a friend. If you are a bus driver you might speed along on your way and leave behind an angry would-be passenger. Whatever the case, mind and body are in close communication and they both reflect each other's condition. Next time you're really angry take a good long look in the mirror!

In terms of human evolution, our ability to understand, control, and ultimately change ourselves will naturally affect all of our outside relationships. Astrology is invaluable to helping us comprehend our inner selves. It is a useful tool in helping us retain our integrity, while cooperating with and living in a world full of other human beings.

Let's go back to our original question: Can astrology predict the future? To know that, we must come to an understanding of what the future is.

In simplest terms the future is the natural next step to the present, just as the present is a natural progression from the past. Although our minds can move from one to the other, there is a thread of continuity between past, present, and future that joins them together in a coherent sequence. If you are reading this book at this moment, it is the result of a real conscious choice you made in the recent past. That is, you chose to find out what was on these pages, picked up the book, and opened it. Because of this choice you may know yourself better in the future. It's as simple as that.

Knowing ourselves is the key to being able to predict and understand our own future. To learn from past experiences, choices, and actions is to fully grasp the present. Coming to grips with the present is to be master of the future.

"Know thyself" is a motto that takes us back to the philosophers of ancient Greece. Mystery religions and cults of initiation throughout the ancient world, schools of mystical discipline, yoga and mental expansion have always been guardians of this one sacred phrase. Know thyself. Of course, that's easy to say. But how do you go about it when there are so many conflicts in our lives and different parts of our personalities? How do we know when we are really "being ourselves" and not merely being influenced by the things we read or see on television, or by the people around us? How can we differentiate the various parts of our character and still remain whole?

There are many methods of classifying human beings into types. Body shapes, muscular types, blood types, and genetic types are only a few. Psychology has its own ways of classifying human beings according to their behavior. Anthropology studies human evolution as the body-mind response to environment. Biology watches physical development and adaptations in body structure. These fields provide valuable information about human beings and the ways they survive, grow, and change in their search for their place in eternity. Yet these branches of science have been separate and fragmented. Their contribution has been to provide theories and data, yes, but no lasting solutions to the human problems that have existed since the first two creatures realized they had two separate identities.

It's often difficult to classify yourself according to these different schemes. It's not easy to be objective about yourself. Some things are hard to face; others are hard to see. The different perspectives afforded to us by studying the human organism from all these different disciplines may seem contradictory when they are all really trying to integrate humankind into the whole of the cosmic scheme.

Astrology can help these disciplines unite to seek a broader and deeper approach to universal human issues. Astrology's point of view is vast. It transcends racial, ethnic, genetic, environmental, and even historical criteria, yet somehow includes them all. Astrology embraces the totality of human experience, then sets about to examine the relationships that are created within that experience.

We don't simply say, "The planets cause this or that." Rather than merely isolating cause or effect, astrology has unified the ideas of cause and effect. Concepts of past, present, and future merge and become, as we shall see a little later on, like stepping-stones across the great stream of mind. Observations of people and the environment have developed the astrological principles of planetary "influence," but it must be remembered that if there is actual influence, it is mutual. As the planets influence us, so we influence them, for we are forever joined to all past and future motion of the heavenly bodies. This is the foundation of astrology as it has been built up over the centuries.

ORDER VS. CHAOS

But is it all written in the stars? Is it destined that empires should thrive and flourish, kings reign, lovers love, and then ... decay, ruin, and natural disintegration hold sway? Have we anything to do with determining the cycles of order and chaos? The art of the true astrologer depends on his ability to uncover new information, place it upon the grid of data already collected, and then interpret what he sees as accurate probability in human existence. There may be a paradox here. If we can predict that birds will fly south, could we not, with enough time and samples for observation, determine their ultimate fate when they arrive in the south?

The paradox is that there is no paradox at all. Order and chaos exist together simultaneously in one observable universe. At some remote point in time and space the Earth was formed, and for one reason or another, life appeared here. Whether the appearance of life on planets is a usual phenomenon or an unrepeated accident we can only speculate at this moment. But our Earth and all living things upon its surface conform to certain laws of physical materiality that our observations have led us to write down and contemplate. All creatures, from the one-celled ameba to a man hurrying home at rush hour, have some basic traits in common. Life in its organization goes from the simple to the complex with a perfection and order that is both awesome and inspiring. If there were no order to our physical world, an apple could turn into a worm and cows could be butterflies.

But the world is an integrated whole, unified with every other part of creation. When nature does take an unexpected turn, we call that a mutation. This is the exciting card in the program of living experience that tells us not everything is written at all. Spontaneity is real. Change is real. Freedom from the expected norm is real. We have seen in nature that only those mutations that can adapt to changes in their environment and continue reproducing themselves will survive. But possibilities are open for sudden transformation, and that keeps the whole world growing.

FREE CHOICE AND
THE VALUE OF PREDICTIONS

Now it's time to turn our attention to the matter of predictions. That was our original question after all: Can astrology peer into the future? Well, astrological prognostication is an awe-inspiring art and requires deep philosophical consideration before it is to be undertaken. Not only are there many grids that must be laid one upon the other before such predictions can be made, but there are ethical issues that plague every student of the stars. How much can you really see? How much should you tell? What is the difference between revealing valuable data and disclosing negative or harmful programing?

If an astrologer tells you only the good things, you'll have little confidence in the analysis when you are passing through crisis. On the other hand, if the astrologer is a prophet of doom who can see nothing but the dark clouds on the horizon, you will eventually have to reject astrology because you will come to associate it with the bad luck in your life.

Astrology itself is beyond any practitioner's capacity to grasp it all. Unrealistic utopianism or gloomy determinism reflect not the truth of astrology but the truth of the astrologer interpreting what he sees. In order to solve problems and make accurate predictions, you have to be *able* to look on the dark side of things without dwelling there. You have to be able to take a look at all the possibilities, all the possible meanings of a certain planetary influence without jumping to premature conclusions. Objective scanning and assessment take much practice and great skill.

No matter how skilled the astrologer is, he cannot assume the responsibility for your life. Only you can take that responsibility as your life unfolds. In a way, the predictions of this book are glancing ahead up the road, much the way a road map can indicate turns up ahead this way or that. You, however, are still driving the car.

What, then, is a horoscope? If it is a picture of you at your moment of birth, are you then frozen forever in time and space, unable to budge or deviate from the harsh, unyielding declarations of the stars? Not at all.

The universe is always in motion. Each moment follows the moment before it. As the present is the result of all past choices and action, so the future is the result of today's choices. But if we can go to a planetary calendar and see where planets will be located two years from now, then how can individual free choice exist? This is a question that has haunted authors and philosophers since the first thinkers recorded their thoughts. In the end, of course, we must all reason things out for ourselves and come to our own conclusions. It is easy to be impressed or influenced by people who seem to know a lot more than we do, but in reality we must all find codes of beliefs with which we are the most comfortable.

But if we can stretch our imaginations up, up above the line of time as it exists from one point to another, we can almost see past, present, and future, all together. We can almost feel this vibrant thread of creative free choice that pushes forward at every moment, actually causing the future to happen! Free will, that force that changes the entire course of a stream, exists within the stream of mind itself—the collective mind, or intelligence, of humanity. Past, present, and future are mere stepping-stones across that great current.

Our lives continue a thread of an intelligent mind

that existed before we were born and will exist after we die. It is like an endless relay race. At birth we pick up a torch and carry it, lighting the way with that miraculous light of consciousness of immortality. Then we pass it on to others when we die. What we call the *unconscious* may be part of this great stream of mind, which learns and shares experiences with everything that has ever lived or will ever live on this world or any other.

Yet we all come to Earth with different family circumstances, backgrounds, and characteristics. We all come to life with different planetary configurations. Indeed each person *is* different, yet we are all the same. We have different tasks or responsibilities or lifestyles, but underneath we share a common currȇnt—the powerful stream of human intelligence. Each of us has different sets of circumstances to deal with because of the choices he or she has made in the past. We all possess different assets and have different resources to fall back on, weaknesses to strengthen, and sides of our nature to transform. We are all what we are now because of what we were before. The present is the sum of the past. And we will be what we will be in the future because of what we are now.

It is foolish to pretend that there are no specific boundaries or limitations to any of our particular lives. Family background, racial, cultural, or religious indoctrinations, physical characteristics, these are all inescapable facts of our being that must be incorporated and accepted into our maturing mind. But each person possesses the capacity for breakthrough, forgiveness, and total transformation. It has taken millions of years since people first began to walk upright. We cannot expect an overnight evolution to take place. There are many things about our personalities that are very much like our parents. Sometimes that thought makes us uncomfortable, but it's true.

It's also true that we are not our parents. You are

you, just you, and nobody else but you. That's one of the wondrous aspects of astrology. The levels on which each planetary configuration works out will vary from individual to individual. Often an aspect of selfishness will be manifested in one person, yet in another it may appear as sacrifice and kindness.

Development is inevitable in human consciousness. But the direction of that development is not. As plants will bend toward the light as they grow, so there is the possibility for the human mind to grow toward the light of integrity and truth. The Age of Aquarius that everyone is talking about must first take place within each human's mind and heart. An era of peace, freedom, and community cannot be legislated by any government, no matter how liberal. It has to be a spontaneous flow of human spirit and fellowship. It will be a magnificent dawning on the globe of consciousness that reflects the joy of the human heart to be part of the great stream of intelligence and love. It must be generated by an enlightened, realistic humanity. There's no law that can put it into effect, no magic potion to drink that will make it all come true. It will be the result of all people's efforts to assume their personal and social responsibilities and to carve out a new destiny for humankind.

As you read the predictions in this book, bear in mind that they have been calculated by means of planetary positions for whole groups of people. Thus their value lies in your ability to coordinate what you read with the nature of your life's circumstances at the present time. You have seen how many complex relationships must be analyzed in individual horoscopes before sensible accurate conclusions can be drawn. No matter what the indications, a person has his or her own life, own intelligence, basic native strength that must ultimately be the source of action and purpose. When you are living truthfully and in harmony with what you know is right, there are no forces, threats, or obstacles that can defeat you.

With these predictions, read the overall pattern and see how rhythms begin to emerge. They are not caused by remote alien forces, millions of miles out in space. You and the planets are one. What you do, they do. What they do, you do. But can you change their course? No, but you cannot change many of your basic characteristics either. Still, within that already existing framework, you are the master. You can still differentiate between what is right for you and what is not. You can seize opportunities and act on them, you can create beauty and seek love.

The purpose of looking ahead is not to scare yourself. Look ahead to enlarge your perspective, enhance your overall view of the life *you* are developing. Difficult periods cause stress certainly, but at the same time they give you the chance to reassess your condition, restate and redefine exactly what is important to you, so you can cherish your life more. Joyous periods should be lived to the fullest with the happiness and exuberance that each person richly deserves.

YOUR HOROSCOPE AND THE ZODIAC

It's possible that in your own body, as you read this passage, there exist atoms as old as time itself. You could well be the proud possessor of some carbon and hydrogen (two necessary elements in the development of life) that came into being in the heart of a star billions and billions of years ago. That star could have exploded and cast its matter far into space. This matter could have formed another star, and then another, until finally our Sun was born. From the Sun's nuclear reactions came the material that later formed the planets—and maybe some of that primeval carbon or hydrogen. That material could have become part of the Earth, part of an early ocean, even early life. These same atoms could well have been carried down to the present day, to this very moment as you read this book. It's really quite possible. You can see how everything is linked to everything else. Our Earth now exists in a gigantic universe that showers it constantly with rays and invisible particles. You are the point into which all these energies and influences have been focused. You are the prism through which all the light of outer space is being refracted. You are literally a reflection of all the planets and stars.

Your horoscope is a picture of the sky at the moment of your birth. It's like a gigantic snapshot of the positions of the planets and stars, taken from Earth. Of course, the planets never stop moving around the Sun even for the briefest moment, and you represent that motion as it was occurring at the exact hour of your birth at the precise location on the Earth where you were born.

When an astrologer is going to read your chart, he or she asks you for the month, day, and year of your birth. She also needs the exact time and place. With this information he sets about consulting various charts and tables in his calculation of the specific positions of the Sun, Moon, and stars, relative to your birthplace when you came to Earth. Then he or she locates them by means of the *Zodiac*.

The Zodiac is a group of stars, centered against the Sun's apparent path around the Earth, and these star groups are divided into twelve equal segments, or *signs*. What we are actually dividing up is the Earth's path around the Sun. But from our point of view here on Earth, it seems as if the Sun is making a great circle around our planet in the sky, so we say it's the Sun's apparent path. This twelvefold division, the Zodiac, is like a mammoth address system for any body in the sky. At any given moment, the planets can all be located at a specific point along this path.

Now where are you in this system? First you look to your *Sun sign*—the section of the Zodiac that the Sun occupied when you were born. A great part of your character, in fact the central thread of your whole being, is described by your Sun sign. Each sign of the Zodiac has certain basic traits associated with it. Since the Sun remains in each sign for about thirty days, that divides the population into twelve major character types. Of course, not everybody born the same month will have the same character, but you'll be amazed at how many fundamental traits you share with your astrological cousins of the same birth sign, no matter how many environmental differences you boast.

The dates on which the Sun sign changes will vary from year to year. That is why some people born near the *cusp*, or edge, of a sign have difficulty determining their true birth sign without the aid of an astrologer who can plot precisely the Sun's apparent motion (the Earth's motion) for any given year. But to help you find your true Sun sign, a Table of Cusp Dates for the years 1900 to 2000 is provided for you on page 17.

Here are the twelve signs of the Zodiac as western astrology has recorded them. Listed also are the symbols associated with them and the *approximate* dates when the Sun enters and exits each sign for the year 1999.

Aries	Ram	March 20–April 20
Taurus	Bull	April 20–May 21
Gemini	Twins	May 21–June 21
Cancer	Crab	June 21–July 23
Leo	Lion	July 23–August 23
Virgo	Virgin	August 23–September 23
Libra	Scales	September 23–October 23
Scorpio	Scorpion	October 23–November 22
Sagittarius	Archer	November 22–December 22
Capricorn	Sea Goat	December 22–January 20
Aquarius	Water Bearer	January 20–February 18
Pisces	Fish	February 18-March 20

In a horoscope the *Rising sign*, or Ascendant, is often considered to be as important as the Sun sign. In a later chapter (see pages 82–84) the Rising sign is discussed in detail. But to help you determine your own Rising sign, a Table of Rising Signs is provided for you on pages 20–21.

THE SIGNS OF THE ZODIAC

The signs of the Zodiac are an ingenious and complex summary of human behavioral and physical types, handed down from generation to generation through the bodies of all people in their hereditary material and through their minds. On the following pages you will find brief descriptions of all twelve signs in their highest and most ideal expression.

ARIES
The Sign of the Ram

Aries is the first sign of the Zodiac, and marks the beginning of springtime and the birth of the year. In spring the Earth begins its ascent upward and tips its North Pole toward the Sun. During this time the life-giving force of the Sun streams toward Earth, bathing our planet with the kiss of warmth and life. Plants start growing. Life wakes up. No more waiting. No more patience. The message has come from the Sun: Time to live!

Aries is the sign of the Self and is the crusade for the right of an individual to live in unimpeachable freedom. It represents the supremacy of the human will over all obstacles, limitations, and threats. In Aries there is unlimited energy, optimism, and daring, for it is the pioneer in search of a new world. It is the story of success and renewal, championship, and victory. It is the living spirit of resilience and the power to be yourself, free from all restrictions and conditioning. There is no pattern you *have* to repeat, nobody's rule you *have* to follow.

Confidence and positive action are born in Aries, with little thought or fear of the past. Life is as magic as sunrise, with all the creative potential ahead of you for a new day. Activity, energy, and adventure characterize this sign. In this sector of the Zodiac there is amazing strength, forthrightness, honesty, and a stubborn refusal to accept defeat. The Aries nature is forgiving, persuasive, masterful, and decisive.

In short, Aries is the magic spark of life and being, the source of all initiative, courage, independence, and self-esteem.

TAURUS
The Sign of the Bull

Taurus is wealth. It is not just money, property, and the richness of material possessions, but also a wealth of the spirit. Taurus rules everything in the visible world we see, touch, hear, smell, taste—the Earth, sea, and sky—everything we normally consider "real." It is the sign of economy and reserve, for it is a mixture of thrift and luxury, generosity and practicality. It is a blend of the spiritual and material, for the fertility of the sign is unlimited, and in this sense it is the mystical bank of life. Yet it must hold the fruit of its efforts in its hands and seeks to realize its fantasy-rich imagination with tangible rewards.

Loyalty and endurance make this sign perhaps the most stable of all. We can lean on Taurus, count on it, and it makes our earthly lives comfortable, safe, pleasurable. It is warm, sensitive, loving, and capable of magnificent, joyful sensations. It is conservative and pragmatic, with a need to be sure of each step forward. It is the capacity to plan around eventualities without living in the future. Steadfast and constant, this is a sturdy combination of ruggedness and beauty, gentleness and unshakability of purpose. It is the point at which we join body and soul. Unselfish friend and loyal companion, Taurus is profoundly noble and openly humanitarian. Tenacity and concentration slow the energy down to bring certain long-lasting rewards.

Taurus is a fertile resource and rich ground to grow in, and we all need it for our ideas and plans to flourish. It is the uncut diamond, symbolizing rich, raw tastes and a deep need for satisfaction, refinement, and completion.

GEMINI
The Sign of the Twins

Gemini is the sign of mental brilliance. Communication is developed to a high degree of fluidity, rapidity, fluency. It is the chance for expressing ideas and relaying information from one place to another. Charming, debonair, and lighthearted, it is a symbol of universal interest and eternal curiosity. The mind is quick and advanced, with a lightning-like ability to assimilate data.

It is the successful manipulation of verbal or visual language and the capacity to meet all events with objectivity and intelligence. It is light, quick wit, with a comic satiric twist. Gemini is the sign of writing or speaking.

Gemini is the willingness to try anything once, a need to wander and explore, the quick shifting of moods and attitudes being a basic characteristic that indicates a need for change. Versatility is the remarkable Gemini attribute. It is the capacity to investigate, perform, and relate over great areas for short periods of time and thus to connect all areas. It is mastery of design and perception, the power to conceptualize and create by putting elements together—people, colors, patterns. It is the reporter's mind, plus a brilliant ability to see things in objective, colorful arrangement. Strength lies in constant refreshment of outlook and joyful participation in all aspects of life.

Gemini is involvement with neighbors, family and relatives, telephones, arteries of news and communication—anything that enhances the human capacity for communication and self-expression. It is active, positive, and energetic, with an insatiable hunger for human interchange. Through Gemini bright and dark sides of personality merge and the mind has wings. As it flies it reflects the light of a boundless shining intellect. It is the development of varied talents from recognition of the duality of self.

Gemini is geared toward enjoying life to the fullest by finding, above all else, a means of expressing the inner self to the outside world.

CANCER
The Sign of the Crab

Cancer is the special relationship to home and involvement with the family unit. Maintaining harmony in the domestic sphere or improving conditions there is a major characteristic in this sector of the Zodiac. Cancer is attachment between two beings vibrating in sympathy with one another.

It is the comfort of a loving embrace, a tender generosity. Cancer is the place of shelter whenever there are lost or hungry souls in the night. Through Cancer we are fed, protected, comforted, and soothed. When the coldness of the world threatens, Cancer is there with gentle understanding. It is protection and understated loyalty, a medium of rich, living feeling that is both psychic and mystical. Highly intuitive, Cancer has knowledge that other signs do not possess. It is the wisdom of the soul.

It prefers the quiet contentment of the home and hearth to the busy search for earthly success and civilized pleasures. Still, there is a respect for worldly knowledge. Celebration of life comes through food. The sign is the muted light of warmth, security, and gladness, and its presence means nourishment. It rules fertility and the instinct to populate and raise young. It is growth of the soul. It is the ebb and flow of all our tides of feeling, involvements, habits, and customs.

Through Cancer is reflected the inner condition of all human beings, and therein lies the seed of knowledge out of which the soul will grow.

LEO
The Sign of the Lion

Leo is love. It represents the warmth, strength, and regeneration we feel through love. It is the radiance of life-giving light and the center of all attention and activity. It is passion, romance, adventure, and games. Pleasure, amusement, fun, and entertainment are all part of Leo. Based on the capacity for creative feeling and the desire to express love, Leo is the premier sign. It represents the unlimited outpouring of all that is warm and positive.

It is loyalty, dignity, responsibility, and command. Pride and nobility belong to Leo, and the dashing image of the knight in shining armor, of the hero, is part of Leo. It is a sense of high honor and kingly generosity born out of deep, noble love. It is the excitement of the sportsman, with all the unbeatable flair and style of success. It is a strong, unyielding will and true sense of personal justice, a respect for human freedom, and an enlightened awareness of people's needs.

Leo is involvement in the Self's awareness of personal talents and the desire and need to express them. At best it is forthrightness, courage and efficiency, authority and dignity, showmanship, and a talent for organization. Dependable and ardent, the Lion is characterized by individuality, positivism, and integrity.

It is the embodiment of human maturity, the effective individual in society, a virile creative force able to take chances and win. It is the love of laughter and the joy of making others happy. Decisive and enthusiastic, the Lion is the creative producer of the Zodiac It is the potential to light the way for others.

VIRGO

The Sign of the Virgin

Virgo is the sign of work and service. It is the symbol of the farmer at harvest time, and represents tireless efforts for the benefit of humanity, the joy of bringing the fruits of the Earth to the table of mankind. Celebration through work is the characteristic of this sign.

Sincerity, zeal, discipline, and devotion mark the sign of the Virgin.

The key word is purity, and in Virgo lies a potential for unlimited self-mastery. Virgo is the embodiment of perfected skill and refined talent. The thread of work is woven into the entire life of Virgo. All creativity is poured into streamlining a job, classifying a system, eradicating unnecessary elements of pure analysis. The true Virgo genius is found in separating the wheat from the chaff.

Spartan simplicity characterizes this sign, and Virgo battles the war between order and disorder. The need to arrange, assimilate, and categorize is great; it is the symbol of the diagnostician, the nurse, and the healer. Criticism and analysis describe this sign—pure, incisive wisdom and a shy appreciation of life's joys. All is devoted to the attainment of perfection and the ideal of self-mastery.

Virgo is the sign of health and represents the physical body as a functioning symbol of the mental and spiritual planes. It is the state of healing the ills of the human being with natural, temperate living. It is maturation of the ego as it passes from a self-centered phase to its awareness and devotion to humanity.

It is humanitarian, pragmatic, and scientific, with boundless curiosity. Focus and clarity of mind are the strong points, while strength of purpose and shy reserve underlie the whole sign. There is separateness, aloofness, and solitude for this beacon of the Zodiac. As a lighthouse guides ships, so Virgo shines.

LIBRA
The Sign of the Scales

Libra is the sign of human relationship, marriage, equality, and justice. It symbolizes the need of one human being for another, the capacity to find light, warmth, and life-giving love in relationship to another human being. It is union on any level—mental, sexual, emotional, or business. It is self-extension in a desire to find a partner with whom to share our joys. It is the capacity to recognize the needs of others and to develop to the fullest our powers of diplomacy, good taste, and refinement.

Libra is harmony, grace, aesthetic sensibility, and the personification of the spirit of companionship. It represents the skill to maintain balances and the ability to share mutually all life's benefits, trials, crises, and blessings. Libra is mastery at anticipation of another's needs or reactions. It is the exercise of simple justice with impartial delicacy.

It is the need to relate, to find a major person, place, or thing to sustain us and draw out our attention. It is growth through becoming awakened to the outside world and other people. It is the union of two loving souls in honesty, equality, mutual cooperation, and mutual accord.

♏

SCORPIO
The Sign of the Scorpion

Scorpio is the sign of dark intensity, swirling passion, and sexual magnetism. It is the thirst for survival and regeneration that are the bases of sexual orientation and the creative impulses for self-expression. No other sign has such a profound instinct for survival and reproduction. Out of the abyss of emotions come a thousand creations, each one possessing a life of its own.

Scorpio is completion, determination, and endurance, fortified with enough stamina to outlive any enemy. It is the pursuit of goals despite any threat, warning, or obstacle that might stand in the way. It simply cannot be stopped. It knows when to wait and when to proceed. It is the constant state of readiness, a vibrant living force that constantly pumps out its rhythm from the depths of being.

Secretive and intimate, Scorpio symbolizes the self-directed creature with a will of steel. It is the flaming desire to create, manipulate, and control with a magician's touch. But the most mysterious quality is the capacity for metamorphosis, or total transformation.

This represents supremacy in the battle with dark unseen forces. It is the state of being totally fearless—the embodiment of truth and courage. It symbolizes the human capacity to face all danger and emerge supreme, to heal oneself. As a caterpillar spins its way into the darkness of a cocoon, Scorpio faces the end of existence, says goodbye to an old way of life, and goes through a kind of death—or total change.

Then, amid the dread of uncertainty, something remarkable happens. From hopelessness or personal crisis a new individual emerges, like a magnificent butterfly leaving behind its cocoon. It is a human being completely transformed and victorious. This is Scorpio.

SAGITTARIUS
The Sign of the Archer

Sagittarius is the sign of adventure and a thousand and one new experiences. It is the cause and purpose of every new attempt at adventure or self-understanding. It is the embodiment of enthusiasm, search for truth, and love of wisdom. Hope and optimism characterize this section of the Zodiac, and it is the ability to leave the past behind and set out again with positive resilience and a happy, cheerful outlook.

It is intelligence and exuberance, youthful idealism, and the desire to expand all horizons. It is the constant hatching of dreams, the hunger for knowledge, travel and experience. The goal is exploration itself.

Sagittarius is generosity, humor, and goodness of nature, backed up by the momentum of great expectations. It symbolizes the ability of people to be back in the race after having the most serious spills over the biggest hurdles. It is a healthy, positive outlook and the capacity to meet each new moment with unaffected buoyancy.

At this point in the Zodiac, greater conscious understanding begins to develop self-awareness and self-acceptance. It is an Olympian capacity to look upon the bright side and to evolve that aspect of mind we call conscience.

CAPRICORN
The Sign of the Sea Goat

Capricorn is the sign of structure and physical law. It rules depth, focus, and concentration. It is the symbol of success through perseverance, happiness through profundity. It is victory over disruption, and finds reality in codes set up by society and culture. It is the perpetuation of useful, tested patterns and a desire to protect what has already been established.

It is cautious, conservative, conscious of the passage of time, yet ageless. The Goat symbolizes the incorporation of reason into living and depth into loving.

Stability, responsibility, and fruitfulness through loyalty color this sector of the Zodiac with an undeniable and irrepressible awareness of success, reputation, and honor. Capricorn is the culmination of our earthly dreams, the pinnacle of our worldly life.

It is introspection and enlightenment through serious contemplation of the Self and its position in the world. It is mastery of understanding and the realization of dreams.

Capricorn is a winter blossom, a born professional with an aim of harmony and justice, beauty, grace, and success. It is the well-constructed pyramid: perfect and beautiful, architecturally correct, mysteriously implacable, and hard to know. It is highly organized and built on precise foundations to last and last and last. It is practical, useful yet magnificent and dignified, signifying permanence and careful planning. Like a pyramid, Capricorn has thick impenetrable walls, complex passageways, and false corridors. Yet somewhere at the heart of this ordered structure is the spirit of a mighty ruler.

AQUARIUS
The Sign of the Water Bearer

Aquarius is the symbol of idealized free society. It is the herding instinct in man as a social animal. It is the collection of heterogeneous elements of human consciousness in coherent peaceful coexistence. Friendship, goodwill, and harmonious contact are Aquarius attributes. It is founded on the principle of individual freedom and the brotherly love and respect for the rights of all men and women on Earth.

It is strength of will and purpose, altruism, and love of human fellowship. It is the belief in spontaneity and free choice, in the openness to live in a spirit of harmony and cooperation—liberated from restriction, repression, and conventional codes of conduct. It is the brilliant capacity to assimilate information instantaneously at the last minute and translate that information into immediate creative action, and so the result is to live in unpredictability.

This is the progressive mind, the collective mind—groups of people getting together to celebrate life. Aquarius is the child of the future, the utopian working for the betterment of the human race. Funds, charities, seeking better cities and better living conditions for others, involvement in great forms of media or communication, science or research in the hope of joining mankind to his higher self—this is all Aquarius.

It is invention, genius, revolution, discovery—instantaneous breakthrough from limitations. It's a departure from convention, eccentricity, the unexpected development that changes the course of history. It is the discovery of people and all the arteries that join them together. Aquarius is adventure, curiosity, exotic and alien appeal. It pours the water of life and intelligence for all humanity to drink. It is humanism, community, and the element of surprise.

PISCES
The Sign of the Fishes

Pisces is faith—undistracted, patient, all-forgiving faith—and therein lies the Pisces capacity for discipline, endurance, and stamina.

It is imagination and other-worldliness, the condition

of living a foggy, uncertain realm of poetry, music, and fantasy. Passive and compassionate, this sector of the Zodiac symbolizes the belief in the inevitability of life. It represents the view of life that everything exists in waves, like the sea. All reality as we know it is a dream, a magic illusion that must ultimately be washed away. Tides pull this way and that, whirlpools and undercurrents sweep across the bottom of life's existence, but in Pisces there is total acceptance of all tides, all rhythms, all possibilities. It is the final resolution of all personal contradictions and all confusing paradoxes.

It is the search for truth and honesty, and the devotion to love, utterly and unquestionably. It is the desire to act with wisdom, kindness, and responsibility and to welcome humanity completely free from scorn, malice, discrimination, or prejudice. It is total, all-embracing, idealistic love. It is the acceptance of two sides of a question at once and love through sacrifice.

Pisces is beyond reality. We are here today, but may be gone tomorrow. Let the tide of circumstances carry you where it will, for nothing is forever. As all things come, so must they go. In the final reel, all things must pass away. It is deliverance from sorrow through surrender to the infinite. The emotions are as vast as the ocean, yet in the pain of confusion there is hope in the secret cell of one's own heart. Pisces symbolizes liberation from pain through love, faith, and forgiveness.

THE SIGNS AND
THEIR KEY WORDS

		Positive	**Negative**
ARIES	self	courage, initiative, pioneer instinct	brash rudeness, selfish impetuosity
TAURUS	money	endurance, loyalty, wealth	obstinacy, gluttony
GEMINI	mind	versatility, communication	capriciousness, unreliability
CANCER	family	sympathy, homing instinct	clannishness, childishness
LEO	children	love, authority, integrity	egotism, force
VIRGO	work	purity, industry, analysis	faultfinding, cynicism
LIBRA	marriage	harmony, justice	vacillation, superficiality
SCORPIO	sex	survival, regeneration	vengeance, discord
SAGITTARIUS	travel	optimism, higher learning	lawlessness, irresponsibility
CAPRICORN	career	depth, responsibility	narrowness, gloom
AQUARIUS	friends	humanity, genius	perverse unpredictability
PISCES	faith	spiritual love, universality	diffusion, escapism

THE ELEMENTS AND
THE QUALITIES OF THE SIGNS

Every sign has both an element and a quality associated with it. The element indicates the basic makeup of the sign, and the quality describes the kind of activity associated with each.

Element	Sign	Quality	Sign
Fire	Aries	Cardinal...........	Aries
	Leo		Libra
	Sagittarius		Cancer
			Capricorn
Earth	Taurus	Fixed..............	Taurus
	Virgo		Leo
	Capricorn		Scorpio
			Aquarius
Air................	Gemini	Mutable	Gemini
	Libra		Virgo
	Aquarius		Sagittarius
			Pisces
Water.............	Cancer		
	Scorpio		
	Pisces		

Signs can be grouped together according to their element and quality. Signs of the same element share many basic traits in common. They tend to form stable configurations and ultimately harmonious relationships. Signs of the same quality are often less harmonious, but share many dynamic potentials for growth and profound fulfillment.

The following pages describe these sign groupings in more detail.

The Fire Signs

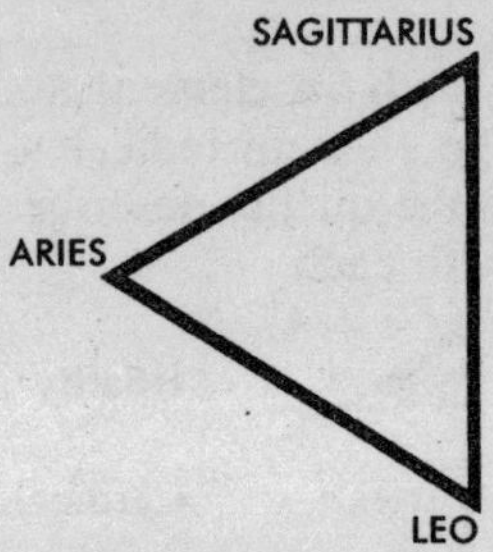

This is the fire group. On the whole these are emotional, volatile types, quick to anger, quick to forgive. They are adventurous, powerful people and act as a source of inspiration for everyone. They spark into action with immediate exuberant impulses. They are intelligent, self-involved, creative, and idealistic. They all share a certain vibrancy and glow that outwardly reflects an inner flame and passion for living.

The Earth Signs

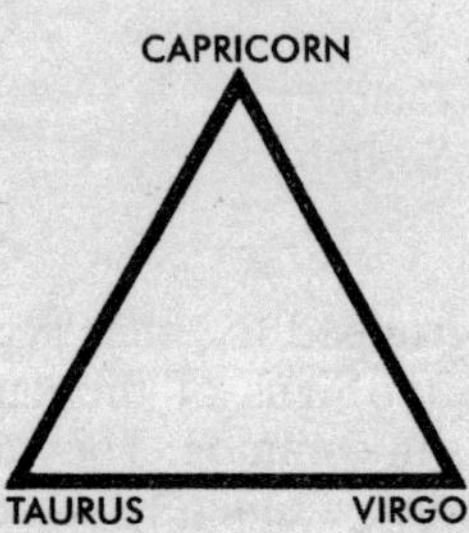

This is the earth group. They are in constant touch with the material world and tend to be conservative. Although they are all capable of spartan self-discipline, they are earthy, sensual people who are stimulated by the tangible, elegant, and luxurious. The thread of their lives is always practical, but they do fantasize and are often attracted to dark, mysterious, emotional people. They are like great cliffs overhanging the sea, forever married to the ocean but always resisting erosion from the dark, emotional forces that thunder at their feet.

The Air Signs

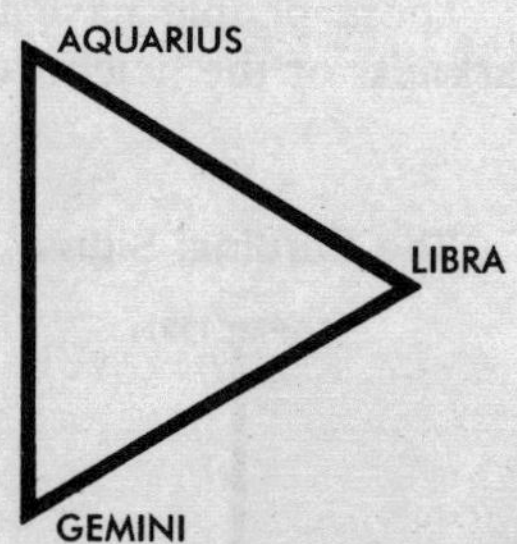

This is the air group. They are light, mental creatures desirous of contact, communication, and relationship. They are involved with people and the forming of ties on many levels. Original thinkers, they are the bearers of human news. Their language is their sense of word, color, style, and beauty. They provide an atmosphere suitable and pleasant for living. They add change and versatility to the scene, and it is through them that we can explore human intelligence and experience.

The Water Signs

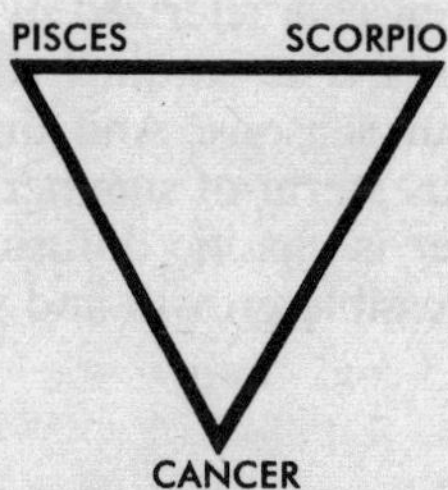

This is the water group. Through the water people, we are all joined together on emotional, nonverbal levels.

The water signs are silent, mysterious types whose magic hypnotizes even the most determined realist. They have uncanny perceptions about people and are as rich as the oceans when it comes to feeling, emotion, or imagination. They are sensitive, mystical creatures with memories that go back beyond time. Through water, life is sustained. These people have the potential for the depths of darkness or the heights of mysticism and art.

The Cardinal Signs

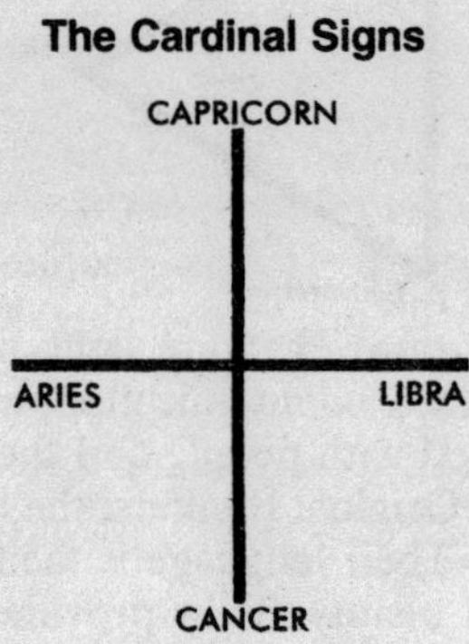

The cardinal signs present a picture of dynamism, activity, tremendous stress, and remarkable achievement. These people know the meaning of great change since their lives are often characterized by significant crises and major successes. The cardinal signs mark the beginning of the four seasons. And this combination is like a simultaneous storm of summer, fall, winter, and spring. The danger is chaotic diffusion of energy; the potential is irrepressible growth and victory.

The Fixed Signs

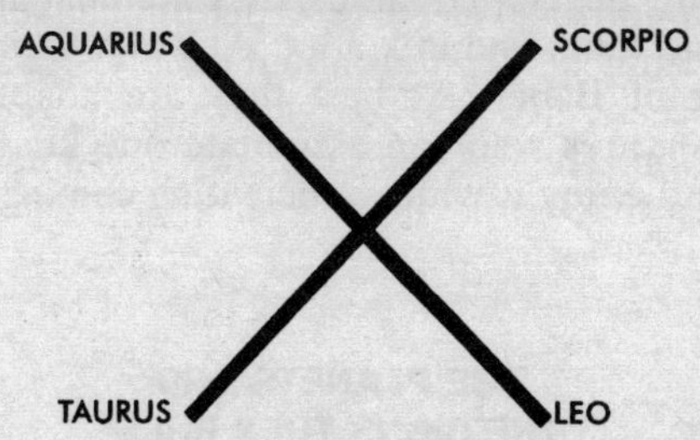

Fixed signs are always establishing themselves in a given place or area of experience. Like explorers who arrive and plant a flag, these people claim a position from which they do not enjoy being deposed. They are staunch, stalwart, upright, trusty, honorable people, although their obstinacy is well-known. Their contribution is fixity, and they are the angels who support our visible world.

The Mutable Signs

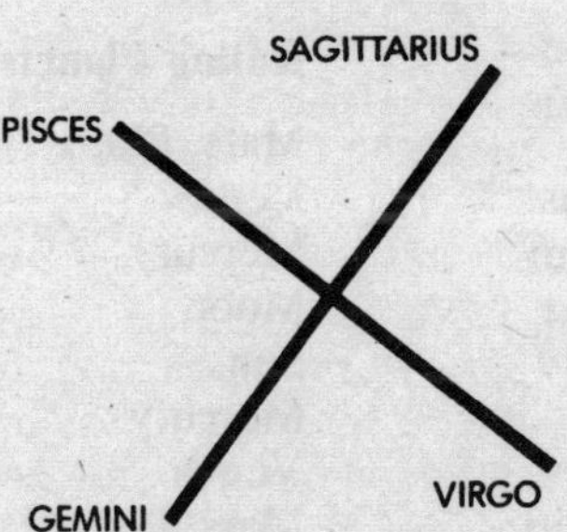

Mutable people are versatile, sensitive, intelligent, nervous, and deeply curious about life. They are the translators of all energy. They often carry out or complete tasks initiated by others. People from mutable signs have highly developed minds; they are imaginative and jumpy and think and talk a lot. At worst their lives are a Tower of Babel. At best they are adaptable and ready creatures who can assimilate one kind of experience and enjoy it while anticipating coming changes.

THE PLANETS AND
THE SIGNS THEY RULE

The signs of the Zodiac are linked to the planets in the following way. Each sign is governed or ruled by one or more planets. No matter where the planets are located in the sky at any given moment, they still rule their respective signs. When they travel through the signs they rule, they have special dignity and their effects are stronger.

Following is a list of the planets and the signs they rule. After you read the definitions of the planets from pages 88 to 96, see if you can determine how the planet ruling *your* Sun sign has affected your life.

Signs	Ruling Planets
Aries	Mars, Pluto
Taurus	Venus
Gemini	Mercury
Cancer	Moon
Leo	Sun
Virgo	Mercury
Libra	Venus
Scorpio	Mars, Pluto
Sagittarius	Jupiter
Capricorn	Saturn
Aquarius	Saturn, Uranus
Pisces	Jupiter, Neptune

THE ZODIAC AND
THE HUMAN BODY

The signs of the Zodiac are linked to the human body in a direct relationship. Each sign has a part of the body with which it is associated.

It is traditionally believed that surgery is best performed when the Moon is passing through a sign *other* than the sign associated with the part of the body upon which an operation is to be performed. But often the presence of the Moon in a particular sign will bring the focus of attention to that very part of the body under medical scrutiny.

The principles of medical astrology are complex and beyond the scope of this introduction. We can, however, list the signs of the Zodiac and the parts of the human body connected with them. Once you learn these correspondences, you'll be amazed at how accurate they are.

Signs	Human Body
Aries	Head, brain, face, upper jaw
Taurus	Throat, neck, lower jaw
Gemini	Hands, arms, lungs, nerves
Cancer	Stomach, breasts, womb, liver
Leo	Heart, spine
Virgo	Intestines, liver
Libra	Kidneys, lower back
Scorpio	Sex and eliminative organs
Sagittarius	Hips, thighs, liver
Capricorn	Skin, bones, teeth, knees
Aquarius	Circulatory system, lower legs
Pisces	Feet, tone of being

THE ZODIACAL HOUSES
AND THE RISING SIGN

Apart from the month and day of birth, the exact time of birth is another vital factor in the determination of an accurate horoscope. Not only do planets move with great speed, but one must know how far the Earth has turned during the day. That way you can determine exactly where the planets are located with respect to the precise birthplace of an individual. This makes your horoscope *your* horoscope.

The horoscope sets up a kind of framework around which the life of an individual grows like wild ivy, this way and that, weaving its way around the trellis of the natal positions of the planets. The year of birth tells us the positions of the distant, slow-moving planets Jupiter, Saturn, Uranus, Neptune, and Pluto. The month of birth indicates the Sun sign, or birth sign as it is commonly called, as well as indicating the positions of the rapidly moving planets Venus, Mercury, and Mars. The day of birth, as well as the time, locates the position of our Moon. And the moment of birth—the exact hour and minute—determines the houses through what is called the Ascendant, or Rising sign.

The illustration on the next page shows the flat chart, or natural wheel, an astrologer uses. The inner circle of the wheel is labeled 1 through 12. These 12 divisions are known as the houses of the Zodiac.

The 1st house always starts from the position marked E, which corresponds to the eastern horizon. The rest of the houses 2 through 12 follow around in a "counterclockwise" direction. The point where each house starts is known as a cusp, or edge.

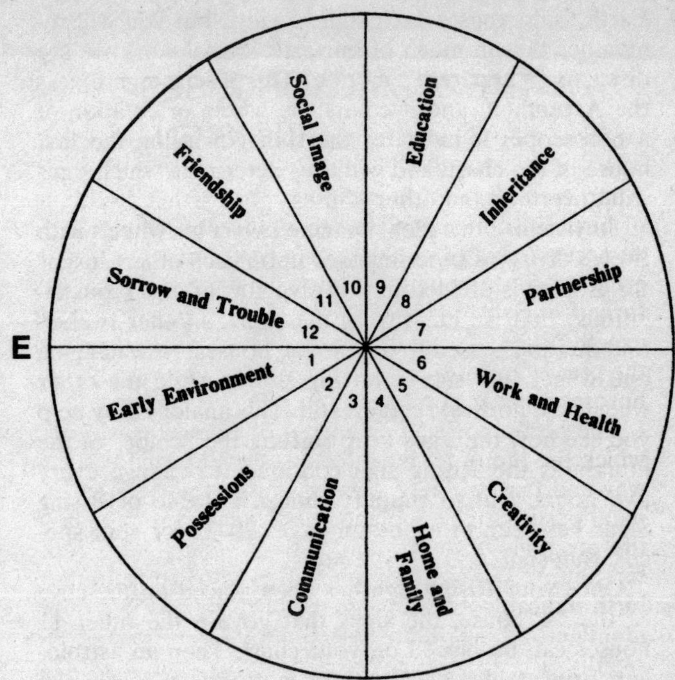

The 12 Houses of the Zodiac

The cusp, or edge, of the 1st house (point E) is where an astrologer would place your Rising sign, the Ascendant. The Rising sign is very important in a horoscope, as it defines your self-image, outlook, physical constitution, early environment, and whole orientation to life. And, as already mentioned, the exact time of your birth determines your Rising sign. Let's see how this works.

As the Earth rotates on its axis once every 24 hours, each one of the 12 signs of the Zodiac appears to be "rising" on the horizon, with a new one appearing about every two hours. Actually it is the turning of the

Earth that exposes each sign to view, but you will remember that in much of our astrological work we are discussing "apparent" motion. This Rising sign marks the Ascendant, and it colors the whole orientation of a horoscope. It indicates the sign governing the first house of the chart, and will thus determine which signs will govern all the other houses.

To visualize this idea, imagine two color wheels with twelve divisions superimposed upon each other. Just as the Zodiac is divided into twelve star groups (constellations) that we identify as the signs, another twelvefold division is used to denote the houses. Now imagine one wheel (the signs) moving slowly while the other wheel (the houses) remains still. This analogy may help you see how the signs keep shifting the "color" of the houses as the Rising sign continues to change every two hours. But to simplify things, a Table of Rising Signs has been provided on pages 20–21 for your specific Sun sign.

Once your Rising sign has been placed on the cusp of the 1st house, the signs that govern the other 11 houses can be placed on your chart. Then an astrologer, using tables of planetary motion, can locate the positions of all the planets in their appropriate houses. The house where your Sun sign is describes your basic character and your fundamental drives. And the houses where the other planets are in your chart suggest the areas of life on Earth in which you will be most likely to focus your constant energy and center your activity.

The illustration on page 83 briefly identifies each of the 12 houses of the Zodiac. Now the pages that follow provide a detailed discussion of the meanings of the houses. In the section after the houses we will define all the known planets of the solar system, with a separate section on the Moon, in order to acquaint you with more of the astrological vocabulary you will be meeting again and again.

THE MEANING OF THE HOUSES

The twelve houses of every horoscope represent areas of life on Earth, or regions of worldly experience. Depending on which sign of the Zodiac was rising on the eastern horizon at the moment of birth, the activity of each house will be "colored" by the zodiacal sign on its cusp, or edge. In other words, the sign falling on the first house will determine what signs will fall on the rest of the houses.

1 The first house determines the basic orientation to all of life on Earth. It indicates the body type, face, head, and brain. It rules your self-image, or the way others see you because of the way you see your self. This is the Ascendant of the horoscope and is the focus of energies of your whole chart. It acts like a prism through which all of the planetary light passes and is reflected in your life. It colors your outlook and influences everything you do and see.

2 This is the house of finances. Here is your approach to money and materialism in general. It indicates where the best sources are for you to improve your financial condition and your earning power as a whole. It indicates chances for gain or loss. It describes your values, alliances, and assets.

3 This is the house of the day-to-day mind. Short trips, communication, and transportation are associated with this house. It deals with routines, brothers and sisters, relatives, neighbors, and the near environment at hand. Language, letters, and the tools for transmitting information are included in third-house matters.

4 This is the house that describes your home and home life, parents, and childhood in the sense of indicating the kind of roots you come from. It symbolizes your present home and domestic situation and reflects your need for privacy and retreat from the world, indicating, of course, what kind of scene you require.

5 Pleasure, love affairs, amusements, parties, creativity, children. This is the house of passion and courtship and of expressing your talents, whatever they are. It is related to the development of your personal life and the capacity to express feeling and enjoy romance.

6 This is the house of work. Here there are tasks to be accomplished and maladjustments to be corrected. It is the house of health as well, and describes some of the likely places where physical health difficulties may appear. It rules routines, regimen, necessary jobs as opposed to a chosen career, army, navy, police—people employed, co-workers, and those in service to others. It indicates the individual's ability to harvest the fruit of his own efforts.

7 This is the house of marriage, partnership, and unions. It represents the alter ego, all people other than yourself, open confrontation with the public. It describes your partner and the condition of partnership as you discern it. In short, it is your "take" on the world. It indicates your capacity to make the transition from courtship to marriage and specifically what you seek out in others.

8 This is the house of deep personal transition, sex as a form of mutual surrender and interchange between human beings. It is the release from tensions and the completion of the creative processes. The eighth house also has to do with taxes, inheritances, and the finances of others, as well as death as the ending of cycles and crises.

9 This is the house of the higher mind, philosophy, religion, and the expression of personal conscience through moral codes. It indicates political leanings, ethical views, and the capacity of the individual for a broader perspective and deeper understanding of himself in relation to society. It is through the ninth house that you make great strides in learning and travel to distant places and come to know yourself through study, dreams, and wide experience.

10 This is the house of career, honor, and prestige. It marks the culmination of worldly experience and indicates the highest point you can reach, what you look up to, and how high you can go in this lifetime. It describes your parents, employers, and how you view authority figures, the condition and direction of your profession, and your position in the community.

11 This is the house of friendships. It describes your social behavior, your views on humanity, and your hopes, aspirations, and wishes for an ideal life. It will indicate what kinds of groups, clubs, organizations, and friendships you tend to form and what you seek out in your chosen alliances other than with your mate or siblings. This house suggests the capacity for the freedom and unconventionality that an individual is seeking, his sense of his connection with mankind, and the definition of his goals, personal and social.

12 This is the house of seclusion, secret wisdom, and self-incarceration. It indicates our secret enemies as well, in the sense that there may be persons, feelings, or memories we are trying to escape. It is self-undoing in that this house acts against the ego in order to find a higher, more universal purpose. It rules prisons, hospitals, charities, and selfless service. It is the house of unfinished psychic business.

THE PLANETS OF THE SOLAR SYSTEM

The planets of the solar system all travel around the Sun at different speeds and different distances. Taken with the Sun, they all distribute individual intelligence and ability throughout the entire chart.

The planets modify the influence of the Sun in a chart according to their own particular natures, strengths, and positions. Their positions must be calculated for each year and day, and their function and expression in a horoscope will change as they move from one area of the Zodiac to another.

Following, you will find brief statements of their pure meanings.

THE SUN

The Sun is the center of existence. Around this flaming sphere all the planets revolve in endless orbits. Our star is constantly sending out its beams of light and energy without which no life on Earth would be possible. In astrology it symbolizes everything we are trying to become, the center around which all of our activity in life will always revolve. It is the symbol of our basic nature and describes the natural and constant thread that runs through everything that we do from birth to death on this planet.

Everything in the horoscope ultimately revolves around this singular body. Although other forces may be prominent in the charts of some individuals, still the

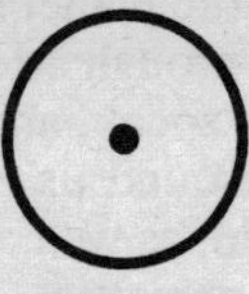

THE SUN

Sun is the total nucleus of being and symbolizes the complete potential of every human being alive. It is vitality and the life force. Your whole essence comes from the position of the Sun.

You are always trying to express the Sun according to its position by house and sign. Possibility for all development is found in the Sun, and it marks the fundamental character of your personal radiations all around you.

It symbolizes strength, vigor, ardor, generosity, and the ability to function effectively as a mature individual and a creative force in society. It is consciousness of the gift of life. The undeveloped solar nature is arrogant pushy, undependable, and proud, and is constantly using force.

MERCURY

Mercury is the planet closest to the Sun. It races around our star, gathering information and translating it to the rest of the system. Mercury represents your capacity to understand the desires of your own will and to translate those desires into action.

MERCURY

In other words it is the planet of mind and the power of communication. Through Mercury we develop an ability to think, write, speak, and observe—to become aware of the world around us. It colors our attitudes and vision of the world, as well as our capacity to communicate our inner responses to the outside world. Some people who have serious disabilities in their power of verbal communication have often wrongly been described as people lacking intelligence.

Although this planet (and its position in the horoscope) indicates your power to communicate your thoughts and perceptions to the world, intelligence is something deeper. Intelligence is distributed throughout all the planets. It is the relationship of the planets to each other that truly describes what we call intelligence. Mercury rules speaking, language, mathematics, draft and design, students, messengers, young people, offices, teachers, and any pursuits where the mind of man has wings.

VENUS

Venus is beauty. It symbolizes the harmony and radiance of a rare and elusive quality: beauty itself. It is refinement and delicacy, softness and charm. In astrology it indicates grace, balance, and the aesthetic sense. Where Venus is we see beauty, a gentle drawing in of energy and the need for satisfaction and completion. It is a special touch that finishes off rough edges.

VENUS

Venus is the planet of sensitivity and affection, and it is always the place for that other elusive phenomenon: love. Venus describes our sense of what is beautiful and loving. Poorly developed, it is vulgar, tasteless, and self-indulgent. But its ideal is the flame of spiritual love—Aphrodite, goddess of love, and the sweetness and power of personal beauty.

MARS

Mars is raw, crude energy. The planet next to Earth but outward from the Sun is a fiery red sphere that charges through the horoscope with force and fury. It represents the way you reach out for new adventure and new experience. It is energy drive, initiative, courage, daring. It is the power to start something and see it through. It can be thoughtless, cruel and wild, angry and hostile, causing cuts, burns, scalds, wounds. It can stab its way through a chart, or it can be the symbol of healthy spirited adventure, well-channeled constructive power to begin and keep up the drive.

MARS

If you have trouble starting things, if you lack the get-up-and-go to start the ball rolling, if you lack aggressiveness and self-confidence, chances are there's another planet influencing your Mars. Mars rules soldiers, butchers, surgeons, salespeople—in general any field that requires daring, bold skill, operational technique, or self-promotion.

JUPITER

Jupiter is the largest planet of the solar system. Planet Jupiter rules good luck and good cheer, health, wealth, optimism, happiness, success, joy. It is the symbol of opportunity and always opens the way for new possibilities in your life. It rules exuberance, enthusiasm, wisdom, knowledge, generosity, and all forms of expansion in general. It rules actors, statesmen, clerics, professional people, religion, publishing, and the distribution of many people over large areas.

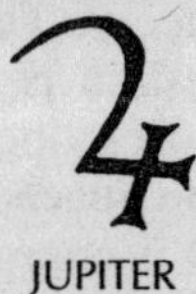

JUPITER

Sometimes Jupiter makes you think you deserve everything, and you become sloppy, wasteful, careless and rude, prodigal and lawless, in the illusion that nothing can ever go wrong. Then there is the danger of your showing overconfidence, exaggeration, undependability, and overindulgence.

Jupiter is the minimization of limitation and the emphasis on spirituality and potential. It is the thirst for knowledge and higher learning.

SATURN

Saturn circles our system in dark splendor with its mysterious rings, forcing us to be awakened to whatever we have neglected in the past. It will present real puzzles and problems to be solved, causing delays, obstacles, and hindrances. By doing so, Saturn stirs our own sensitivity to those areas where we are laziest.

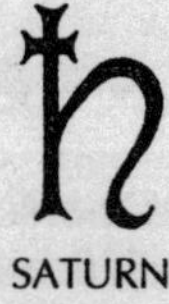

SATURN

Here we must patiently develop method, and only through painstaking effort can our ends be achieved. It brings order to a horoscope and imposes reason just where we are feeling least reasonable. By creating limitations and boundary, Saturn shows the consequences of being human and demands that we accept the changing cycles inevitable in human life. Saturn rules time, old age, and sobriety. It can bring depression, gloom, jealousy, and greed, or serious acceptance of responsibilities out of which success will develop. With Saturn there is nothing to do but face facts. It rules laborers, stones, granite, rocks, and crystals.

THE OUTER PLANETS: URANUS, NEPTUNE, PLUTO

Uranus, Neptune, and Pluto are the outer planets. They liberate human beings from cultural conditioning, and in that sense are the lawbreakers. In early times it was thought that Saturn was the last planet of the solar system—the outer limit beyond which we could never go. The discovery of the next three planets beyond Saturn ushered in new phases of human history, revolution, and technology.

URANUS

Uranus rules unexpected change, upheaval, revolution. It is the symbol of total independence and asserts the freedom of an individual from all restriction and restraint. It is a breakthrough planet and indicates talent, originality, and genius in a horoscope. It usually causes last-minute reversals and changes of plan, unwanted separations, accidents, catastrophes, and eccentric behavior. It can add irrational rebelliousness and perverse bohemianism to a personality or a streak of unaffected brilliance in science and art.

URANUS

Uranus rules technology, aviation, and all forms of electrical and electronic advancement. It governs great leaps forward and topsy-turvy situations, and always turns things around at the last minute. Its effects are difficult to predict, since it rules sudden last-minute decisions and events that come like lightning out of the blue.

NEPTUNE

Neptune dissolves existing reality the way the sea erodes the cliffs beside it. Its effects are subtle like the ringing of a buoy's bell in the fog. It suggests a reality higher than definition can usually describe. It awakens a sense of higher responsibility often causing guilt, worry, anxieties, or delusions. Neptune is associated with all forms of escape and can make things seem a certain way so convincingly that you are absolutely sure of something that eventually turns out to be quite different.

NEPTUNE

It is the planet of illusion and therefore governs the invisible realms that lie beyond our ordinary minds, beyond our simple factual ability to prove what is "real." Treachery, deceit, disillusionment, and disappointment are linked to Neptune. It describes a vague reality that promises eternity and the divine, yet in a manner so complex that we cannot really fathom it at all. At its worst Neptune is a cheap intoxicant; at its best it is the poetry, music, and inspiration of the higher planes of spiritual love. It has dominion over movies, photographs, and much of the arts.

PLUTO

Pluto lies at the outpost of our system and therefore rules finality in a horoscope—the final closing of chapters in your life, the passing of major milestones and points of development from which there is no return. It is a final wipeout, a closeout, an evacuation. It is a subtle but powerful catalyst in all transformations that occur. It creates, destroys, then recreates. Sometimes Pluto starts its influence with a minor event or insignificant incident that might even go unnoticed. Slowly but surely, little by little, everything changes, until at last there has been a total transformation in the area of your life where Pluto has been operating. It rules mass thinking and the trends that society first rejects, then adopts, and finally outgrows.

PLUTO

Pluto rules the dead and the underworld—all the powerful forces of creation and destruction that go on all the time beneath, around, and above us. It can bring a lust for power with strong obsessions.

It is the planet that rules the metamorphosis of the caterpillar into a butterfly, for it symbolizes the capacity to change totally and forever a person's lifestyle, way of thought, and behavior.

THE MOON

Exactly how does the Moon affect us psychologically and psychically? We know it controls the tides. We understand how it affects blood rhythm and body tides, together with all the chemical fluids that constitute our physical selves. Astronauts have walked upon its surface, and our scientists are now studying and analyzing data that will help determine the age of our satellite, its origin, and makeup.

THE MOON

But the true mystery of that small body as it circles our Earth each month remains hidden. Is it really a dead, lifeless body that has no light or heat of its own, reflecting only what the gigantic Sun throws toward it? Is it a sensitive reflecting device, which translates the blinding, billowing energy from our star into a language our bodies can understand?

In astrology, the Moon is said to rule our feelings, customs, habits, and moods. As the Sun is the constant, ever shining source of life in daytime, the Moon is our nighttime mother, lighting up the night and swiftly moving, reflecting ever so rapidly the changing phases of behavior and personality. If we feel happy or joyous, or we notice certain habits and repetitive feelings that bubble up from our dark centers then vanish as quickly as they appeared, very often it is the position of the Moon that describes these changes.

THE MOON IN ALL SIGNS

The Moon moves quickly through the Zodiac, that is, through all twelve signs of our Sun's apparent path. It stays in each sign for about 2¼ days. During its brief stay in a given sign, the moods and responses of people are always colored by the nature of that sign, any planets located there at that time, or any other heavenly bodies placed in such a way that the Moon will pick up their "vibration" as well. It's astonishing to observe how clearly the Moon changes people's interests and involvements as it moves along.

The following section gives brief descriptions of the Moon's influence in each sign.

MOON IN ARIES

There's excitement in the air. Some new little thing appears, and people are quick and full of energy and enterprise, ready for something new and turning on to a new experience. There's not much patience or hesitation, doubt or preoccupation with guilty self-damning recriminations. What's needed is action. People feel like putting their plans into operation. Pleasure and adventure characterize the mood, and it's time for things to change, pick up, improve. Confidence, optimism, positive feeling pervade the air. Sick people take a turn for the better. Life stirs with a feeling of renewal. People react bravely to challenges, with a sense of courage and dynamism. Self-reliance is the key word, and people minimize their problems and maximize the power to exercise freedom of the will. There is an air of abruptness and shortness of consideration, as people are feeling the courage of their convictions to do something for themselves. Feelings are strong and intuitive, and the mood is idealistic and freedom-oriented.

MOON IN TAURUS

Here the mood is just as pleasure loving, but less idealistic. Now the concerns are more materialistic, money-oriented, down-to-earth. The mood is stable, diligent, thoughtful, deliberate. It is a time when feelings are rich and deep, with a profound appreciation of the good things the world has to offer and the pleasures of the sensations. It is a period when people's minds are serious, realistic, and devoted to the increases and improvements of property and possessions and acquisition of wealth. There is a conservative tone, and people are fixed in their views, needing to add to their stability in every way. Assessment of assets, criticism, and the execution of tasks are strong involvements of the Taurus Moon when financial matters demand attention. It is devotion to security on a financial and emotional level. It is a fertile time, when ideas can begin to take root and grow.

MOON IN GEMINI

There is a rapid increase in movement. People are going places, exchanging ideas and information. Gossip and news travel fast under a Gemini Moon, because people are naturally involved with communication, finding out things from some, passing on information to others. Feelings shift to a mental level now, and people feel and say things that are sincere at the moment but lack the root and depth to endure much beyond the moment. People are involved with short-term engagements, quick trips. There is a definite need for changing the scene. You'll find people flirtatious and talkative, experimental and easygoing, falling into encounters they hadn't planned on. The mind is quick and active, with powers of writing and speaking greatly enhanced. Radio, television, letters, newspapers, magazines are in the spotlight with the Moon in Gemini, and new chances pop up for self-expression, with new people involved. Relatives and neighbors are tuned in to you and you to them. Take advantage of this fluidity of mind. It can rescue you from worldly involvements and get you into new surroundings for a short while.

MOON IN CANCER

Now you'll see people heading home. People turn their attention inward to their place of residence under a Cancer Moon. The active, changeable moods of yesterday vanish, and people settle in as if they were searching for a nest of security. Actually people are retiring, seeking to find peace and quiet within themselves. That's what they're feeling when they prefer to stay home rather than go out with a crowd of people to strange places. They need the warmth and comfort of the family and hearth. Maybe they feel anxious and insecure from the hustle and bustle of the workaday world. Maybe they're just tired. But it's definitely a time of tender need for emotional sustenance. It's a time for nostalgia and returning to times and places that once nourished deeply. Thoughts of parents, family, and old associations come to people. The heritage of their family ties holds them strongly now. These are personal needs that must be fed. Moods are deep and mysterious and sometimes sad. People are silent, psychic, and imaginative during this period. It's a fruitful time when people respond to love, food, and all the comforts of the inner world.

MOON IN LEO

The shift is back out in the world, and people are born again, like kids. They feel zestful, passionate, exuberant and need plenty of attention. They're interested in having a good time, enjoying themselves, and the world of entertainment takes over for a while. Places of amusement, theaters, parties, sprees, a whole gala of glamorous events, characterize this stage of the Moon's travel. Gracious, lavish hosting and a general feeling of buoyancy and flamboyance are in the air. It's a time of sunny, youthful fun when people are in the mood to take chances and win. The approach is direct, ardent, and strong. Bossy, authoritarian feelings predominate, and people throw themselves forward for all they're worth. Flattery is rampant, but the ego is vibrant and flourishing with the kiss of life, romance, and love. Speculation is indicated, and it's usually a time to go out and try your hand at love. Life is full and rich as a summer meadow, and feelings are warm.

MOON IN VIRGO

The party's over. Eyelashes are on the table. This is a time for cleaning up after the merrymakers have gone home. People are now concerned with sobering up and getting personal affairs straight, clearing up any confusions or undefined feelings from the night before, and generally attending to the practical business of doctoring up after the party. People are back at work, concerned with necessary, perhaps tedious tasks—paying bills, fixing and adjusting things, and generally purifying their lives, streamlining their affairs, and involving themselves with work and service to the community. Purity is the key word in personal habits, diet, and emotional needs. Propriety and coolness take the place of yesterday's devil-may-care passion, and the results are a detached, inhibited period under a Virgo

Moon. Feelings are not omitted; they are merely subjected to the scrutiny of the mind and thus purified. Health comes to the fore, and people are interested in clearing up problems.

MOON IN LIBRA

Here there is a mood of harmony, when people strive to join with other people in a bond of peace and justice. At this time people need relationships and often seek the company of others in a smooth-flowing feeling of love, beauty, and togetherness. People make efforts to understand other people, and though it's not the best time to make decisions, many situations keep presenting themselves from the outside to change plans and offer new opportunities. There is a general search for accord between partners, and differences are explored as similarities are shared. The tone is concilatory, and the mood is one of cooperation, patience, and tolerance. People do not generally feel independent, and sometimes this need to share or lean on others disturbs them. It shouldn't. This is the moment for uniting and sharing, for feeling a mutual flow of kindness and tenderness between people. The air is ingratiating and sometimes lacks stamina, courage, and a consistent, definite point of view. But it is a time favoring the condition of beauty and the development of all forms of art.

MOON IN SCORPIO

This is not a mood of sharing. It's driving, intense, brooding—full of passion and desire. Its baser aspects are the impulses of selfishness, cruelty, and the pursuit of animal drives and appetites. There is a craving for excitement and a desire to battle and win in a bloodthirsty war for survival. It is competitive and ruthless, sarcastic and easily bruised, highly sexual and touchy, without being especially tender. Retaliation, jealousy, and revenge can be felt too during this time. Financial involvements, debts, and property issues arise now. Powerful underworld forces are at work here, and great care is needed to transform ignorance into wisdom, to keep the mind from descending into the lower depths. During the Moon's stay in Scorpio we contact the dark undercurrents swirling around and get in touch with a magical part of our natures. Interest lies in death, inheritance, and the powers of rebirth and regeneration.

MOON IN SAGITTARIUS

Here the mind climbs out of the depths, and people are involved with the higher, more enlightened, and conscious facets of their personality. There's a renewed interest in learning, education, and philosophy, and a new involvement with ethics, morals, national and international issues: a concern with looking for a better way to live. It's a time of general improvement, with people feeling more deeply hopeful and optimistic. They are dreaming of new places, new possibilities, new horizons. They are emerging from the abyss and leaving the past behind, with their eyes gazing toward the new horizon. They decide to travel, or renew their contacts with those far away. They question their religious beliefs and investigate new areas of metaphysical inquiry. It's a time for adventure, sports, playing the field—people have their eye on new possibilities. They are bored with depression and details. They feel restless and optimistic, joyous and delighted to be alive. Thoughts revolve around adventure, travel, liberation.

MOON IN CAPRICORN

When the Moon moves into Capricorn, things slow down considerably. People require a quiet, organized, and regularized condition. Their minds are sober and realistic, and they are methodically going about bringing their dreams and plans into reality. They are more conscious of what is standing between them and success, and during this time they take definite, decisive steps to remove any obstacles from their path. They are cautious, suspicious, sometimes depressed, discouraged, and gloomy, but they are more determined than ever to accomplish their tasks. They take care of responsibilities now, wake up to facts, and wrestle with problems and dilemmas of this world. They are politically minded and concerned with social convention now, and it is under a Capricorn Moon that conditioning and conformity elicit the greatest responses. People are moderate and serious and surround themselves with what is most familiar. They want predictable situations and need time to think deeply and deliberately about all issues. It's a time for planning.

MOON IN AQUARIUS

Spontaneity replaces the sober predictability of yesterday. Now events, people, and situations pop up, and you take advantage of unsought opportunities and can expect the unexpected. Surprises, reversals, and shifts in plans mark this period. There is a resurgence of optimism, and things you wouldn't expect to happen suddenly do. What you were absolutely sure was going to happen simply doesn't. Here there is a need for adventure born from a healthy curiosity that characterizes people's moods. Unrealistic utopias are dreamed of, and it is from such idealistic dreams that worlds of the future are built. There is a renewed interest in friendship, comradeship, community, and union on high planes of mental and spiritual companionship. People free each other from grudges or long-standing deadlocks, and there is a hopeful joining of hands in a spirit of love and peace. People don't feel like sticking to previous plans, and they must be able to respond to new situations at the last minute. People need freedom. Groups of people come together and meet, perhaps for a common purpose of having dinner or hearing music, and leave knowing each other better.

MOON IN PISCES

Flashes of brilliant insight and mysterious knowledge characterize the Moon's passage in Pisces. Sometimes valuable "truths" seem to emerge which, later in the light of day, turn out to be false. This is a time of poetry, intuition, and music, when worldly realities can be the most illusory and unreliable of all. There are often feelings of remorse, guilt, or sorrow connected with a Pisces Moon—sorrow from the childhood or family or past. Confusion, anxiety, worry, and a host of imagined pains and sorrows may drag you down until you cannot move or think. Often there are connections with hospitals, prisons, alcohol, drugs, and lower forms of escape. It is a highly emotional time, when the feelings and compassion for humanity and all people everywhere rise to the surface of your being. Mysteries of society and the soul now rise to demand solutions, but often the riddles posed during this period have many answers that all seem right. It is more a time for inner reflection than positive action. It is a time when poetry and music float to the surface of the being, and for the creative artist it is the richest source of inspiration.

MOON TABLES

CORRECTION FOR NEW YORK TIME, FIVE HOURS WEST OF GREENWICH

Atlanta, Boston, Detroit, Miami, Washington,
Montreal, Ottawa, Toronto, Bogota,
Havana, Lima, Santiago........................Same time

Chicago, New Orleans, Houston, Winnipeg,
Churchill, Mexico City ....Deduct 1 hour

Albuquerque, Denver, Phoenix, El Paso,
Edmonton, Helena........................Deduct 2 hours

Los Angeles, San Francisco, Reno,
Portland, Seattle, Vancouver ....Deduct 3 hours

Honolulu, Anchorage, Fairbanks, Kodiak... Deduct 5 hours

Nome, Samoa, Tonga, Midway ....Deduct 6 hours

Halifax, Bermuda, San Juan, Caracas,
La Paz, Barbados ....Add 1 hour

St. John's, Brasilia, Rio de Janeiro,
Sao Paulo, Buenos Aires, Montevideo.......Add 2 hours

Azores, Cape Verde Islands...................Add 3 hours

Canary Islands, Madeira, Reykjavik ....Add 4 hours

London, Paris, Amsterdam, Madrid, Lisbon,
Gibraltar, Belfast, Rabat ....Add 5 hours

Frankfurt, Rome, Oslo, Stockholm, Prague,
Belgrade....................................Add 6 hours

Bucharest, Beirut, Tel Aviv, Athens, Istanbul,
Cairo, Cape Town, Johannesburg ....Add 7 hours

Moscow, Leningrad, Baghdad, Addis Ababa,
Dhahran, Nairobi, Teheran, Zanzibar ....Add 8 hours

Bombay, Calcutta, Sri Lanka .... Add 10 ½ hours

Hong Kong, Shanghai, Manila, Peking,
Perth ....Add 13 hours

Tokyo, Okinawa, Darwin, Pusan ....Add 14 hours

Sydney, Melbourne, Port Moresby, Guam ....Add 15 hours

Auckland, Wellington, Suva, Wake...........Add 17 hours

1999 MOON SIGN DATES—NEW YORK TIME

JANUARY		FEBRUARY		MARCH	
Day Moon Enters		Day Moon Enters		Day Moon Enters	
1. Cancer	3:16 am	1. Virgo	8:38 pm	1. Virgo	5:06 am
2. Cancer		2. Virgo		2. Virgo	
3. Leo	5:32 am	3. Virgo		3. Libra	1:35 pm
4. Leo		4. Libra	4:57 am	4. Libra	
5. Virgo	10:50 am	5. Libra		5. Libra	
6. Virgo		6. Scorp.	4:07 pm	6. Scorp.	0:23 am
7. Libra	7:54 pm	7. Scorp.		7. Scorp.	
8. Libra		8. Scorp.		8. Sagitt.	0:47 pm
9. Libra		9. Sagitt.	4:39 am	9. Sagitt.	
10. Scorp.	7:50 am	10. Sagitt.		10. Sagitt.	
11. Scorp.		11. Capric.	4:11 pm	11. Capric.	0:55 am
12. Sagitt.	8:24 pm	12. Capric.		12. Capric.	
13. Sagitt.		13. Capric.		13. Aquar.	10:33 am
14. Sagitt.		14. Aquar.	0:58 am	14. Aquar.	
15. Capric.	7:30 am	15. Aquar.		15. Pisces	4:31 pm
16. Capric.		16. Pisces	6:41 am	16. Pisces	
17. Aquar.	4:12 pm	17. Pisces		17. Aries	7:14 pm
18. Aquar.		18. Aries	10:07 am	18. Aries	
19. Pisces	10:41 pm	19. Aries		19. Taurus	8:10 pm
20. Pisces		20. Taurus	0:30 pm	20. Taurus	
21. Pisces		21. Taurus		21. Gemini	9:06 pm
22. Aries	3:26 am	22. Gemini	2:55 pm	22. Gemini	
23. Aries		23. Gemini		23. Cancer	11:34 pm
24. Taurus	6:53 am	24. Cancer	6:10 pm	24. Cancer	
25. Taurus		25. Cancer		25. Cancer	
26. Gemini	9:30 am	26. Leo	10:45 pm	26. Leo	4:23 am
27. Gemini		27. Leo		27. Leo	
28. Cancer	11:58 am	28. Leo		28. Virgo	11:35 am
29. Cancer				29. Virgo	
30. Leo	3:17 pm			30. Libra	8:50 pm
31. Leo				31. Libra	

Summer time to be considered where applicable.

1999 MOON SIGN DATES—NEW YORK TIME

APRIL		MAY		JUNE	
Day Moon Enters		**Day Moon Enters**		**Day Moon Enters**	
1. Libra		1. Scorp.		1. Capric.	
2. Scorp.	7:50 am	2. Sagitt.	2:37 am	2. Capric.	
3. Scorp.		3. Sagitt.		3. Aquar.	8:38 am
4. Sagitt.	8:08 pm	4. Capric.	3:13 pm	4. Aquar.	
5. Sagitt.		5. Capric.		5. Pisces	6:02 pm
6. Sagitt.		6. Capric.		6. Pisces	
7. Capric.	8:40 am	7. Aquar.	2:41 am	7. Pisces	
8. Capric.		8. Aquar.		8. Aries	0:09 am
9. Aquar.	7:25 pm	9. Pisces	11:17 am	9. Aries	
10. Aquar.		10. Pisces		10. Taurus	2:44 am
11. Aquar.		11. Aries	3:54 pm	11. Taurus	
12. Pisces	2:36 am	12. Aries		12. Gemini	2:49 am
13. Pisces		13. Taurus	4:57 pm	13. Gemini	
14. Aries	5:47 am	14. Taurus		14. Cancer	2:15 am
15. Aries		15. Gemini	4:08 pm	15. Cancer	
16. Taurus	6:08 am	16. Gemini		16. Leo	3:08 am
17. Taurus		17. Cancer	3:40 pm	17. Leo	
18. Gemini	5:40 am	18. Cancer		18. Virgo	7:13 am
19. Gemini		19. Leo	5:38 pm	19 Virgo	
20. Cancer	6:28 am	20. Leo		20. Libra	3:11 pm
21. Cancer		21. Virgo	11:16 pm	21. Libra	
22. Leo	10:07 am	22. Virgo		22. Libra	
23. Leo		23. Virgo		23. Scorp.	2:19 am
24. Virgo	5:05 pm	24. Libra	8:30 am	24. Scorp.	
25. Virgo		25. Libra		25. Sagitt.	2:52 pm
26. Virgo		26. Scorp.	8:06 pm	26. Sagitt.	
27. Libra	2:47 am	27. Scorp.		27. Sagitt.	
28. Libra		28. Scorp.		28. Capric.	3:13 am
29. Scorp.	2:14 pm	29. Sagitt.	8:38 am	29. Capric.	
30. Scorp.		30. Sagitt.		30. Aquar.	2:20 pm
		31. Capric.	9:07 pm		

Summer time to be considered where applicable.

1999 MOON SIGN DATES—NEW YORK TIME

JULY Day Moon Enters		AUGUST Day Moon Enters		SEPTEMBER Day Moon Enters	
1. Aquar.		1. Aries	11:48 am	1. Taurus	
2. Pisces	11:35 pm	2. Aries		2. Gemini	0:26 am
3. Pisces		3. Taurus	4:10 pm	3. Gemini	
4. Pisces		4. Taurus		4. Cancer	3:11 am
5. Aries	6:22 am	5. Gemini	6:58 pm	5. Cancer	
6. Aries		6. Gemini		6. Leo	6:30 am
7. Taurus	10:23 am	7. Cancer	8:54 pm	7. Leo	
8. Taurus		8. Cancer		8. Virgo	10:58 am
9. Gemini	0:01 pm	9. Leo	10:57 pm	9. Virgo	
10. Gemini		10. Leo		10. Libra	5:17 pm
11. Cancer	0:28 pm	11. Leo		11. Libra	
12. Cancer		12. Virgo	2:23 am	12. Libra	
13. Leo	1:27 pm	13. Virgo		13. Scorp.	2:09 am
14. Leo		14. Libra	8:25 am	14. Scorp.	
15. Virgo	4:40 pm	15. Libra		15. Sagitt.	1:36 pm
16. Virgo		16. Scorp.	5:41 pm	16. Sagitt.	
17. Libra	11:20 pm	17. Scorp.		17. Sagitt.	
18. Libra		18. Scorp.		18. Capric.	2:14 am
19. Libra		19. Sagitt.	5:33 am	19. Capric.	
20. Scorp.	9:31 am	20. Sagitt.		20. Aquar.	1:39 pm
21. Scorp.		21. Capric.	6:00 pm	21. Aquar.	
22. Sagitt.	9:49 pm	22. Capric.		22. Pisces	9:52 pm
23. Sagitt.		23. Capric.		23. Pisces	
24. Sagitt.		24. Aquar.	4:50 am	24. Pisces	
25. Capric.	10:09 am	25. Aquar.		25. Aries	2:35 am
26. Capric.		26. Pisces	0:51 pm	26. Aries	
27. Aquar.	8:55 pm	27. Pisces		27. Taurus	4:52 am
28. Aquar.		28. Aries	6:10 pm	28. Taurus	
29. Aquar.		29. Aries		29. Gemini	6:22 am
30. Pisces	5:28 am	30. Taurus	9:42 pm	30. Gemini	
31. Pisces		31. Taurus			

Summer time to be considered where applicable.

1999 MOON SIGN DATES—NEW YORK TIME

OCTOBER		NOVEMBER		DECEMBER	
Day Moon Enters		Day Moon Enters		Day Moon Enters	
1. Cancer	8:32 am	1. Virgo	11:08 pm	1. Libra	0:30 pm
2. Cancer		2. Virgo		2. Libra	
3. Leo	0:14 pm	3. Virgo		3. Scorp.	10:36 pm
4. Leo		4. Libra	6:58 am	4. Scorp.	
5. Virgo	5:41 pm	5. Libra		5. Scorp.	
6. Virgo		6. Scorp.	4:47 pm	6. Sagitt.	10:28 am
7. Virgo		7. Scorp.		7. Sagitt.	
8. Libra	0:53 am	8. Scorp.		8. Capric.	11:15 pm
9. Libra		9. Sagitt.	4:16 am	9. Capric.	
10. Scorp.	10:02 am	10. Sagitt.		10. Capric.	
11. Scorp.		11. Capric.	5:01 pm	11. Aquar.	12:00 pm
12. Sagitt.	9:20 pm	12. Capric.		12. Aquar.	
13. Sagitt.		13. Capric.		13. Pisces	11:19 pm
14. Sagitt.		14. Aquar.	5:47 am	14. Pisces	
15. Capric.	10:05 am	15. Aquar.		15. Pisces	
16. Capric.		16. Pisces	4:22 pm	16. Aries	7:31 am
17. Aquar.	10:18 pm	17. Pisces		17. Aries	
18. Aquar.		18. Aries	10:58 pm	18. Taurus	11:46 am
19. Aquar.		19. Aries		19. Taurus	
20. Pisces	7:34 am	20. Aries		20. Gemini	0:40 pm
21. Pisces		21. Taurus	1:27 am	21. Gemini	
22. Aries	0:42 pm	22. Taurus		22. Cancer	11:53 am
23. Aries		23. Gemini	1:15 am	23. Cancer	
24. Taurus	2:26 pm	24. Gemini		24. Leo	11:33 am
25. Taurus		25. Cancer	0:30 am	25. Leo	
26. Gemini	2:34 pm	26. Cancer		26. Virgo	1:35 pm
27. Gemini		27. Leo	1:20 am	27. Virgo	
28. Cancer	3:10 pm	28. Leo		28. Libra	7:15 pm
29. Cancer		29. Virgo	5:12 am	29. Libra	
30. Leo	5:48 pm	30. Virgo		30. Libra	
31. Leo				31. Scorp.	4:37 am

Summer time to be considered where applicable.

1999 FISHING GUIDE

	Good	**Best**
January	3-4-5-17-24-28-30-31	1-2-9-29
February	1-2-3-16-23-27-28	8
March	1-2-3-10-28-29-30	4-5-17-24-31
April	16-22	1-2-3-9-27-28-29-30
May	2-3-8-15-22-29-30-31	1-27-28
June	13-20-25-26-27-30	1-2-7-28-29
July	1-6-13-25-28-29-30	20-26-27-31
August	11-19-23-24-25-26-29	4-27-28
September	2-9-17-22-25-26	23-24-27-28
October	22-23-24-26-27-31	2-9-17-21-25
November	16-20-23-24-29	8-21-22-25-26
December	7-16-20-21-22-24-25	19-23

1999 PLANTING GUIDE

	Aboveground Crops	**Root Crops**
January	1-20-21-25-29	2-8-9-10-11-12-16
February	17-21-25-26	4-5-6-7-8-12-13
March	20-21-24-25-31	4-5-6-7-11-12-16
April	17-21-27-28-29	1-2-3-4-8-9-12-13
May	18-19-25-26-27-28	1-5-6-10-14
June	14-15-21-22-23-24	1-2-6-7-10-11-29
July	18-19-20-21-22-26-27	3-4-8-12-31
August	15-16-17-18-22-23	4-5-8-9-27-28-31
September	11-12-13-14-18-19-23-24	1-4-5-27-28
October	10-11-12-16-17-21	2-8-25-29-30
November	8-12-13-17-18-21-22	5-6-7-25-26
December	9-10-14-15-19	2-3-4-5-23-29-30-31

	Pruning	**Weeds and Pests**
January	2-11-12	4-5-6-7-13-14
February	7-8	1-2-3-9-10-14-15
March	6-7-16	2-9-10-14
April	3-4-12-13	5-6-10-11-15
May	1-10	2-3-7-8-12-30-31
June	6-7	4-5-8-9-12
July	3-4-12-31	1-2-6-10-29
August	8-9-27-28	2-6-7-10-29-30
September	4-5	2-3-7-8-9-26-30
October	2-29-30	4-5-6-7-27-31
November	7-25-26	1-2-3-23-24-27-28-29-30
December	4-5-23-31	7-25-26-27-28

1999 PHASES OF THE MOON—NEW YORK TIME

New Moon	First Quarter	Full Moon	Last Quarter
Dec. 18 ('98)	Dec. 26 ('98)	Jan. 1	Jan. 9
Jan. 17	Jan. 24	Jan. 31	Feb. 8
Feb. 16	Feb. 22	March 2	March 10
March 17	March 24	March 31	April 8
April 15	April 22	April 30	May 8
May 15	May 22	May 30	June 6
June 13	June 20	June 28	July 6
July 12	July 20	July 28	Aug. 4
Aug. 11	Aug. 18	Aug. 26	Sept. 2
Sept. 9	Sept. 17	Sept. 25	Oct. 1
Oct. 9	Oct. 17	Oct. 24	Oct. 31
Nov. 7	Nov. 16	Nov. 23	Nov. 29
Dec. 7	Dec. 15	Dec. 22	Dec. 29

Each phase of the Moon lasts approximately seven to eight days, during which the Moon's shape gradually changes as it comes out of one phase and goes into the next.

There will be a partial solar eclipse during the New Moon phase on February 16 and August 11.

There will be a lunar eclipse during the Full Moon phase on July 28.

Use the Moon phases to connect you with your lucky numbers for this year. See the next page (page 112) and your lucky numbers.

LUCKY NUMBERS
FOR ARIES: 1999

Lucky numbers and astrology can be linked through the movements of the Moon. Each phase of the thirteen Moon cycles vibrates with a sequence of numbers for your Sign of the Zodiac over the course of the year. Using your lucky numbers is a fun system that connects you with tradition.

New Moon	First Quarter	Full Moon	Last Quarter
Dec. 18 ('98)	Dec. 26 ('98)	Jan. 1	Jan. 9
8 5 1 5	8 8 6 4	5 4 9 2	2 3 7 4
Jan. 17	Jan. 24	Jan. 31	Feb. 8
4 0 1 4	4 2 2 9	4 5 7 8	8 3 9 6
Feb. 16	Feb. 22	March 2	March 10
6 0 7 5	5 3 3 8	1 0 2 6	6 3 9 4
March 17	March 24	March 31	April 8
4 7 5 7	5 5 1 3	3 0 8 5	5 2 6 0
April 15	April 22	April 30	May 8
0 9 7 2	1 7 9 0	4 5 2 8	8 3 6 4
May 15	May 22	May 30	June 6
4 2 0 1	6 8 9 4	8 0 7 2	2 5 3 3
June 13	June 20	June 28	July 6
3 0 9 6	8 5 6 1	5 4 8 9	2 9 9 7
July 12	July 20	July 28	August 4
7 6 3 5	6 1 9 6	2 7 0 8	8 8 6 5
August 11	August 18	August 26	Sept. 2
6 2 4 5	5 9 0 7	6 9 5 3	3 0 9 6
Sept. 9	Sept. 17	Sept. 25	Oct. 1
6 8 9 4	4 1 7 3	0 9 4 4	2 1 7 9
Oct. 9	Oct. 17	Oct. 24	Oct. 31
9 1 5 2	2 8 3 0	7 7 5 4	5 1 3 4
Nov. 7	Nov. 16	Nov. 23	Nov. 29
4 8 5 2	6 9 7 1	7 8 7 4	4 6 7 2
Dec. 7	Dec. 15	Dec. 22	Dec. 29
2 8 5 9	9 3 1 6	5 3 9 2	8 3 7 4

ARIES
YEARLY FORECAST: 1999

Forecast for 1999 Concerning Business
Prospects, Financial Affairs, Health,
Travel, Employment, Love and Marriage
for Persons Born with the Sun
in the Zodiacal Sign of Aries,
March 21–April 20.

This year promises to be a challenging and fulfilling one for those of you born under the influence of the Sun in the zodiacal sign of Aries, whose ruler is Mars, the planet of drive and initiative. There will be opportunities this year to put life on a much firmer footing all around. You arc likcly to bc making key decisions which will shape your future for a long period ahead. After several years of having had to make personal sacrifices of one kind and another, much greater personal fulfillment is highlighted in 1999. Your earning capacity also is likely to be strengthened this year. You may need to cut back on luxury spending somewhat, but the overall picture indicates greater financial success and security for the future. Challenges of a more personal nature are likely to inspire you. This will not be a year for rushing in blindly where new ventures are concerned, however. Patience and planning together are more likely to ensure success. Where business matters are concerned, do not expect opportunities simply to fall into your lap. You are likely to have to work hard to find a break or a new opening. Endurance will be your key to success here, and it is likely to be important to keep an eye to the future. Financially, it should be easier to make money this year once you find your niche. However, overspending can be a problem. You are advised to set a firm budget early in the year and stick to it. As with business prospects, it is likely to be more important this year to look to the long-term future where finances are concerned. In regard to health, your tendency to work too hard to achieve your aims can potentially leave you feeling washed out a lot of the time. It is advisable to plan your life so that much of your spare time is given over to rest and relaxation. This way you will have a chance to recharge your batteries on a regular basis and avoid creating or exacerbating problems through too much stress and strain. Where travel is concerned, you are likely to undertake overseas voyages more in relation to work than in connection with personal and social plans. Routine occupational affairs are likely to be easier going this year, largely due to the lack of contention in the work place. Where marriage and romance are concerned, you are likely to feel less disposed toward sharing and caring than you have done in recent years. This is a year when you are likely to need more support and understanding from your partner as you go forth to fulfill your personal aims and ambitions.

Professional Aries people are advised to look a long way ahead into the future this year. New involvements are likely to be slow in coming to fruition. In fact, you are likely to have to work quite hard to make changes and find breakthroughs even where existing business interests are concerned. Patience is not a natural Aries trait, yet it will be important to work on developing a degree of it this year. If you are taking on a new role, bear in mind that it may take quite some time to start to feel that you really understand what is required of you. Markets are likely to need thorough testing before you invest in any major, new endeavor. The need to take your time where business matters are concerned cannot be overemphasized. Try not to be too quick to judge slow and gradual growth as a sign of failure. It is likely that truly worthwhile and substantial rewards can be reaped only in the longer term. This will probably become more obvious to you once the first quarter of the year has passed by. You are likely to be tempted to invest in unusual areas of business or in ventures that seem ahead of their time. A desire to keep your feet firmly on the ground means that you may not feel so able merely to trust your intuition and leap at one of the extraordinary opportunities that will crop up during the first few months of the year. You probably will be wise in the fall to give ventures that seem too good to be true a wide berth until you have more solid, empirical information and clear statistics to go on. You Aries people involved in banking and other big business and those with interests in the plumbing and building trades are likely to win larger contracts and meet with considerable success between March 2 and August 29.

Where finances are concerned, this will not be a year for taking too many big risks. On the one hand, you appear to have fortune on your side, making it easier to earn money in larger quantities more quickly. On the other hand, you are also at risk this year of spending too much too fast. The key to your success is to pace yourself. Gains made during the summer months are probably best invested right away or else utilized to pay off any existing debts. During the period between August 25 and October 23 everything in relation to money is likely to move more slowly. This means that property transactions can be delayed, perhaps due to a lack of easy cash flow from the other person involved. Payments due to you also can be delayed for one reason or another during this period. It will be well to plan ahead from the start of the year. Aim to maintain a surplus of funds in your bank account so that you can easily cover periods when you are awaiting payments that are slower than you would normally expect. The overall emphasis this year will be on working to build up your future financial security. It will be an ideal year for opening up a savings account to which you are able to make regular payments. It does not necessarily matter if your contributions are small. The accent is more on gradual accumulation of wealth.

Where health matters are concerned, the focus is likely to be more on your partner's health than on your own during the early part of the year. The worry and burden of this situation should dwindle away quite soon, however, as your loved one completes this final period of healing and regains better health. Be careful not to burn yourself out in relation to your own hectic pace of life, however. Freed from certain restrictions on your personal plans this year, you are likely to want to make up for lost time; but it is not wise to try to do too much too soon. Aim for even and steady progress. Making more of an effort to keep your home tidy is likely to be beneficial to your overall health also, trivial as it may seem. You are likely to have more chance to be both mentally calm and physically relaxed if you come home regularly to orderly and peaceful surroundings. You Aries people with constantly noisy neighbors may find that the desire to move to somewhere more serene and tranquil is likely to become more pressing. Doing so should bring a sense of relief and the ability to relax more, both of which ought to help to remove tension and enhance your overall sense of well-being.

Travel opportunities this year are most likely to crop up in connection with work and professional matters. Unless you plan ahead, you may not find time to get away for an extended vacation break. Weekends spent in a different environment from your usual surroundings can compensate in that case. The period between September 3 and October 17 is most favored for long-distance travel, but prepare well ahead for any trip made during this time. Rushing around at the last minute may lead to some kind of calamity that can easily be avoided if you have planned thoroughly.

Where routine occupational affairs are concerned, it should be mostly a case of business as usual this year. Colleagues are likely to be quite laid-back. Any opposition from them is probably going to have most to do with differing attitudes to the work itself. You Aries people like to push ahead and get things done. Associates at work probably will not have your kind of enthusiasm at the start of the year. Give them time, as this tendency is likely to fade away as the months roll on. Any sense that overall change is afoot in your area of work is probably accurate. However, you are unlikely to see massive changes taking place overnight in 1999. This looks like more of a long haul, a gradual process.

Where love and marriage are concerned, this will be a year when the concept of togetherness is not likely to mean so much to you. As you work to fulfill your own personal ambitions, a greater sense of personal strength should develop, making you even more self-sufficient than usual. You can, however, find yourself feeling more isolated and lonely as a greater degree of responsibility keeps you away from those you have been closest to. Long-term partners will tend to be understanding and provide the kind of comforting support you need when time is short and you do not want to go through lengthy explanations or debates. For you single Aries people, the accent this year will be more on personal interests and achievements than on relationships. This does not mean, however, that there will be an entire lack of romantic involvement for you throughout the year. The periods between January 1 to 26 and June 4 to July 5 are likely to be especially fruitful for love and romance.

ARIES
DAILY FORECAST: 1999

1st Week/January 1–7

Friday January 1st. You are likely to begin this new year in a fairly serious mood. Plans for future travel may already be forming in your mind. It can be fun discussing these with close relatives. In fact, part of your plans may be a desire to visit those friends and kinsfolk that live a long way off or abroad. On this holiday, you can reflect on how much you have learned about yourself these last few years.

Saturday the 2nd. The mere idea of getting back into the swing of work is irritating. However, a boss or other important authority figure may be nagging you to get cracking. Your workplace seems to lack harmony and can appear quite ugly to your eyes. A partner seems to be in a bad mood just now, so take care not to quarrel over trifles. Just turn a deaf ear to provocative remarks.

Sunday the 3rd. Feelings of being stiff or sore can slow you down a lot. You may feel like just relaxing at home this morning. A parent can be quite demanding and a burden at times. Although you long to start on some personal hobby later in the day, you may find yourself uninspired. Young folks may bring in their friends and create chaos everywhere. Try to keep such gatherings from getting too noisy.

Monday the 4th. At last you can get a break from social and family matters and get on with your own interests. Studies and research projects that have been occupying you can be renewed with intensity. You can enjoy some serious reading and interesting conversations with a friend or a fellow student. News about a legal matter should settle your mind. An older relative may get in touch from overseas.

Tuesday the 5th. You should feel steadier and more in touch with your own needs. However, the problems of friends or loved ones can arouse your sympathy. This may mean giving up precious time to help them out. A spiritual group of people can help you to be more creative. An outing to the theater is likely to be a serious rather than a frivolous occasion. It can give you much food for thought.

Wednesday the 6th. This should be a far better day for professional matters. You may be inclined to make a few subtle alterations to the day-to-day running of your workplace. Although this can arouse some opposition, your boss seems to approve. All sorts of new ideas can present themselves now, as well as fresh insights into career situations. Your health may improve too.

Thursday the 7th. You may find that you have to cut back on your activities in order to get on with a task that has been hanging fire. Your interest in health matters is greater than usual. Feelings of consideration and benevolence may mean that you want to devote some time to people you know in the hospital or in an institution. Those of you with pets may tend to worry about them.

Weekly Summary

There seems to be some conflict in you just now in regard to home and family matters. This can be due to the fact that you don't feel quite up to doing all the little duties and taking on all the responsibilities you did in the past. Perhaps you would be wise to sit down and see where you can cut back. Other relatives should be encouraged to take on their share of duties too. But try to be tactful rather than forceful when dealing with the subject.

You may feel a great need to deal with the children and get them under some sort of control. They seem to be acting as if the place were just for them and their friends and you have no rights of your own. In fact, you seem to be feeling either guilty or martyred or both. Take some time to get on with your own interests and hobbies if you can. You will find that young ones respond to control better on Monday and leave you a bit more free.

The latter part of the week can be a good deal easier. You are likely to get down to some clearing out both at home and at work. It can be a good time to restructure your daily routines and habits from both a health and an efficiency standpoint. Try not to take on too much or promise to do more than you can manage.

2nd Week/January 8–14

Friday the 8th. Groups of spiritually minded friends can get you enthusiastic about a cause. You may find this a good day for some quite out-of-the-ordinary entertainment and activities. A partner can be full of bright ideas for a special night out. Or you can enjoy mulling over vacation plans and ideas together. You tend to feel caring and loving toward others and seek to please them.

Saturday the 9th. A boss seems to be getting you down. You can find yourself having to assume a position of leadership at work. Partners may tend to be grumpy and irritable at times. This doesn't do a lot for your own temper, so a few cross words can result. However, this should clear the air in the long run. Try to be as diplomatic as you can when it comes to a professional or legal matter.

Sunday the 10th. You seem to feel a bit hampered by a personal disability or ailment this morning. Or you may just not be in the mood to deal with other people's hang-ups. This can make you appear cold and rejecting, so don't be surprised if your partner gets into a bit of a sour mood. Later in the day you may hear some disturbing news about a friend. Get on the phone to find out how you can help.

Monday the 11th. Unexpected events can mean spending some of your savings or tapping into investments.

However, you seem ready to help out a friend with a business venture or other professional move. A party that comes up tonight can be a bonus for single Aries people. You can have an exciting encounter with someone attractive. However, don't count on its lasting very long at this stage.

Tuesday the 12th. Some good fortune can come from certain private investments. You may be delighted with your dividends and bonuses. Generally this is a very fortunate day for money matters and speculation. Some of you may find you are to receive a tax refund or benefit from some inheritance. Eating out and theatrical entertainment can be expensive but well worth every penny. Celebrate with your loved one.

Wednesday the 13th. Dreaming of faraway places can be fun, but you Aries people need more action and adventure. Some of you may decide to enroll on a course of spiritual enlightenment or a healing seminar. Unusual social events can be most enjoyable. You and a loved one seem inclined to be a bit outrageous at times. Your feelings can run deep over some idealistic cause, and you may recruit friends to join you.

Thursday the 14th. Foreign friends may turn up or get in contact out of the blue. This can really cheer and enliven you. A loved one can be a very stimulating friend and companion these days. You will feel very happy and enjoy being on your own more than usual. You may find that your previous efforts are now gaining some recognition publicly and professionally.

Weekly Summary

Although relationships and feelings are very much highlighted, you can find that things tend to be a bit strained at the start of the week. Despite all your efforts to be understanding, you may find a partner or loved one unresponsive, even downright ungrateful and quarrelsome. You need to see just why you are provoking this reaction. Maybe you have been too cool, withdrawn, and neglectful of late.

Money matters can take a real turn for the better just after the weekend. You can find this a good time to put certain schemes and plans into operation at last. Investments seem to be paying some good dividends. Generally this can be a good time to speculate a little with a few private deals and behind-the-scenes wheelings and dealings. Take care on Monday, however, when you may find that you have some sudden and unexpected expenses.

Some of you Aries people may now be considering enrolling in various kinds of courses or studies. You are thinking deeply and seriously about life these days and may be attracted to various self-help or healing weekends and courses. Many of you will be interested in ways of getting your ideals into action now.

3rd Week/January 15–21

Friday the 15th. Don't get too carried away with ideas and plans for the future. You are sure to be very energetic and enthusiastic, which can help you to get to grips with a legal matter that may need a prompt decision. A partnership is likely to prove lively but rewarding although you may not always see eye-to-eye. You can get other people inspired with your own visions and ideals.

Saturday the 16th. Maybe you will come down to earth with a bump now. Practical matters need to be sorted out without further delay. Professional situations seem to be speeding up. This may be helped by the fact that you have a new car or other piece of equipment to help you out. This can be a good day for buying any items you need for the office, but take care not to be too impulsive. Try to find some bargains.

Sunday the 17th. Although others seem to be set against some of your professional dreams, your faith in yourself now can be rewarded by success. This can be a very good day for you, especially if you have been waiting for some results from an exam or interview. Some of you may start a new job tomorrow. This is a good day to prepare, sort out your personal needs, and deal with practical issues.

Monday the 18th. Now it can seem as if many of the goals you dream about are becoming realities. This can be a good time for meeting with groups of people who want to help you with various charitable or spiritual matters. You are ready to get going with various reforms and changes, especially in educational matters. The day will be good for working with a team of like-minded friends and engaging in cooperative activities.

Tuesday the 19th. Your diplomatic and practical actions will help out with a tricky group situation. Although it goes against the grain, you can help to avert an angry scene with a partner by using some self-control. This can be a time for making a few compromises over your personal demands and desires and respecting the needs of others which are equally valid. You will find doing so advantageous in the long run.

Wednesday the 20th. You may have to take some time off to deal with a bit of private study or research. However, it can turn out to be a frustrating task. Matters beyond your control will hold you up. You will need to take care when traveling, as you can find yourself caught up in a massive traffic jam. Don't allow students or teachers to manipulate and control you. You must make your own decisions.

Thursday the 21st. This can turn out to be a very good day for professional activities. You can find that a letter, some private communication, or a deal made behind closed doors turns out to be most advantageous. A younger person can give you some good tips. Salespeople, especially those traveling, will find that hospitals and privately run institutions are good targets for your sales pitch.

Weekly Summary

You may be involved in learning some new techniques or dealing with newly acquired machinery at work. However, although this may mean making extra effort, you are likely to benefit in the long run. Your leadership qualities may be called upon if any disputes arise. You are going to need to exercise all your self-control in order to keep matters from reaching boiling point at times. This week is good for making decisions and having debates and meetings. But be cautious; you usually tend to be too impulsive.

Your interest in group activities can be important this week. You are likely to get together after the weekend with friends or others who share your beliefs and ideals. This can lead to your taking on and organizing several activities, mainly pleasurable and fun. Some of you can be involved in dealing with the finances of some group activity just now. If so, take care to check things out thoroughly.

You may be busy now with an interesting research matter concerning prisons, hospitals, or other such institutional bodies. This can mean a lot of traveling in order to get all your material and information.

4th Week/January 22–28

Friday the 22nd. Spend the morning enjoying some peace and quiet. It will be a good time to do yoga or meditation. A visit to a friend in a nursing home or hospital can be your good deed for the day. You may feel highly spiritual and inclined to help out with various charitable groups. But some of you may be feeling confused and unsure of your goals just now, so you will need to turn your thoughts inward.

Saturday the 23rd. This seems like a good time to get to grips with a lot of ideas that have been brewing in your mind. Many personal goals and projects can suddenly be achieved. You may need to put some effort into any studies or research work. Other people will exert a highly magnetic influence over you. You should make a good impression at an interview or when meeting prospective employers.

Sunday the 24th. This may be a morning for flare-ups and upsets with a partner. Everyone you meet will seem to be challenging you. Take care not to be too cutting in return. You need to be a little more tactful at times and less severe and exacting. However, a loved one may try to soothe and relax you, so try not to be too grumpy. A very special friendship may be going through a difficult time.

Monday the 25th. Be very wary when dealing with tax or insurance matters. You may find that sudden demands on your purse catch you unawares. Try not to be too upset when some financial scheme refuses to get off the ground. You can find that you are changing your outlook on a group situation or a certain friendship. Maybe the time has come to break away altogether if you can do it without hurting feelings.

Tuesday the 26th. This is likely to be a much happier and more cheerful morning. Your sense of humor will help a lot when dealing with a friend or loved one. You need to speak with a partner about a professional or legal matter. Try not to be too impatient if you don't get the result you hoped for. The later hours of the day should be the best time for any social activities.

Wednesday the 27th. Having a good time with neighbors can mark a special occasion. You are getting to be quite a leading light in your local area just now. If you are interested in educational reforms, you can find this a good day for putting your point across to a group of people or a board. However, you need to be sure that you have all the right facts at your fingertips in case of challenge.

Thursday the 28th. You tend to be overoptimistic about the outcome of some private deal. Your sensible and reliable attitude toward a partner will make it easier to persuade him or her that you know what you are doing. Maybe you are feeling less defensive now. This will help you to relax and enjoy the company of a lover. Money matters and private enterprises are likely to prosper.

Weekly Summary

When it comes to sorting out your own personal plans and ideas, you can find things subject to change this weekend. You Aries people always seem to have too many irons in the fire. This can lead to getting a bit muddled over what to do next. You may need to spend a little time alone figuring out just what you really want to do. Your personal need just now is to impress your ideas on others and get yourself organized. But others keep challenging you and frustrating your desire to get ahead.

After the weekend, a lot of changes may suddenly occur, wrecking your financial plans. Be careful of any speculative ventures. It may also be wise not to listen to a friend's advice. Some people may not have your best interests at heart but hope to feather their own nests. However, things will improve by Tuesday, when a little private deal can increase your bank balance.

Of late you seem to be taking a good deal of interest in local matters. You may be participating in some educational improvement scheme or simply devoting your tireless energies to helping the local school. Try not to take on too many things at a time.

5th Week/January 29–February 4

Friday the 29th. If you intend to meet a lover, be prepared for feelings and desires to be strong. You can get quite swept off your feet, but this always appeals to you ardent Aries people. You are likely to put a lot of energy into a secret or private plan to make some money. Visiting museums and getting intensely involved in research projects also can inspire you.

Saturday the 30th. This can be a very pleasant time for family matters. You may want to expand your residence or get busy with some decorating this morning. However, be careful not to fall or injure yourself in some way. You can find that noisy, lively children get you down later on. You will have to keep as detached and uninvolved as you can if you are to accomplish all you set out to do.

Sunday the 31st. It may seem at times as if no one is to be trusted. You can find a group of fellow students acting a little mysteriously. Be careful not to get involved in drugs or alcohol. A Full Moon always seems to bring out the worst in everyone, and this day will be no exception. Be prepared for some disruptive happenings when out socially or when you are with a group of friends.

Monday February 1st. The morning is probably your best time for settling down to hobbies or creative goals. You are likely to feel disciplined, orderly, and in control. A good deal can be achieved. Your imagination may run amok at times. If your interest is in crime or medical research, this can be somewhat unpleasant. Try to keep as detached and factual as you can about important matters.

Tuesday the 2nd. This will probably turn out to be a very busy and energetic day. You can find yourself kept on the go at work. Take care of your health, for something you eat can have an adverse effect on you. Be particularly wary of shellfish. If you are leading a certain group of people, you may find that your revolutionary attitude is stirring up a hornet's nest.

Wednesday the 3rd. You may change your mind completely about a certain project on which you have been working. On the whole, you should be feeling very much more positive. Lots of wonderful ideas and inspirations can illuminate you at present. A phone call from a friend may change your direction in life in some way. Meetings with groups of like-minded people will be rewarding as well as informative.

Thursday the 4th. You are likely to take on too many duties and to try to accomplish too much at work. The morning is likely to be hectic, but you may feel you have little tangible to show for it. People in need may ask for your help. If you work with animals, especially horses, you probably will find the morning a bit of a trial. Later in the day, things will get more relaxed. A friend's sympathy can help you to calm down.

Weekly Summary

The week will start off on a somewhat energetic and active note. Some of you busy Aries people may want to begin to do some decorating and renovations to your house. You are likely to feel a real desire to make your home look beautiful and attractive. This can be a favorable time for getting down to preparations and plans of this sort. However, take care not to rush about in an effort to get everything finished in a morning. Saturday may find you feeling stiff or sore if you do.

Your weekend is likely to be taken up with various problems concerning children. You may be quite upset to find that a child has been deliberately deceiving you. Or it may be that a problem at school has been concealed. This seems a good time to get to the bottom of it all. However, try to be as tactful and compromising as you can. You may find that an authority figure has differing views on the matter from those you hold.

This will be a really busy week for you, so slow the pace down and deal with things in more detail after the weekend. You will be feeling so energetic and full of marvelous ideas that you may be trying to take on too many tasks each day.

6th Week/February 5–11

Friday the 5th. You are likely to feel very deeply about someone just now and need to tell the person. A date or important meeting can be the time to declare yourself; otherwise you could burst. Some of you may feel deeply moved by a visit to an art exhibit or by hearing some stirring music. Students need to take care not to get too carried away by political debates. Tempers can run high.

Saturday the 6th. A partner may seem quite cold or reserved at times. You may tend to feel somewhat withdrawn yourself and may prefer to be alone for a while. This is not an easy time for getting along with others. Those of you Aries people who deal with the public can find yourselves in some awkward and irritating situations. Energy levels are likely to be low, so take things easy.

Sunday the 7th. If you are dealing with other people's money you may have to be a lot more careful than usual. You can find that someone has been trying to cheat you or confuse you. A certain group of people seem to be acting in an unreliable fashion, and this can make you angry. However, you will be inclined to try to keep the peace for once, which can be the best move at such a trying time. A short walk can calm you down.

Monday the 8th. It seems that no matter how many good ideas you come up with, someone influential is blocking your goals. You may have to deal with a friend about a financial matter. It will not be easy to get your message across to a group leader. In the end, you are just going to have to spell things out, even if others get upset. Meetings with relatives don't appear to be very helpful, so avoid them if possible.

Tuesday the 9th. At last, it will feel as if a breakthrough is occurring on a joint money matter. The morning is the best time for any private wheeling and dealing. If you are in therapy, you can discover a lot about your unconscious motives and feelings, but this should be very liberating. Later in the day, you may enjoy studying books of a spiritual nature and engaging in charitable group activities.

Wednesday the 10th. Teamwork or team discussion can help you to understand some research work. You students can find friends helpful in getting you motivated with your work. You may tend to feel a little lazy at times and need someone to wake up your enthusiasm. You seem to take life quite seriously and to look at things more deeply. Your whole philosophy seems to be undergoing an upheaval.

Thursday the 11th. This is a very favorable day for applying yourself to study matters. You should feel a lot better organized, disciplined, and ready to commit yourself. At last, you may be able to get your personal plans and ideas in motion. An older friend or sibling can come up with some useful advice. Don't be too proud to listen. Teachers may find that a staff meeting helps to iron out some hidden problems.

Weekly Summary

You don't appear to take a relationship issue lightly this week. There seem to be some serious issues at stake for some of you Aries people. Jealousy and possessiveness are not usually your problems, but this week may see a touch of the green-eyed monster. Although it isn't easy to be detached with loved ones, try to cultivate a philosophical attitude toward certain matters. If you probe or interfere too much into other people's lives you may find that they react by rejecting you.

Dealing with joint finances seems to be a very frustrating business this weekend. You may have to fill out a lot of paperwork connected with taxes, insurance, or inheritance matters. As this is never a favorite occupation for you active Aries people, you can get very irritable. However, you will find things going more smoothly by Tuesday morning and get a lot accomplished. This can be a favorable time for any private money matters too.

Those of you who are now embarked on a new course of study will find that you are enjoying meeting new faces and going new places. At first you may find it a little hard to settle, especially if you are a mature student. Religious or philosophical studies can appeal to many of you these days.

7th Week/February 12–18

Friday the 12th. A lot of unflagging, persistent effort and hard work can achieve wonders. Professionally you have a lot going for you now. A quick decision can save the day when it comes to a career situation. You tend to lead others and inspire them with your dynamism and enthusiasm for the job. Generally, you will feel cheerful and very determined to do well. The results can be amazing, even to you.

Saturday the 13th. This ought to be a good day for you to sit back and have a rest after all your efforts of yesterday. You and a loved one can enjoy some special and private time together. Make the most of a rare occasion. Your efforts at work seem to be creating a most favorable impression although you may not yet be aware of it. Those who deal with the public will find it easier and more enjoyable.

Sunday the 14th. Don't let a few hiccups in your schedule frustrate you now. Last-minute hitches may occur this morning but should sort out by the afternoon. However, you still seem to be rather unsure of a particular financial commitment. You may stand to lose a lot if things go wrong. It would be better to wait and seek advice. Spiritual interests can really absorb some of you, but others will be in the mood for Valentine romance.

Monday the 15th. Although a lot seems to be going on that you didn't expect, you will manage to concentrate on your goals. You can find that a philosophical group of people has a transforming effect on your ideas. You can learn to be much more detached than usual about life. Traveling with friends will help a journey to be more lively and interesting. Research or medical team-work can yield some surprising discoveries.

Tuesday the 16th. This should be a good day for making a start on a personal project or ambition. You can put a recent decision about a money matter into action now; you will see some good results. An influential friend can help you to get ahead, so don't be afraid to make use of the person's talents or know-how. Some of your plans for the future may still be secret; they are best kept that way for just a little while.

Wednesday the 17th. Although you may be inclined to keep to yourself at present, you will feel cheerful and busy. You appear to have a lot of plans and ideas for ways of using a recent inheritance or other windfall. Travel can figure in these plans, and you may want time to think it all through. Those of you who are planning retirement may be considering going to live abroad.

Thursday the 18th. This is likely to be a relaxed and peaceful morning. It can be a good time for yoga and meditation or other spiritual interests. Lazy times spent with a loved one can make you feel happy and good-tempered. You have a very determined approach to life now and mean to make your hopes and wishes come true. This may take work and patience, but for once you are ready to make some real efforts.

Weekly Summary

This seems to be a very goal-orientated time for you Aries people. Professional and career matters are very important this week, and you should be very motivated, very busy. A lot of energy may go into sports events or anything that requires a lot of effort and hard work. However, you are prepared to train and to work at what has to be done. You can take things a little easier on Saturday and give yourself a little breathing space before starting off again.

A team of people may acknowledge you as its leader

now. This can mean a lot of new responsibilities and decisions. But you aren't daunted by such matters and will feel ready to forge ahead. Working with friends or with a group of people seems to be the best way to achieve all your highly personal goals and hopes now. After the weekend will be a good time for socializing with your friends. Someone may have some especially good news for you then.

This can be a good time for those of you who are near retirement age to sort out your plans for the future. However, even younger people may feel a need to withdraw from extrovert activities and have some time for a little contemplation and reflection on the way their lives are shaping up.

8th Week/February 19–25

Friday the 19th. You may get a bit carried away by some news you receive from abroad. An in-law can have an unusual proposition to make. Be prepared for some unexpected happenings in a group situation. You can get very much involved in a reform or crusade in which you take a personal interest. However, this may be a good time also for some work on self-transformation and inner reform too. Visit your local library.

Saturday the 20th. Things still seem a little dicey where group financial matters are concerned. If you are involved in charitable concerns and activities with others, make sure that all your dealings are aboveboard. Any undeclared income can now prove to be a problem. You really need to straighten out your personal cash flow muddles also. Too many demands seem to be confusing you.

Sunday the 21st. Getting to grips with money matters is the only way to get things cleared up once and for all. You are likely to wake up and put all your efforts into accounts and other matters. Find some time if you can for reading the sort of things you enjoy; give yourself a little space. You are not contemplative by nature, but this is a good time to think things over quietly. A religious gathering can inspire you.

Monday the 22nd. This is a very favorable day for putting into action any personal plans and ideas. You really can't go wrong. Everyone seems to be charmed by your personality, your attitude, and your proposals. A conversation or a little trip with a loved one can make you feel very relaxed and happy. A benevolent attitude toward others means that you will receive a lot of love back. The evening can be very quiet.

Tuesday the 23rd. Spiritual friends may have some deep and absorbing conversations with you. You can find that a journey to some exotic place teaches you a great deal and can change you in some way. Travels at this time can make you feel free, happy, and fulfilled. In many ways this is a time for making dreams and wishes come true. This is a good time for educational and study matters. You may hear of an interesting summer program.

Wednesday the 24th. Don't give away any secrets if you can help it. You really need to exercise a little caution about certain ideas that are not yet ripe for action. An engagement may still need to be kept from the public gaze. You seem to enjoy mystifying your friends these days. A blind date should turn out very well. You are likely to enjoy feeling glamorous and may want to be seen with attractive people tonight.

Thursday the 25th. You can feel very happy in the company of family at present. The home atmosphere will be peaceful and relaxing just now, and a lazy morning will do you a lot of good. However, that doesn't mean you are going to stay still for long. You always like to be on the go and this day will be no exception. You can feel very confident deep down about a romantic situation. A small gift of flowers or candy will be received with enthusiasm.

Weekly Summary

This can turn out to be a time for dealing with some of your own very personal affairs. You need to find a little time for yourself in order to work out certain plans that have been brewing quietly away in your mind. It may be time also for some study and reading that you want to do for yourself alone. You will be in a chatty and good-humored mood, and this can make encounters with others fun. Others will find your personality magnetic and inspiring.

The weekend may turn out to be a tense and trying time for you financially. You don't seem to be too clear about some of your investments or resources. It may be a good idea to get to grips with it all and try to clear up any misunderstandings that have arisen, especially if a friend is involved. This is definitely not a good time to allow any double-dealing on your part or that of another.

Things will seem to clear up after the weekend, thanks to talking it all through sensibly and honestly. A touch of good humor also can help. You can enjoy parties and entertainment in your local area this week. Neighbors seem to be in a jolly and carefree mood and want to share their good fortune.

9th Week/February 26–March 4

Friday the 26th. You may want to spend the day in the privacy of your study. You seem to have a lot of plans and ideas brewing that are still unformed. Try a brainstorming session with a relative who can help. Some of your plans may revolve around moving or improving your present home. This is a good day for reading, writing, or just being at home with the family. A parent may have a lot of fascinating family gossip for you.

Saturday the 27th. The morning tends to get off to a slow start. You may feel time dragging. It can be a good day for lovers; romance is decidedly on the cards, for any Aries married or single. You may be enjoying a celebration, an engagement, or a special date. But one way and another, there are sure to be stars in your eyes and a loved one can do no wrong. Your generosity and charm go a long way toward impressing others too.

Sunday the 28th. Having to part with a lover can be upsetting for you. A child may go off on a church school trip or stay with friends for the first time. Doting parents can feel bereft, but you need to let go. Unexpected events are likely to occur when planning some entertainment or event for the day. You will be wise simply to expect the unexpected and laugh it all off. By evening, you will be ready to relax at home.

Monday March 1st. Now should be a good time for buckling down to some spring cleaning and other daily activities and tasks. You can pay attention to all sorts of details and get things cleared up and thoroughly organized. Your working day will go well, and you should find co-workers steady and supportive. However, take care not to attempt to lay down the law too much. Use the carrot instead of the stick approach.

Tuesday the 2nd. Don't force yourself to go ahead with something when you really feel tired or out of sorts. Rome wasn't built in a day. However, good advice is likely to be wasted on you at present. You seem to have some sort of bee in your bonnet and are determined to get certain tasks done at work even if it means driving yourself or others to the limit. Those who are musical will give their all at a concert.

Wednesday the 3rd. It may not be too easy to get off a letter or make a call to a partner just now. You can spend a lot of time wrangling over issues with a lawyer. A business meeting is likely to be something of a trial for your nerves. However, you seem determined to compromise and keep the peace with others even if it means talking all night. It may be better to travel alone rather than with a partner.

Thursday the 4th. A more sympathetic attitude from a friend can cheer you up. You may feel a bit lazy and laid-back about certain personal matters. However, meeting with a group of motivated people seems to galvanize you into action again. In your desire to keep things on an even keel, you may have to play the hypocrite. This is not a role in which you Aries people will feel at all comfortable.

Weekly Summary

Despite a slow start to the weekend, you now will at last find some time to get on with your creative activities. Your imagination seems to be working overtime just now, and all sorts of ideas should be flooding in. Those of you who are involved in film, writing, and photography hobbies and interests can find that all the right ingredients come together to produce the sort of atmosphere you want. Make the most of Saturday when the setup should be just right.

After the excitement and various disruptions of the weekend, you may find yourself back in your usual boring and routine activities again. However, you seem ready to apply yourself steadily and carefully to the tasks that need doing. This is just as well, as a good deal of backlog seems to need sorting, sifting, and eliminating. You may have to undertake a journey to visit someone in a nursing home or hospital during the week. There is no doubt that your energetic presence can be very therapeutic and cheering.

On the whole, your relationships with a partner or others close to you in life may not always be easy. No matter what you say, you cannot seem to make yourself understood. A friend may act as an intermediary, and this can help to sort out a quarrel or estrangement.

10th Week/March 5–11

Friday the 5th. You are likely to enjoy taking the floor at a party or other social activity. You can really charm and entertain your friends with your liveliness and sense of fun. It is a good day for any group activities. There should be a lot of harmonious and happy feeling. Everyone seems ready to compromise and keep the peace. An interesting item may arrive by mail.

Saturday the 6th. Things don't seem to be moving in regard to joint financial ventures. You may find that funds are short when it comes to a cooperative business or financial project. Certain bills may have to be paid soon, especially those concerning taxes, insurance, and so on. You really need to buckle down to some hard work or overtime and try to earn a bit extra. Or you may have to take a second job.

Sunday the 7th. A burst of energy and enthusiasm this morning can help you to tackle a financial matter head-on, even on a Sunday. Someone influential may have to be approached carefully and a private deal struck on a business matter. You may need to keep all this under your hat for the time being. A group of people may have a lot of confidential things to discuss with you tonight, perhaps at your home.

Monday the 8th. Generally, this will prove to be a relaxed and easy day. Nothing very exciting or interesting is likely to occur. You may feel like reading some travel magazines and planning your vacation or doing some useful research and getting in a little study. Any trips you make at this time are likely to be humdrum and uneventful. The mail may bring word about a family event.

Tuesday the 9th. Some of you may enjoy a trip to the shore or enjoy activities on the water if the weather permits. You can feel very cheerful and expansive and in the mood to be outdoors. Team sports of all kinds can be most enjoyable and improve you physically. This is a good time for dealing with foreigners and their customs. You can learn a good deal and broaden your outlook and perhaps improve your language skills.

Wednesday the 10th. This is most likely to be a day for enjoying being by yourself. You don't seem to feel the need for company even when traveling. However, some of you Aries people may meet charming and romantic individuals while on a journey. Such meetings can well transform your lives and outlooks. The day will be good for studies involving art or music. Some of you will be performing in public.

Thursday the 11th. A certain job that you are involved in is bringing in a more steady income. Try not to get too carried away and make too many plans on how to spend it. A cautious approach is best at present. You may be given a lot more extra work and responsibility, but you are sure to be up to it. At present your work seems to involve a good deal of communicating with others.

Weekly Summary

At the start of this week, you are likely to be very much preoccupied by the funds you share with others. It doesn't seem to be as easy to negotiate a loan or get a mortgage as you were hoping. Dealing with officials and red tape can be most frustrating to an impatient Aries person. However, try to deal with it all in an organized and disciplined manner. Be very cautious about any risks and speculative matters at this time.

You may be prepared to go on some trips this week. These can include friends or a team of people with whom you plan to spend some exciting time touring about on a sports activity. Water seems to play a large part in your adventures now. However, others of you may enjoy just planning and considering a future expedition to some exotic place. Wednesday will see you feeling a bit too lazy to do anything that active.

Your professional life seems to be plodding along on a rutlike but determined course this week. You may feel as if you would like to have a change but probably are glad of the steady cash you are earning now. Your lively sense of humor can help to cheer fellow workers up at least.

11th Week/March 12–18

Friday the 12th. Some sudden last-minute financial backing can put life into a professional venture. You can find yourself very busy at your work, especially if you are involved in banking or real estate. You can be highly expressive and imaginative when giving a talk or lecture. This is a good time for those involved in photography, filming, or charitable work.

Saturday the 13th. The morning may give you some problems in dealing with a female co-worker. You may have to be as diplomatic as possible when dealing with certain issues. It would be foolish to take everything too personally. Later in the day, you may find that a friendship you have relied on is cooling down. Some sort of misunderstanding seems to have arisen and driven you apart. Try to remain calm and objective.

Sunday the 14th. Although things seem to be improving in a friendship or group situation, you may still feel a lot of anger and dismay. Unexpected flare-ups can spoil an evening out. Try hard to hold on to your sense of humor and ability to see the funny side of it all. This is a good time for those traveling or studying. You can learn a great deal that can help your personal transformation process.

Monday the 15th. Now you can really relax and begin to shine in a social situation. No matter where you go or what you do, you cannot fail to win love and support. This can be a good time for lovers. You will not only feel happy together, but also be good friends; and that's what counts in the end. This is a good time to have a party or other celebration, perhaps a really lavish affair.

Tuesday the 16th. If you can get some time off, try to sit down quietly on your own and put your mind to personal finances. These can do with a little juggling and sorting. Some of you may find that red tape is keeping you from benefiting from a tax refund or sizeable inheritance. However, with a little effort and energy, you can get the wheels rolling in your direction.

Wednesday the 17th. A lot can be done if you just sit down quietly and plan your next moves. This can be a good day for making private decisions and mulling over ideas for a new start on some personal or private project. It is a good time for spiritual practices such as yoga and meditation. You are feeling unusually withdrawn, contemplative, and peaceful just now. Make the most of it.

Thursday the 18th. Now you can begin to get going on certain personal plans and ideas. You can use your influence with friends to persuade them to back a really grand venture. However, don't expect quick results or a speedy response. You can find this a wonderful time for travel, sport, and outdoor activities. You are likely to feel quite rejuvenated with the coming of spring.

Weekly Summary

Now you may feel as if you are getting to grips with a professional situation. Your energies and enthusiasm in the job seem renewed. Your primary need can still be in sorting out the groundwork of a scheme or business proposition, You do need to use all your charm and put all your efforts into getting backing for a career matter during the first couple of days of this period.

Social expectations are high now, and you may be planning a birthday party or other jolly celebration that will take place soon. Being with your buddies can be very enjoyable and pleasant this weekend, no matter how you intend to spend it. Some of you may have a very delightful romantic encounter with someone you meet socially. You need to be sure you don't get too carried away when watching your favorite team playing on Sunday.

After all the weekend's fun and games, you will need to find a little space when you can sit down quietly alone. This may make a welcome break from your usual hectic lifestyle. You may just feel a little tired and need the break. Or you may use the time to plan a whole new lot of ventures and experiences to launch yourself into. Spiritual interests will also be important this week.

12th Week/March 19–25

Friday the 19th. Unexpected visits from a friend can mean that your plans for the day change rapidly. A spiritual leader or preacher may have a stirring message for you. You can find that a child has been quietly working away and achieving good results. Social activities are favored. You may be asked to take some sort of leading role or give a talk or lecture. Be sure you are adequately prepared.

Saturday the 20th. A long-lost lover may come back into your life and stir up old memories. You can find that a person much younger or much older than yourself can create a lot of strong feeling in you. Financially, this can be a time of reckoning for some of you. Old debts may resurface and need to be paid off. You may at times feel as if you work only to pay the tax collector.

Sunday the 21st. A social event may turn out to be quite costly. But it is sure to be worth every penny if you and your friends have fun. You may sadly realize that money is disappearing like water these days. You may have thought you were better off, only to find that it was a hopeful dream when you look at your bank statement. Be careful not to be too gullible and fall for someone's sob story.

Monday the 22nd. A neighborhood get-together can make you feel quite special. You will enjoy a great deal of popularity with friends. Certain people from overseas may write to give you good news. You may be planning to go to see some religious sites and spiritual places with a group of like-minded people. Things you study and absorb now seem to be like revelations.

Tuesday the 23rd. You seem to keep making new plans and changing your goals and direction. But then everything is so new and interesting to you right now. Take care not to let the cat out of the bag about a certain bit of secret information. Teachers can enjoy taking a group of children to a museum or gallery, but expect to deal with a lot of mischievousness and chatter. Keeping them interested can be hard.

Wednesday the 24th. Plans to sell or renovate a property can come to fruition now. You may need to take the lead in sorting out a family problem. Older people can need some sympathy and care. You will tend to feel compassionate and open to beautiful things. A desire for life to be more peaceful and happy can make you feel a bit sentimental at times, especially about the past.

Thursday the 25th. A lot of effort may have to be put into straightening out family finances just now. You may find that there is more to sort out than you supposed in connection with an inheritance or estate with which you are involved. Your plans still need to be kept in the dark when it comes to a business venture. Private meetings and exchanges must be very carefully conducted; there are nosy people everywhere.

Weekly Summary

You seem to have some plans afoot concerning various financial transactions this week. You will be wise not to discuss these with everyone until everything becomes more clear. Just now you may need to consolidate a merger or sort out some uncertain monetary deals. However, it seems as if a nest egg is going to come in useful. You can find a lot of demands on your resources now, and this may worry you a bit; but it will all even out in the end.

Local activities can make this a very busy weekend. You are likely to find yourself coming and going much of the time. This can be a good week for shopping expeditions with relatives. Having a good gossip and sharing a few secrets together can be entertaining. Meeting a brother or sister again can be a strange experience for some of you. What you can now find is that old enmities are forgotten and you are becoming friends once more.

After the weekend, your mind may turn to family matters. You seem to be sorting out a lot of practical things these days. Everyone seems to look to you to be provider and handyman all mixed together. However, you will be in a kindly and detached mood this week and ready to be obliging.

13th Week/March 26–April 1

Friday the 26th. This can be a really frustrating day for those of you who are hoping to make progress with a favorite sport or hobby. You may find that you have run out of cash just when you plan a good time with friends or the kids. Or a children's entertainer may not turn up on time. However, you are not a born leader for nothing. Your powers of invention will help you to keep everyone happy.

Saturday the 27th. Things can go well as long as you watch your purse strings. If you are involved in the theatrical and entertainment industries, you can achieve some sort of fame, or notoriety, depending which you prefer. Something you particularly want to do is likely to prove quite costly, and you may have to forgo the desire. Children can be very rowdy and annoying and have to be reined in.

Sunday the 28th. If you take things slowly, a lot can be achieved. This is a good time to settle down to some boring but necessary tasks. You may get really angry about a money matter. Try to keep things in perspective. Having to go in to work on your day off can make you feel irritable and tense. But some extra pay will make it worth the bother. By evening, you will be more relaxed.

Monday the 29th. You may be in the mood for a massive clearing out at home or at work. Sorting out closets, drawers, and desks can give you a satisfied feeling. You can enjoy a journey to a far-off place. Your values can be greatly changed by the kind of sights you see right now. This day will be good for dealing with financial matters of all kinds if you can get all the information you need.

Tuesday the 30th. You seem to be quite the daydreamer and far from reality now. This makes it hard to concentrate on your day-to-day routine tasks. Machinery you are using at work can develop peculiar problems that aren't easy to clear up. Generally, this can turn out to be a chaotic day for any sort of discussions or communications. Phone messages can become garbled or misunderstood.

Wednesday the 31st. A more caring and understanding approach to a mate or spouse can work wonders. You feel you are beginning to understand one another at a deeper level. There may be some financial matters to work out with a friend or group of people with whom you are involved. This is a good time to make a definite statement to others about yourself and your life's direction.

Thursday April 1st. An evening out with a mate or spouse will be be very special. You may be celebrating an anniversary or just want to enjoy one another's company. You should feel expansive, benevolent, and generous. Splendid opportunities can arise for you through others. On the whole, you can feel lucky now and ready to have fun. Passover will make some of you quite contemplative.

Weekly Summary

Although the week can begin on a slightly frustrating note, things will soon begin to clear up and become more positive for you. Children can occupy you Aries parents more than usual just now. You feel very benevolent and easygoing with offspring or any children in your care. If you have disabled children to care for, this can be a special week when you may put a lot of effort into helping them have some fun. Perhaps you can go on a trip some place.

Getting to grips with your daily tasks and activities can make this a busy weekend. But you are going to be in the mood to be organized, disciplined, and thorough. Fellow workers may upset you over some money matters. But on the whole, you seem to be enjoying a fairly harmonious and cooperative period in your daily working life. Part of this is because you are feeling more fit and more cheerful, and others can relax around you,

The week will end on a most delightful note. You and a mate or spouse can be feeling a lot of pleasure and joy in each other's company. This can be due to many reasons, but the main thing is that you, yourself, are feeling a lot happier and want to spread your kindness and goodwill to others.

14th Week/April 2–8

Friday the 2nd. A certain business or financial setback can seem a bit confusing or make you overanxious. But you need to try to get to grips with it if you can. Seeing an official may at least help you to straighten out any legal matters or red tape involved. Be careful what you buy. Secondhand goods could be especially tricky. Advertisements may be misleading too, so read them with care.

Saturday the 3rd. There seems to be a need to keep on and on trying to sort out the financial situation of a certain company or group of people. You may have to put in a lot of effort and get little thanks for it. It is really hard to remain detached from it all when the situation is still so highly irritating. Naturally, all these emotional storms and suppressed feelings take it out of you.

Sunday the 4th. This Easter Sunday will not be all worship and pleasure. A confab with someone behind the scenes can help to throw some light upon a tax or insurance problem. You may have to read up a little on the legal aspects of your situation. Salespeople or buyers can probably have an intutive feel of what is right for the market just now. You can enjoy going shopping for little secret gifts that you mean to save for a special occasion.

Monday the 5th. You may have long been planning to get off on a splendid and exotic vacation. For some of you, this can be your day for setting off to the ocean or a lake. Air as well as sea travel should go well and be enjoyable. You can relax now and be quiet and peaceful in your own little space. Students may really enjoy just taking off with a load of books to the reference library.

Tuesday the 6th. You can really expand and be yourself. Those of you who are abroad may feel that you want to stay there forever. If you are involved in examinations or other studies, this should be a most favorable time for understanding some very complex subjects. Your whole outlook on life appears to be opening up and transforming. This can be a good time for teachers and public speakers.

Wednesday the 7th. This is a very good day for professional and career matters. You may have to shoulder some new responsibilities, but these don't bother you. In fact, you will be more ambitious than ever and ready to improve your abilities. Those of you working with older people can find them easier to deal with. In fact, a lot of practical advice may come from an older person with whom you work.

Thursday the 8th. Try not to get too carried away by your newfound exuberance and good spirits. You may take on or promise too much and regret it later. However, this should be a cheerful and busy day for you professionally. You can have an amusing and good-humored approach when dealing with customers or clients, although they may be as demanding as usual.

Weekly Summary

There may be some problems facing you at the start of this period. Your financial troubles do not seem over quite yet, despite all your efforts and hard work. Maybe you have been a bit too trusting, especially of friends or of a spiritual group of people. If you are dealing with funds for charities, you may feel a certain amount of disillusion with the more mundane attitudes of others. However, not everyone is as idealistic and humanitarian as you.

Those of you who have been yearning and planning for a really good vacation somewhere abroad should get off on a good start now. Whatever your circumstances, make this a time for a trip somewhere, preferably near some water. You may be able to indulge in some sailing or other adventure sport. Try to keep life simple and relax as much as you can with loved ones in beautiful and refreshing places.

Wednesday can be a good time for professional interests. At this point, you are sure to have found your feet and should have settled to a fairly steady rhythm. You are inclined to be expansive and benevolent, but this may lead you into making promises you cannot keep, so be wary.

15th Week/April 9–15

Friday the 9th. A boss or other authority figure may challenge your personal decisions and your leadership. This can be upsetting to your pride and ego. However, you will be wise to keep your opinions to yourself at work. This is not a day for making waves. Tact and compromise are your best weapons. You may in fact find it better to work alone at home if the nature of your work permits.

Saturday the 10th. Luckily your present philosophical outlook helps you to cope with a lot of hassles over finances. You seem to be trying hard to suppress your fury at some sort of official interference. Trying to sort out taxes, insurance, or joint business matters is hard work just now. You may become a little bored with a spiritual or charitable group of people.

Sunday the 11th. This is likely to be a far better day for social activities. Unusual friends or different sorts of pursuits can make this a challenging but interesting day. You can enjoy team sports as a participant or spectator. A group meeting will be very lively and jolly tonight. You can be sure something unexpected will occur to liven up the proceedings. You probably will take an active role.

Monday the 12th. A lack of funds may mean that you have to forgo a social activity in the morning. The afternoon and evening are likely to be spent in seclusion. You may even take some work home and get it done in the privacy of your own study. This can be a good time to apply yourself conscientiously to dealing with your bills, debts, and other obligations. An overlooked bill may come to light.

Tuesday the 13th. Take care of your health, especially now. Any colds and chills you may have felt coming on can lay you low for a while. But don't feel too sorry for yourself; this is nature's way of giving you a rest. You may hear some upsetting news from a grandparent or uncle. A journey you have been planning can run into a few minor problems, but they can be easily dealt with.

Wednesday the 14th. Private conversations behind closed doors may take place this morning. If you feel you have certain matters weighing on your mind, you may need to consult a priest or counselor. Later in the day you can begin to feel a lot more like yourself and may be more inclined to get out and about to see neighbors or friends. You should be a lot more relaxed and chatty.

Thursday the 15th. This ought to turn out to be a very favorable day for you personally. You can find that your life is transformed by a spiritual group to which you belong. You may take a journey with them or enjoy some sort of deep and penetrating discussion. Therapy groups can work especially well. You should be feeling confident and full of optimism about your future goals.

Weekly Summary

Although a group of humanitarian or spiritually inclined people have been supportive in the past, you may feel a bit bored with them this weekend. If you have in some way become involved in working on their finances or other responsibilities, it can all seem a burden now. However, a bit of effort applied in the right quarters, a word in the right official ear, can work wonders. You are sure to be very popular with everyone this week.

If a certain ailment has been brewing quietly away and left neglected, it just may lay you low for a while this week. Take heed of any warning signals, and slow down your pace a bit. You Aries people tend to burn yourselves out in your enthusiasms. Use any spare time to relax alone and study, read, contemplate, or meditate. You will feel the benefits of just a few hours of such therapy and are sure to bounce back in no time at all.

The latter part of this week can see you concerned with your own personal needs. You can enjoy pleasant and harmonious conversations with loved ones. Your whole outlook on life will now be more loving, caring, and empathetic; this naturally attracts the love and care of others for you.

16th Week/April 16–22

Friday the 16th. This may seem like a good time to make a whole new start in a highly personal situation. You can enjoy just doing your own thing this morning. The afternoon may be spent helping out a sick or elderly friend. You probably have a great deal of work to catch up on. Try not to exhaust yourself too much; your own health is still not quite what you would wish.

Saturday the 17th. Finances seem to be subject to various changes. If you are involved with banks or the stock market, expect lots of surprises and shocks. A sudden bill or expense you have not planned for can really throw your budget into disorder. Some of you may decide to change your wills or take your business to another banking firm. You can take the weekend to think it over.

Sunday the 18th. A cheerful chat with a neighbor can be very pleasant. You may even have a little party or other enjoyable social activity with local friends. Lots of new and inspired ideas can be bubbling up inside you now. The day is good for writing activities and for the study of music or art. Teachers and students alike can benefit from this Sunday's harmonious energies.

Monday the 19th. You need to watch a tendency to push your own philosophies and ideas down others' throats. However, if you can keep a sense of balance and detachment, you are sure to find that others are interested and inspired. There is no doubt that your confidence and easy friendliness are making you a popular figure wherever you go. Use any opportunities for advancement of your aims.

Tuesday the 20th. A parent may not be very easy to share your ideas with just now. Family finances do seem to be a trial to you still. You may find that getting a mortgage or loan is not too easy. You seem to be coming up against a wall of frustration over a property matter. Repairs to the home can prove costly and slow to get done. You may find that nerves can upset your stomach.

Wednesday the 21st. Some of your natural exuberance can be knocked out by a family problem. A lot of relatives may come to see you, which can be exhausting. Noisy repairs in the neighborhood tend to be disruptive and annoying. However, you can really enjoy a talk with a friend tonight. A lecture or speech you make will impress a group you belong to.

Thursday the 22nd. This should be a good day for creative matters as long as you are practical. You may feel a little disappointed with a bank official or other influential person. You don't seem to be getting much help or sympathy from such quarters. However, try not to lose your temper; it will only make things worse. A child may be taking advantage of your good nature. It is time to draw the line.

Weekly Summary

Lately you have been feeling as if you were being bugged by money matters. There does seem to be a lot of fluctuating and change in your circumstances. This may especially affect you if you are in business or trying to buy new property. At times you may really wonder whether any people know what they are talking about. Certain pharmaceutical or chemical corporations can prove tricky and troublesome to get money from.

Sunday can prove to be an immensely enjoyable day for you if you spend time with local friends and neighbors. Relatives also may get in touch and add to the party or the festivity. You may find this a good chance to catch up on local gossip and get to know your neighbors a lot better. But be careful not to lay down the law too much on Monday when dealing with a local matter. Political attitudes can do more harm than good.

Getting family and property issues sorted out this week will need a cool head. Keep your volatile temper under strict control, and try to use tact and diplomacy. On the whole, you can be optimistic about a property matter. But be sure of all the facts and figures.

17th Week/April 23–29

Friday the 23rd. This can be a really active and enjoyable day for you. You will have some new ideas about fund-raising activities. This may be to help children's charities or other good causes. Team games can be very lively. Lots of outdoor activities will be good for your health and general fitness. Those of you who enjoy writing will feel inspired. Your personal experiences will do to start with.

Saturday the 24th. You can get quite confused by a friend's odd reactions. You may tend to get a bit irate with a pretty hopeless set of people with whom you have become friendly of late. Take care not to get involved with those on a drink or drugs scene. Things may not be all they seem. Many of your hopes and wishes seem now to be somewhat fanciful and foolish.

Sunday the 25th. You can put a lot of effort into routine activities this weekend. There may be certain special tasks that you like to handle yourself. Dealing with accounts may be one of these. You may have to figure out just how much you can afford for a vacation. You should be feeling quite energetic and can enjoy a tough workout in a gym, or maybe yoga for those more elderly.

Monday the 26th. Some of you Aries people may have a very fascinating romantic encounter at work. You may find that someone you have been longing to chat with is ready to be approached. Taking pets on a journey may not be a very good idea. Those who have birds should take care that they do not escape. This is a good day for talking or writing about your beliefs and philosophies.

Tuesday the 27th. A romantic attitude toward a partner is just what is needed. You may arrange to take a loved one to the movies or a romantic dinner for two. You can enjoy being with a special person whose conversation you particularly enjoy. There seems to be a good deal of loverlike chitchat on the menu. A child may seem to become more mature and sensible suddenly; conversations can be very encouraging.

Wednesday the 28th. Things now seem to be going swimmingly in a partnership. You can have so much to tell one another. New insights and revelations about a mate or spouse keep the relationship alive and interesting. Those who are dealing with legal matters can have a successful day. A breakthrough can occur. You are likely to receive mixed news of a divorce settlement or other such issue.

Thursday the 29th. Your feelings are running very deep. In many ways your emotional reactions toward a long-drawn-out money matter are likely to be explosive. But you will be wise not to try to get revenge on those you feel are plotting against you. Those of you who are in therapy can have a need to deal with hidden anger. Those involved with banks and insurance companies are likely to be very busy.

Weekly Summary

You Aries people tend to be very active and enjoy athletic activities a good deal. This can be a very good week for such things as watching your favorite team games, participating in gym workouts and sports of all kinds. Your luck should hold out in all you tackle just now. Generally this is a creative time. Those of you who are more studious can also find that you are energetic and ready to apply your mind to writing or artistic pursuits.

Your daily routines are a little easier to get on with this weekend. You seem less likely to be interrupted and more inclined to buckle down to life's necessary tasks. Try not to spend too much time in idle and pleasant chitchat on Monday. You seem to be finding certain people at work something of a distraction from duty. On the whole, you should have a busy but satisfying time at work. People seem more inclined to work as a team.

A mate or spouse can be really involved with you in some spiritual group situation. You may want to share all your goals and ideals together now. This can be a good time for talking over with your partner all that you value, all that you personally aspire to do.

18th Week/April 30–May 6

Friday the 30th. Things always look worst at the time of the Full Moon, so don't be too anxious or overzealous about a money matter. You may be wise to seek some expert advice on a building project. A bank manager may be willing to advance you a loan. You will need to use all your charisma to work on someone. Giving a talk or lecture to a group of people will come off very well.

Saturday May 1st. Things are likely to be quite unpredictable in regard to business. You may be awaiting a decision or some news about a current financial situation. However, you seem to be highly optimistic that the outcome will be in your favor. Your sense of humor and cheerful attitude can help to keep others from losing faith. Dealings with a brother or sister can be pleasant and productive.

Sunday the 2nd. This can be a favorable time for religious and spiritual activities. You can find yourself really enlightened by what a priest or church leader has to say. Meditating with a group can be most uplifting. Those of you who are engaged in charitable work may have some traveling to do in connection with your activities. You tend to take a broader and more compassionate view of life at present.

Monday the 3rd. Your feel-good factor certainly does everyone else a lot of good too. You may be enjoying a well-earned vacation abroad right now. Or you may just be having a break and taking a trip somewhere with a group of friends. Any sort of research or study is favored. Those of you who are interested in archaeology can make interesting finds. Sports activities and interests can claim your attention.

Tuesday the 4th. You enjoy teaching students at present. Subjects such as art and music can be important this morning. Youngsters may be particularly interested in what you have to say. The latter part of the day can be a time for working on some business deals. You probably are very much involved in certain exciting financial moves. This can be a good time for making long-term decisions.

Wednesday the 5th. A lot of good, disciplined work can be done. You can feel that you are getting some results in good, hard cash. Those of you who are involved in real estate or the building trades should be doing steady and reliable work now. You find that an older person has some helpful advice concerning a professional matter. You may have a lot of ambitious plans for the future of your career.

Thursday the 6th. Although an influential person seems ready to back a personal venture, you may be having second thoughts. Keep cool, and do not jump in where angels fear to tread. Try not to stick your neck out too much when dealing with an authority figure. However, your natural leadership is sure to win you rewards and even some sort of promotion. You can bask in well-deserved attention.

Weekly Summary

It isn't quite the time to relax about a joint money matter yet. You can start the week feeling a bit anxious about it all. However, if you talk it through with a friend or a group of associates, you will soon begin to find that light at the end of the tunnel. You seem to be very sure of your ideas and innovations in certain financial areas and prepared to back them to the hilt. But you seem likely also to have the backing of others who have faith in you.

A meeting on Sunday can have a very deep and transforming impact on you. This may be of a spiritual and religious nature. Or you may just feel that a certain book you read or talk you attend enlightens your mind. All in all, you can find your views and philosophies much broadened and clarified. Make good use of all you are learning, and write it down if necessary. It may be helpful at some later time when you feel down.

This is likely to be a splendid time for your professional interests. You seem to feel more serious and inclined to buckle down to the more sober and practical side of things as much as the visions and ideas. The combination of both these factors can certainly make you popular with the public and your boss.

19th Week/May 7–13

Friday the 7th. A partner may be in a somewhat feisty mood this morning. However, you can have a good, straightforward talk together about a work-related problem. Your energetic approach toward a legal matter can soon help to straighten things out. However, later this afternoon, you may find some unexpected and upsetting developments arising over a social engagement.

Saturday the 8th. Things can be changed quite a lot. You may find that matters are working out better than you expected in connection with a planned surprise party. A neighborhood affair should be very lively and cheer you and a loved one up. You are decidedly in the mood to have some fun and a bit of a fling. But a partner seems to get on your nerves for some reason that you cannot figure out.

Sunday the 9th. You may become quite excited about a romantic engagement or meeting tonight. This can be a good day for those of you who want to pop the question. Your feelings will be ardent, and there is no way you can stop yourself from expressing them. A friendship will be especially warm and loving. You are likely to be able to express yourself with unusual clarity just now.

Monday the 10th. You may have a lot of far-reaching ideas for a future business deal or property investment. But you really should consult those more cautious or less visionary than yourself. This will be a good thing in some ways and can check your usual impulsiveness. Taking time off to visit an older person in a hospital or nursing home can be your good deed for the day.

Tuesday the 11th. Plans for a shopping spree may have to be forgotten. You may find that a friend is not feeling well enough to come with you. Be very careful of being cheated when buying goods. Take all the receipts and file them away carefully. This is not a good time to speculate or gamble with your personal finances. You may be confused about the fine print on some document.

Wednesday the 12th. This is a favorable time for decorating the house and putting things in order. You want to keep on good terms with family members just now, which can make you a much more sympathetic listener than usual. You may be able to apply your philosophy or spiritual ideals to a certain family situation. A parent will be glad of your affection and warmth. In-laws may get in touch with you later in the day.

Thursday the 13th. Unexpected invitations to social affairs tonight can make you feel cheerful. You are in a lively and happy mood these days, with energy bursting out all over. Spring is definitely your season. But you may have to keep quiet about a money matter when with a partner lest you cause a bit of a rumpus and an adverse reaction. You can work out any such financial problems by yourself.

Weekly Summary

Socially, this can be a pretty hectic week. You may spend a lot of time with a great many friends, teams, or groups of people. They all seem to want to get you involved. So really this is your time to be a bit selective and make up your mind where you want to be. For some of you Aries people, this can be a very romantic time. You may be having an engagement party or just enjoying insightful conversations with a loved one.

You may have to withdraw from all this socializing a little over the weekend. This can be due to the fact that you still have to keep an eye on your budget. Or you may just feel that you have had enough and need a little time alone to recuperate and reflect on other things. You may be disillusioned by someone about a particular spiritual matter. Check things out for yourself; don't be too gullible.

Your personality seems to be blooming and unsquashable after your slightly introverted weekend. You are in much too exuberant a mood to keep out of the way for too long. This can be a happy time for you. Many of your personal interests and desires can be attended to and personal philosophies put into action.

20th Week/May 14–20

Friday the 14th. If you still find that a particular financial tie or other obligation feels wrong, you will be wise to say goodbye and get out of it. You may feel too tired to go out to a movie tonight. You will be more inclined to curl up on the sofa with a video. Get in some shopping, especially for practical and useful articles. You may be considering buying a new car too.

Saturday the 15th. Financially things can take a turn for the worse in some ways. You really seem impatient now to get out of a company or group involvement. This is a good time to do just that and to make a fresh start. Perhaps a child is acting in an antisocial manner. You may have to consult an expert or a teacher about this kind of behavior in order to get at the root of the matter.

Sunday the 16th. Neighbors can act in a very helpful and sympathetic manner on this day of rest. You may learn that a particular film you want to see has come to your local movie theater. It may be important to consider with care your cast-iron view of life. Maybe some things need to become more adaptable. Otherwise you can be too judgmental about a friend's mistakes.

Monday the 17th. You can be in a very warmhearted and benevolent mood. Local people may enjoy a little gathering or party in your home. You may meet someone from your past. It can give you quite a shock to see how much friends or relatives have changed. A mate or spouse will be in a lively mood. Between you, you can make others feel welcome.

Tuesday the 18th. Get on with some decorating or do-it-yourself activities around the home. You are in the mood now to make things look brighter and fresher. Family relationships can be very harmonious and calm. You can really enjoy having relatives for an extended visit, especially those you haven't seen for a while. You can make some extra cash if you put your mind to it.

Wednesday the 19th. Having a business meeting in your home may not be too good an idea. You can find yourself getting more and more irate with a parent or other family member. A partner may seem to be getting too enthusiastic about some home decorating schemes. You are likely to be irritable and a bit touchy. It may be better to stay in your shell and not provoke others.

Thursday the 20th. This can be a quite inspired time for those of you who are creative. You can put a lot of your ideas into a moneymaking venture now. Some of you will find that you are having to change many of your old value systems. This will not be an easy day for those with children. They may tend to be rude, idle, or even a little withdrawn. You may want to consult a child specialist.

Weekly Summary

You seem to be running into some difficult problems with your personal finances just now. It may seem hard at times to track just where it has all gone, but it seems as if some of your savings have vanished into thin air. You may discover that a lot has been spent on social or charitable matters. Some may have been lent to a so-called friend who has since disappeared. The moral is: don't be too trusting at present.

This is likely to be a good week for getting together with your neighbors and acquaintances. You may find that local affairs and local politics claim your attention more than usual. Repairs to gas mains, sewers, and so on can be creating quite a disturbance. You may feel like joining others and making some sort of protest. However, good humor and a sense of fun can turn all your local activities into a party at times.

If you have been planning some decorating and other home beautifying activities, this can be your time for getting down to it. You ought to enlist the help of other members of the family but are more likely to be impulsive and get going on it alone. In this case, carelessness and rush may lead to accidents.

21st Week/May 21–27

Friday the 21st. You may act as arbitrator or leader in a group matter. This can be a very enjoyable time for you socially. You tend to feel expansive and gregarious. There may be a clash of interests. You will feel like getting on with some creative work rather than socializing. However, a partner can make the ultimate decision. To keep the peace, give in.

Saturday the 22nd. A boss may be playing some sort of power game with you just now. You find that it is hard to get any sort of reforms or changes into your daily work schedule. However, it is worth the struggle to do so, as it can increase efficiency all around. You may have to see a doctor or a dentist about a health matter. This can be a good day for any accounting work.

Sunday the 23rd. This should be a far more pleasant day than yesterday. You will feel in harmony with the family and enjoy simply relaxing at home. Craft work and dressmaking activities will be rewarding. You are more inclined now to appreciate and enjoy the simple everyday routines of life. Dealing with various details around the home can freshen it up and make it look attractive and cozy.

Monday the 24th. A long chat with a partner or a spouse can help to clarify a lot of things. You and your mate can enjoy a social get-together with a friend or neighbor. Local charitable or church activities can keep you busy. You may have to give a talk to some local people. This should go over very well and help to raise funds for any schemes in which you are involved.

Tuesday the 25th. Your relationships seem to be going through quite a transformation. You may feel that it is easier to be friendly and detached from others. A philosophical attitude will help when dealing with legal matters. You will find that you are doing a lot of talking and traveling around of late. This may be for various spiritual or creative purposes.

Wednesday the 26th. This turns out to be a quite trying day for dealing with a mate or spouse; your personal needs and desires may clash badly. You can find that you have been too optimistic about a legal situation. You may need to watch that you don't lose your temper with someone in a big way at present. A family member seems to be especially provoking just now.

Thursday the 27th. You need to get down to some work on a joint money matter. Books can require balancing or some sort of muddle straightened out. You may decide to make a will or revise an insurance plan. Don't get too worried and anxious if a certain financial matter isn't panning out as you were hoping. Red tape and other official matters may need to be dealt with first.

Weekly Summary

This can be a good week for dealing with daily matters and activities. You should be able to get a good many personal affairs cleared up and sorted out. At work, you may feel that certain everyday routine methods can do with a little streamlining and tidying up. This should greatly help you and co-workers to deal with things more efficiently. But you may discover that it is harder than you think to shake people out of habitual ways of doing things.

There seems to be a good deal to discuss and hammer out with others this week. You may have to call meetings of business partners to sort out various legal and constitutional matters. Or you may simply be trying to get across to a mate or spouse something you truly believe in. Being with other people who are on your spiritual or philosophical wavelength is truly wonderful. But you can find that there are many who don't see things your way at all.

Toward the end of this week, you can find that the focus shifts to your old problem of financial worries and confusion. Maybe it is time to grab the bull by the horns and try to straighten out any recent muddles in both personal and family finances. Friends seem to be taking advantage of your kindness.

22nd Week/May 28–June 3

Friday the 28th. Those of you who are considering moving may have a shock over a money matter. Or you may have to try to take a firm stand on the furnishings and equipment you were hoping to buy. You may start to get angry and try bullying or manipulative tactics to get things going, leading to unpleasant scenes. Students can find themselves frustrated when trying to do some research.

Saturday the 29th. Friends will be on your spiritual and philosophical wavelength. Discussing some deep subjects and sorting the world out between you can be very enjoyable. An outing or trip you take may be with a group of people whose company you find fascinating. Being at the seashore can be especially pleasant. Or you may want to go to a concert or film together.

Sunday the 30th. Be careful when challenging a teacher or other authority figure. You may well be in the right, but you need to be tactful about it. This holiday weekend is not an easy time for travel. You tend to act in an exaggerated or careless manner toward others, and it can arouse some hostility. However, a friend may come to your aid and help to smooth things out.

Monday the 31st. This is likely to be a much more favorable day for a journey or for continuing travels. You can be in a gregarious and friendly mood now. Although you may still meet some difficult, even dangerous, characters, you seem to be able to handle such confrontations with ease. Being cheerful and good-humored can get you a long way when dealing with an irate family member.

Tuesday June 1st. This can turn out to be a quiet day for you. You may spend it considering your professional and career goals and interests. Use any spare time to plan the future a little more carefully. Those who are at work can find things going along in a fairly routine, even humdrum, manner. However, it will give you a break from your usual hectic lifestyle.

Wednesday the 2nd. This can be a good day for making progress in professional matters. You feel ambitious and goal-oriented. But better yet, you will have the discipline and patience to apply yourself with more care to your tasks. If you are involved in banking, real estate, or other financial matters, you can make a lot of progress with official matters, taxes, and so on.

Thursday the 3rd. A business partner is likely to get a little jumpy about your desire to be more expansive. You may feel that you are paying a good deal of money for certain services that are not up to standard. This will not be an easy day for dealing with loved ones. Everyone may seem very irritable and lacking in humor. In the afternoon, you can feel a great need to escape and get out on your own.

Weekly Summary

Things seem to be testing you out in regard to a business venture or a property move this week. You may feel somewhat dubious about putting money into schemes that may be shaky or uncertain. Make sure that you do your research; don't just accept a situation at face value. You may be occupied with bills, costly repairs to a car, or tax matters that need special attention.

For those of you who enjoy travel and adventure, and what Aries person doesn't, this can be your week. On the whole, you seem to enjoy being with friends or groups of spiritually inclined people these days. You may decide to vacation near, or even on, the sea, for water seems to fascinate you. Take care at the time of the Full Moon on Sunday when you are likely to have confrontations with authority figures, maybe even have a brush with the law.

For those of you who work, the rest of the week can go forward on a calmer and more peaceful note. Generally, you Aries people are able to deal with the public and the world out there in such a way as to make others see you as reliable and supportive. But Thursday may see a few setbacks and challenges again. On the whole, however, you enjoy that kind of thing.

23rd Week/June 4–10

Friday the 4th. A good honest talk with a mate or spouse can really clear the air again. You should get straight to the point when dealing with some very personal issues. Driving can give you great pleasure, but try not to exceed the speed limit. The day is good for any social activities or outings. Teachers will find students eager to learn.

Saturday the 5th. This should be an auspicious day for you and a mate or spouse. You can feel a lot of warmth and goodwill in one another's company. An enjoyable evening out can give you a chance to discuss things and have some time together without contending with obstreperous kids or other demands. You may enjoy driving around in a new car. Salespeople can have a more lucrative day than usual.

Sunday the 6th. It may be necessary for students to get their heads down and do some work at home. You may need to do some private work on the side to earn a bit of extra cash. You can deal very efficiently with any situation that presents itself. Sunday shoppers may need to go out and get in some necessities and practical items for the home. Do not be tempted by slashed prices to buy doubtful goods.

Monday the 7th. A child may seem to be a bit secretive about something. You can find that an influential person you meet socially can really wake you up and give you lots of new ideas. Salespeople and those who travel short distances can do very well. You should be on the go a good deal. New and innovative technology such as computers can be absorbing and keep you entranced.

Tuesday the 8th. You are likely to be very attractive to others these days. For some of you Aries people, a new lover can seem both glamorous and ideal. You may enjoy meeting in a secluded place for a chat or a bit of intrigue. Children can be delightful companions. They can give you a lot of love and make you feel good about yourself. Buying new clothes for yourself or others can be fun.

Wednesday the 9th. Unexpected events can make this a lively and quite exciting day. Some of you may be acting in a very impatient and rebellious manner toward a group of people with whom you are involved. Naturally this can create a bit of a storm at times. However, if you can keep calm and remain detached, things can right themselves again by the end of the day. The evening can bring peace and love.

Thursday the 10th. If you keep an open mind this morning, things can work out very well for you personally. You certainly seem to be more confident than usual and sure of yourself and your aims. Later on in the day, you may feel that a new love is completely changing all your old values and needs. You yourself can be very attractive to others, perhaps more than you think. Someone may ask you for a date.

Weekly Summary

Social events and group activities can make the start of this week particularly busy and cheerful. You are likely to be feeling lively and ready to participate in whatever is going on, from team sports to group outings. Your whole attitude toward other people is far more humorous and open-minded now. This, of course, will help a lot when dealing with friends and acquaintances as well as with partnership issues.

You may find that you have to meet someone in secret over the weekend. But the experience seems to be very enlivening and exciting for you. Some of you Aries people may find that an authority figure is prepared to listen to something you have kept hidden and private for a while. It can be a great release to let go of such things.

Personal interests and activities can take you out and about a good deal after the weekend. You may be inclined to act somewhat rashly or impulsively when dealing with others, so be sure to look before you leap into any situation. There is no doubt that you now feel very confident of your own abilities. You are ready to defy all comers.

24th Week/June 11–17

Friday the 11th. A canceled event this evening can be quite upsetting. You may need to take a more aggressive approach toward someone who owes you money, even if it is a friend. The day can be good for straightening out paperwork and other matters, especially anything to do with tax forms and ledgers. Some of you may get a bit of a shock when you see the state of your bank balance right now.

Saturday the 12th. A sympathetic neighbor will be willing to listen to your problems. A conversation with a loved one can change your whole perspective. You may have to reverse your views on certain moral problems. Try not to be too judgmental but more compassionate when talking to a friend in need. This can be a good time for buying books, stationery, and unusual art objects.

Sunday the 13th. Help may come from an unexpected quarter. You may decide to make a fresh start in a new neighborhood. Some of you Aries people will even be entering into a new business or personal relationship. Certainly things begun now will continue to do very well. You can spend money on some practical appliances for the home, such as vacuum cleaners and refrigerators.

Monday the 14th. You are likely to be on the go a good deal. Getting lots of personal errands seen to may be necessary if you are going off on a trip soon. You should have a happy day, especially if you are meeting a lover. Your feelings can be very deep and very intense. Nor are you likely to have any difficulty in expressing your happiness and joy. The evening can be all your heart desires.

Tuesday the 15th. The safety and security of your home may occupy your mind. This can be a good day for dealing with any practical matters that need to be dealt with around the house. This is a good time for planning any structural alterations or future changes that you have had in mind. Cost may be the major setback to your plans. Older people in the family can enjoy a chat with you.

Wednesday the 16th. Don't get too carried away with enthusiasm; you may have all sorts of schemes of a do-it-yourself nature. But a partner needs to be considered too. Make sure your tastes agree. You can feel somewhat irresolute and unsure of yourself when dealing with a lover later in the day. A child may try to cover up some mischief, But you seem to be able to ferret out the truth.

Thursday the 17th. A meeting with a lover can be very special. But although your feelings run deep, you seem to have some reserve, doubt, or suspicion. Try to be detached and calm about it all. Children may be in need of some practical help and guidance with their work. You may need to arrange for some extra tuition for them. Although you may make a slow start, the day will be good for creative work.

Weekly Summary

This week can turn out to be very busy for you. There will be lots of comings and goings. You can find yourself paying a good many social calls on neighbors and acquaintances in your local area. You may have a lot of shopping to catch up on. Or there may be errands to run for others who are ill and in need of some help. This can also be a good week for catching up on correspondence, phone calls, and other communications.

Your desire to improve your home seems to be more practical than ornamental this week. You may feel a real need to make life easier by buying various useful gadgets and items to help with the housework. Those of you who are involved in real estate, either buying or selling, may come to some sort of agreement or conclusion this week. In fact, you may be saying goodbye to a place where you have lived for a long time.

The week is likely to end on a creative note for many of you Aries people. You will be fascinated with art, music, or other forms of expression. However, you may tend to feel that you are not good enough at what you do and give up before you have begun. You need to be more persevering and less judgmental.

25th Week/June 18–24

Friday the 18th. You can have a wonderful day with children and partners. This can be a good time to go out and enjoy some athletic activity together. This is also a day for horseplay and fun and games rather than sitting around in an armchair. Everyone seems to be in a lively and energetic mood. Your energies can also be put into creative activities that require a lot of effort.

Saturday the 19th. You need to be sensible if you are feeling tired or under the weather. Maybe it is time to take a break and not attempt to do so much. If you can get organized, you can get a lot of routine work done. You may feel sad or rejected by a loved one. A child may seem depressed and have you worried. Be careful when buying clothes or food. You can pay too much and be dissatisfied with your purchase.

Sunday the 20th. Things seem a whole lot better and more positive now. You can get a good deal of writing, phoning, and gossiping into the day. This is a good day for travel, especially for personal enjoyment. You can find that a new computer is extremely helpful when you have lots of writing to do. Buying and selling cars can take up a large part of the day for some of you.

Monday the 21st. You are more inclined to be considerate and helpful toward a mate or spouse. This can certainly improve your relations with others in your life. You may be influenced by some philosophy or by a spiritual group to which you belong. Now seems to be the time to practice what you preach. Legal matters may need some research before you can go ahead with confidence.

Tuesday the 22nd. This can be a very loving and romantic day for many of you. You can be friends as well as lovers with a person close to you. Just being at home with loved ones can be very relaxing. You may find that a brother or sister is acting oddly. However, you will be wise to keep silent on the subject. Try to be more detached and tolerant when dealing with a parent.

Wednesday the 23rd. You may tend to be too exuberant when dealing with other people. This may not go over too well in an interview. Legal matters need careful attention. You can be very excitable in your reactions to a child. Try to be calmer and less reactionary. You may be imagining too much and blowing a family matter out of all proportion. Try to see the other person's viewpoint.

Thursday the 24th. Although you seem to have had a recent financial windfall, you also can have some major bills to contend with. A love affair may run into a bit of bother. Someone seems to be cooling down quite suddenly. This can be quite upsetting and hurtful. On the other hand, you may feel that someone is being too possessive; you may need to raise a few barriers.

Weekly Summary

Your health can be a matter of some concern at the start of this weekly period. It may be time to see a dentist or a specialist about various aches and pains. A child or pet can also be causing you some concern. If this is the case, you will be wise to investigate and seek some expert advice. Some of you may be considering going on some kind of crash diet, but be sure not to overdo it.

If you are involved in a separation or divorce, you may find that it isn't always easy to remain amicable with a former mate or spouse. Legal wrangles over children and possessions can now be ironed out in a more civilized fashion, but you may find feelings running high on Wednesday morning. However, those of you who are still happily involved in a relationship can find this a time for sharing similar entertainment, friends, and other pleasant activities.

This seems to be a week when you can be inclined to fall for a sob story or get conned in some way financially. Be very wary of all salesmen and get-rich-quick schemes. It is not a good time for any sort of gambles or risky ventures. Caution is not natural to you, but you will need to exercise it now.

26th Week/June 25–July 1

Friday the 25th. A family meeting or discussion can help you to get to grips with finances. If you are planning a move or the purchase of a new car, you will need to have a confab about it. This is a good day for those in therapy. You can feel ready to discuss a great many hidden matters with insight and understanding.

A brother or sister can be helpful. Generally, you will feel closer to family members.

Saturday the 26th. If you are going on an unusual journey, you may need to get up with the birds. Be very careful that your memory doesn't fail you and let you leave an important task undone. This can be a day for carelessness both in speech and when out driving. You really will need to keep your wits about you, especially if you are feeling tired. Pull over to the side to rest occasionally.

Sunday the 27th. Being in different surroundings and with different kinds of people can be very stimulating. You will really enjoy being with loved ones somewhere pleasant, even if it is just a day trip with the children. You will be in the mood to enjoy yourself and to relax thoroughly. This can do you a lot of good and put you in a very amicable and friendly mood.

Monday the 28th. The morning can be a happy time for those on vacation or traveling someplace. You can enjoy being with others and should be in a gregarious and cheerful mood. Students will do very well. You can feel very confident about yourself if you are involved in some sports competition. However, you may feel that a parent is not being fully supportive later in the day.

Tuesday the 29th. Now it can be a lot easier to be disciplined and determined. Your ambitious but sensible attitude toward a professional matter should bring some good rewards. Those seeking jobs or having interviews can make a good impression. Dealing with officials such as auditors and tax collectors is likely to go well and be helpful for your business or personal finances.

Wednesday the 30th. Events this morning can certainly make you feel ready to stand up for your rights. You may feel that your personal space is being trampled on by some very annoying people. A lucky breakthrough in a money matter needs to be viewed with care. Don't go crazy and make too many promises just because you suddenly find you have some spare cash.

Thursday July 1st. This is not an easy day for those working with campers or students, especially children. You may find that you cannot easily keep the peace or any sort of law and order. Be prepared to get tough. You can find that it is hard to communicate what you think and feel to a lover. There simply isn't enough detachment on the part of either of you just now.

Weekly Summary

This can be a week when many of you Aries people head off to the sun and seashore and have a well-earned vacation. You really do need that dose of sunshine just for yourself. Many of you will enjoy traveling with a group or joining a group of friends. Self-improvement vacations may be quite appealing now. It can be worth the long and possibly trying journey to get to your particular haven. Then you and loved ones can really sit back, relax, and enjoy yourselves.

Professional matters are likely to go smoothly and well during the week. You can find that partners are energetic and more than helpful, ready to put their all into an enterprise. Just now, you feel a lot happier about work and business matters. But there still seems to be the odd problem when dealing with an authority figure who may be trying to undermine you in some way.

Dealing with spiritual groups of people can tend to be a bit trying for your sense of proportion. You may begin to wonder what on earth they are all talking about. You may even feel that you are in a social situation or with a gathering of people who are just unreal, even a bit ridiculous at times.

27th Week/July 2–8

Friday the 2nd. You really feel like getting out and about. Although you enjoy being with children, you long for adult companionship at times. However, cramming in too many social events can be like eating too many sweets. Relax as much as you can. Put your energies into hobbies and creative work if possible. Loved ones may appear to be very detached, but you cannot figure out why.

Saturday the 3rd. The morning promises to be very lively and companionable. A partner will be in a cheerful and energetic mood. A friendly attitude helps to keep eveyone happy. Churchgoers can enjoy a special event, possibly a picnic or dinner. You can find this a very good day for spiritual matters of all kinds. Meditation can be deep and teach you a good deal. Reading a good book will broaden your outlook.

Sunday the 4th. Just being at home with the family this holiday can make you feel calm, stable, and secure. You don't seem to be in the mood to try anything new or different. You may decide to visit an older person, perhaps a parent, in a nursing home or hospital. You are likely to find that the person is in a comfortable and relaxed environment. An older child can show a lot of maturity and wisdom.

Monday the 5th. Friends may feel you are being a bit coy about certain personal matters. It isn't like you to keep secrets, but maybe this is the best policy just now. A surprise party may be in the offing for someone. The day is good for group activities, especially with people who are into healing, spiritual, and charitable activities. It is good also for those with photography and filming hobbies.

Tuesday the 6th. Teaching or simply chatting with children can be really enjoyable. You may have some original ideas for keeping young people interested and entertained. Be prepared to have your schedule or timetable rearranged at the drop of a hat. You may be called upon to make a journey to see a parent or an in-law. Those who want to catch up on hobbies and correspondence can find the time.

Wednesday the 7th. This morning, you may spend some time with a lover and feel relaxed and happy. But you will have to get moving later on to catch up with other meetings, appointments, and social engagements. You may get things into a bit of a muddle at times. Be especially careful not to drink and drive. Because of roadwork or other matters you can do nothing about, traveling can be chaotic.

Thursday the 8th. Dealing with youngsters can take a lot of energy and self-control. You may be taking a group of them on an outing. If so, it can be important to show them just who is in charge. Some news about a personal money matter can make you feel really dispirited. A creative project or some writing work you have done may not be as successful as you hoped.

Weekly Summary

You are likely to find the tempo of the week varied and swift to change. At the start of the period, you are likely to be in a restless frame of mind and looking for ways of getting out and about. This can lead to your committing yourself to too many social activities and engagements. It will take some fast footwork if you are to be in ten places at once. But you will feel energetic and ready for fun.

This burst of frenetic activity may mean that you are in a more withdrawn or spiritual mood over the weekend. Those of you who are involved with various religious rituals or ceremonies may be called upon to be present at them. They can have a profound and calming effect upon you and also make you aware of where your duties and obligations lie. For those whose path is more individual, this can be a good time for meditation and yoga.

Putting across your personal interests and ideas to

others can be fine, but try to remain detached. You may have to keep readjusting your attitude whenever you meet other people. There seems to be a constant flow of meetings, encounters, and interesting private chats for you to deal with.

28th Week/July 9–15

Friday the 9th. You may wonder where all your cash has gone lately. It may be that you have spent a lot more than usual on enjoyable activities and entertainment of various kinds. Also, children may have been more demanding. The morning is likely to be spent working on accounts and pondering these mysteries. Later hours in the day should be good for group meetings and local gatherings.

Saturday the 10th. A trip you are obliged to take can give you a lot of problems. You need to be sure that your car is in good shape before taking to the road. Be wary; don't try speeding where you shouldn't, or you will have a brush with the law. Friends may have a lot of interesting information and local gossip to pass on. Money matters need to be thought over carefully.

Sunday the 11th. A really enjoyable morning can set you up for the day. You may meet a loved one or reread a letter or get a call from a sweetheart. The rest of the day may be well spent at home, dealing with repairs, do-it-yourself activities, or just clearing out closets. You are likely to be feeling happy, cheerful, and energetic. Now you can assess your real values in life.

Monday the 12th. Those of you who want to buy a new home, perhaps for your retirement, can do well. You should be able to get a bargain or two when out shopping for practical smaller items too. Generally this will be a good time to get down to some work around the home. You are likely to be in an organizing mood. You should be able to think of ways of saving money too.

Tuesday the 13th. This is a good time to make a new start in a new home. Or you can be in the mood to make an existing property look fresher and more attractive. You can get on very well with a parent. As the day goes on, it may be important to spend some time with a child. The youngster may have a few secrets or revelations to share and will welcome some positive help.

Wednesday the 14th. This ought to be a splendid time to make progress in some hobby or creative activity. You may find it hard to keep up with any research or study, however. Anxieties about money matters can prevent you from enjoying yourself as much as you would like. You may feel that a friend is undermining your position in a group situation or financial involvement.

Thursday the 15th. It may be a good idea to take some time off and simply rest and relax. You really should try to find time to do something personal and creative just for yourself. Those of you who like the theater may want to book some seats for a show tonight. Children will prove less trying than usual. Generally it is likely to be a quiet but positive day.

Weekly Summary

Although it seems likely that you will have a good deal of traveling to do this week, you may find that getting around is a problem. This may be due to road repairs, gas mains being installed, or simply a breakdown with your car. So be prepared, and check your engine; plan routes if you can to avoid trouble spots. Saturday is a time to take particular care. But after this, travel can be much smoother, even enjoyable.

You seem to have a good many practical and useful plans up your sleeve. These may include home improvements of various kinds. Some of you may even be considering moving into a new home. But those of you who have older houses to care for can find yourselves spending quite a bit on renovation and repair. However, you will be wise to deal with it constructively and sensibly. In the long run, you can only be improving your property.

Those of you who are creative will find some time after the weekend to devote to your interests and hobbies too. You may have to put in some extra hours of research or investigation in order to find the best way of tackling certain subjects. Don't try to take on too much, or you will get yourself in a muddle.

29th Week/July 16–22

Friday the 16th. This is a good day for getting ahead with some routine work. You can enjoy dressmaking and cooking and may even earn a bit of cash with such activities. Co-workers are likely to be ready for a laugh and to be more laid-back than usual. However, a cheerful atmosphere will make work far easier and happier. Doing your homely, everyday tasks with a loved one can bring a sense of contentment.

Saturday the 17th. Things seem to be going ahead very steadily, especially if you are at work. You should find that you are making good progress with certain jobs that you have set for yourself to accomplish. Your health is likely to be stable, and you can be calm and philosophical about life just now. An elderly person whom you have been worrying about should now seem a lot more settled and contented, which will ease your mind.

Sunday the 18th. Relationships with friends and loved ones are likely to be tender and caring now. You may have a strange conversation with someone you have just met. Religious activities and studies can make a slow but definite change in your life. You may find your understanding of another person is growing daily. A friend may let you down on a social commitment. The excuse may not be at all acceptable.

Monday the 19th. A mate or spouse may have some surprise entertainment lined up for you, or vice versa. You will enjoy being with friends at some group event. Conversations with students and other young people can be very probing and revealing. You are likely to want to have answers to some very deep questions. This day is good for research work or political debates, which can arise from current news events.

Tuesday the 20th. A legal matter may need some clarification. It may concern shared property or a divorce settlement. You can at times feel somewhat at odds with a parent or an older child. Business and joint finances seem to be in a state of some confusion or upheaval now. However, you will cheer up when you get your regular paycheck or some other payment for recent work.

Wednesday the 21st. Your somewhat abrasive or irritable attitude is not helping much when dealing with a teenager or small child. You can put some of it down to the fact that you are still agitated about a business or financial matter. A good, honest talk with a young person should help to clear the air. Company officials can find that a meeting with shareholders results in a definite decision at last.

Thursday the 22nd. This can turn out to be a somewhat uneventful day. You may be quite grateful for a break from all the annoyances of the last few days. Make the most of the calm, and try to clear up as many bills and other financial matters as you can. Those who are in therapy may feel that little is understood or experienced just now. Reading psychology books and doing research can make the day more productive than expected.

Weekly Summary

At the start of the week, you are likely to be busy with your usual daily routine activities at home and at work. You may feel a lot happier and more productive now.

Colleagues seem to be better able to get going and to cooperate with you than before. Naturally this means that you all can work in a more organized and efficient way. Those of you who do piecework should be earning quite a steady wage, but it can be a struggle at times.

You can find that your relationships with others are undergoing some dramatic changes this weekend. Those of you who are involved in divorce proceedings should be able to deal with things in a friendly way. However, a youngster may be causing some fresh problems between you that need sorting out. You are likely to find that other people take sides in any dispute. This can be a bit upsetting at times.

The week can end on a flat and humdrum note. But of late you have had enough excitement to last you a while. Make use of any spare time or an uneventful day to get a few monetary matters resolved. You probably need a more honest appraisal of your current situation.

30th Week/July 23–29

Friday the 23rd. This can be a very favorable time for dealings with houses and land. A parent may help you out if you are buying your first home. Seeing an expert in some business area can really help you get a feel of it. Your confidence should be good, which can help you to take a leading role in a joint business venture. Someone at work may be acting in an overbearing or hypocritical manner. Try to shrug it off.

Saturday the 24th. A sudden call from abroad may mean packing your bags and setting off. You are ready to be adventurous and can feel a need for stimulating companions as well. You students will discover that your mind is flashing with brilliant insights and ideas this weekend. Working with a team of people on some foreign project can be most interesting. You are sure to learn a great deal very fast.

Sunday the 25th. Those who are on vacation at present can be really enjoying their adventures. What you see and experience will have a very wonderful effect upon you, broadening your mind and ideas. This can be a good time for meetings with religious people, working in religious communities, and so on. You should be feeling very positive and confident now. Those in publishing and legal activities can make place for expansion.

Monday the 26th. This can turn out to be a red-letter day for a professional matter. You seem to be enjoying organizing colleagues and employees. An office party can be the occasion when you meet a new romance. Those of you who are involved in craft work, dress-making, and cooking can do very well financially. However, take care when signing any contracts; read the fine print.

Tuesday the 27th. You are likely to be a bit confused about what to do with yourself now. A lot of interesting options seem to be available. This is a good time for creative activities as long as you do not spread yourself too thin. Be wary of a youngster in your life. He or she may not be as straightforward or trustworthy as you have been hoping. You need to beware of confidence tricksters and con men these days.

Wednesday the 28th. It will be wise to keep as detached as possible now when dealing with friends. Gossip can be very harmful to reputations, and you will be wise to steer clear of it. You can find that an older child is going through a difficult period. It may be necessary to prop up an ailing business with some of your personal capital. But be sure that owners of jointly held funds are in agreement.

Thursday the 29th. You may feel as if you have had your share of surprise events. However, you can hear some sad news about a friend now. If you have had enough of a certain group of people, you may be better off getting away from their company. Dealing with a personal debt or financial setback can be most frustrating. You may run into some sort of official interference in the course of the day.

Weekly Summary

The week can start off in a very cheerful and expansive way. You may be enjoying a vacation somewhere or traveling for other reasons. All you see and experience seems to be making a beneficial impression on you. Those of you who enjoy working in a kibbutz, an ashram, or other religious community can find that you are gaining a spiritual dimension to life as well. Good companions also help to make your travels stimulating and exciting.

You can find that professional matters are working well on a day-to-day basis. But all the same, you may need to rethink some of your ideas and strategies. Be especially careful when dealing with salespeople, using a firm's car, or signing contracts. You are likely to run up against some crafty people and uncertain situations. Check information and identities before making any commitments.

You may need to examine certain group commitments you are now involved with. It may be that you are finding the people you mix with too old, too boring, or just frustrating in some way. Friendships can also be a source of sadness for some of you this week.

31st Week/July 30–August 5

Friday the 30th. You may feel that someone is not being honest at work. The person can seem nice on the surface but act like an enemy behind your back. All the same, you seem ready to take it in your stride. A relative in the hospital is sure to be glad of a friendly visit. Your sense of humor can be outrageous but cheering. A lover may be becoming too possessive or manipulating you. Let the relationship cool for a little while.

Saturday the 31st. You may be more accident-prone than usual when traveling. Seeing a relative or a friend in the hospital may be quite emotional. However, you are likely to be very cheerful and philosophical. This kind of attitude rubs off on others and does them good. A more regulated and sensible attitude toward a money matter can get you back on an even keel. The evening can be quiet but pleasant.

Sunday August 1st. This should turn out to be a pleasant day for meetings with brothers and sisters. You should find that a call from a relative can clear your mind about a certain secret worry. The afternoon can be spent in dealing with others in a very compassionate and caring way. You seem to know intuitively all the right things to say just now. A church service may be held outdoors.

Monday the 2nd. It may be hard to put one over on you. You are likely to be a force to be reckoned with. You will be bursting with positive energies and ready to make changes in many personal matters in your life. Some of you Aries people may be about to embark on a journey you have always longed to make. Generally, you are in a creative and enthusiastic mood and eager to see and do new things.

Tuesday the 3rd. Although you may think you have worked things out with care, you can find yourself in trouble when it comes to arranging accommodation or rent matters. You may be at odds with a relative. However, a phone call or letter can put things right. Don't allow past memories to trouble you. This can be a day for wallowing in nostalgia and old photo albums; you may be in for some surprises.

Wednesday the 4th. Be prepared to deal with some very odd situations when you are out socially tonight. Meeting famous people can make some of you quite starry-eyed. A person you encounter now may seem to be the lover of your dreams. This can make you feel very excited. But try not to be too impulsive or to jump into a relationship too fast. Tomorrow you may sober up to reality.

Thursday the 5th. A realistic and sensible approach to a debt or other money matter can help a lot. A letter you receive this morning can have some good news about a financial transaction. The day is good for signing contracts and agreements. Those of you who are interested in a new car can enjoy doing the rounds of the dealers. You should be able to find a good bargain if you do some negotiating.

Weekly Summary

It will be important, not to mention wise, to keep quiet about a certain development this week. You may be trying to come to some private arrangement with a relative and need to keep the details under your hat. Some of you may be making retirement plans and working out pensions and other details. This will be a good week for those who want to be involved in healing or charitable activities.

You may burst out of your chrysalis in a big way this weekend. It can be a good time to get various personal plans and ideas into action. Your particular brand of caring, warmth, and honest sympathy can be very helpful to others. You seem to have a quite detached attitude as well. This will help if you are dealing with those who are down and out. Be sure to find a little time to do something you enjoy doing this weekend. You deserve a break.

Your mind is likely to turn toward your possessions and your personal finances this week. You may decide that it is time to have a massive clearing out mentally and physically. To your surprise, you may find that you do not need half as much as you thought. Financially you still seem to find a certain group commitment draining your resources.

32nd Week/August 6–12

Friday the 6th. This is a splendid day for any sort of writing activity. You can feel quite imaginative and inspired. Teachers at camp or in summer school can enjoy dealing with a class in music. Dancing and craft work can also be rewarding pursuits. A trip to the shore or near some water is likely to make you feel much more calm and tranquil than you have felt in a while.

Saturday the 7th. Unusual activities and social events can really excite and stimulate you. You may be kept busy running about on all sorts of errands; unexpected matters will crop up. A child may have some sort of accident or injury. Take great care when driving, as this is a time of sudden mishaps. Maybe you would be wiser to stay in and write letters or make phone calls.

Sunday the 8th. This can turn out to be an especially peaceful and relaxing day. You may be able to take time off from work or other pursuits and enjoy being at home with the family. Just doing various little daily chores can be soothing. Polishing up your possessions, putting a stamp collection together, or other detailed work is just what the doctor ordered. You may start a child collecting stamps or coins.

Monday the 9th. You are likely to feel quite calm and sensible, no matter what turns up. You are going to need this attitude when certain creative ventures begin to go wrong. You may find that a child is feeling a little depressed. Try a bit of homespun philosophy and common sense to sort the problems out. An older person may give you some anxious moments by showing signs of illness.

Tuesday the 10th. The morning can be spent pleasantly chatting with a brother or sister. You may have a lot of old memories flooding over you. It may be a good idea to write some of these down. Those who keep a diary can be catching up on it now. The afternoon can be spent studying, engaging in a favorite sport or hobby. Your interests are likely to lie in the spiritual rather than mundane.

Wednesday the 11th. You will need to work very hard to get a creative project off the ground, as it can call for a good deal of planning and groundwork. However, some sort of red tape or other official intervention can be causing you delays in getting going. Naturally this can be irritating and frustrating. But be patient and a new start can yet be made. The results will be worth the effort.

Thursday the 12th. If you settle down to routine work and activities, you can feel quite peaceful. You may want to make your office look a bit more attractive. This can be a good day for cooking, craft work, dressmaking, and anything that requires detailed attention. Quite a lot of cash can be earned this way. You may have to put a great deal of sustained effort into it all, however.

Weekly Summary

You will have more interaction than usual with your neighbors this week. This can be a good time for getting together on social occasions, such as barbecues and local fairs and so on. In fact, you may have some sort of common charitable aim. Making new friends among local folks can be a bonus for those of you who may have just moved into a new neighborhood. It can take some time to get used to new surroundings.

Home can be the most relaxing place for you this weekend. You can really enjoy getting busy with all your various household chores and do-it-yourself activities. Just concentrating on various projects around the house can actually be very soothing to your spirit. Some of you may be talking about old times with an older family member or telling your own tales to a younger one.

A quite creative mood can seize you after the weekend, but you may run into all sorts of obstacles. Not being the world's most patient person, you can find this highly irritating. However, don't burst a blood vessel trying to achieve everything at once. Sports activities especially need to be handled with care.

33rd Week/August 13–19

Friday the 13th. Don't let the date alarm you. This can, in fact, turn out to be a very constructive and useful day. You are likely to be energetic and dedicated to finishing off tasks for once. You will find that workmates also are ready to keep going until a particular job is done and out of the way. Your attitude toward money matters tends to be pragmatic these days.

Saturday the 14th. If you like dressing up and creating illusions, you are sure to enjoy a masked ball or fancy dress party tonight. You will find that a movie or theatrical production is well worth seeing. Be wary of promises made by a lover, who may be trying to string you along. Try to stay aboveboard when dealing with a child. Children are sure to know if you are trying to fool them and will react accordingly.

Sunday the 15th. A partner or spouse can be helpful and friendly. You seem to be a little detached about your relationships at present, which probably is a good thing. It may be that you and a mate could do with some space in your relationship. A journey will be all the more enjoyable if you have a loving friend or partner with you. A religious figure can make a deep impression on you and others.

Monday the 16th. This is likely to be a very loving and pleasant day. You and a loved one may feel that it is time to declare your feelings for each other to the world. You may enjoy buying an engagement ring together. Take care not to talk too much to someone who may misconstrue your words, especially if you are dealing with members of the press. You may let a joke get out of hand, making someone very uncomfortable.

Tuesday the 17th. If you try to take on too many things or have too many irons in the fire, you can get in a muddle. Relax and take things one at a time. This is not an easy time for those in therapy work or medicine. You can find that things get a trifle chaotic. Dealing with children can also be a bit of a trial. However, keep a good sense of humor going, and all will be resolved in the end.

Wednesday the 18th. If you plunge into everything headlong, you can wind up feeling exhausted by the end of the day. It may be a good idea to try to take an occasional break, phone a friend, or just take it all slower. You cannot finish a certain task all in one day, so why try? You are likely to be very intense and even a bit emotional about a recent change. Take it easy; all will work out for the best.

Thursday the 19th. A loved one can give you a pretty emotional time this morning. You may feel possessive or jealous, or you may be the victim of another's manipulative techniques. Later in the day, you will be inclined to see things more sympathetically and compassionately. It may be best to sit down and have a long and serious talk with a lover or a child and get to the bottom of any problem.

Weekly Summary

Most of this week can be taken up trying to get to the bottom of a relationship issue. You may be dismayed to find that a partner has not been altogether straight with you on certain issues. It will be a good idea to be as open as you can about anything that either of you has been doing in secret. Otherwise all sorts of misunderstandings and confusion can arise. Your friendly but detached attitude is certainly the best way to tackle any issues that arise now.

Things can get quite heavy and involved when it comes to joint finances this weekend. You seem to be putting a great deal of effort and concentration into saving a business or just propping up family finances for a bit longer. Maybe you need to stop trying so hard. This is not a good time to gamble with your hard-earned money. You Aries people who are involved in banking or money markets may wonder whether you are coming or going sometimes. However, matters will begin to settle and be more normal again by Thursday.

You can end the week feeling a lot better about life and a lot more philosophical. A trip taken purely for pleasure will make you feel much better.

34th Week/August 20–26

Friday the 20th. If you are interested in crime, the occult, or psychology, you can really get involved in some in-depth reading. This can be a good time for writers and researchers, and creative activities in general. Taking a trip with a loved one can give you a real boost. Children will have a good time on vacation and are likely to be well-mannered and well-behaved. They can entertain themselves.

Saturday the 21st. When at your best, you Aries people can be immensely warm and lovable. The sort of magnanimous mood you are in now will bring children, lovers, and all others flocking to your side. This should be a very pleasant and happy day. If you are enjoying a vacation, you can relax and let life pass you by. Those who are seeking to publish some writing or poetry can get some encouraging news.

Sunday the 22nd. You seem to be giving some thought to a professional situation. Positive and practical action seems to be your keynote. Generally, things seem to be going well financially. You can feel generous and lighthearted with your cash now. This can be a good day to buy some interesting large items for home or business. The odd wager on the horses can pay off handsomely.

Monday the 23rd. You can feel quite settled and practical about a career matter. You may also find that you are very busy sorting out various complex problems. Children can be very changeable and annoying. They and their friends may keep popping in and out and creating a major disturbance to your routine and tranquility. However, you will be able to keep your temper better than usual.

Tuesday the 24th. If you aren't wary, you are likely to find yourself faced with all sorts of demands on your purse. Be careful not to be conned by salesmen into buying some awful white elephant of an object that you will later regret. You may find that a social outing that has been heavily publicized is a bit of a disappointment. It isn't very easy to be good-humored and tolerant with children and demands that you consider excessive.

Wednesday the 25th. A broad-minded view can help you to come to terms with a friend's dour attitude. You may find that you have to be much more stern and unyielding with a child or adolescent. Trying to make progress with a piece of creative writing can be a chore rather than a pleasure. However, if you keep yourself strictly at the task, inspiration will flow again. Ignore the ringing of the telephone.

Thursday the 26th. This can be a busy time for many of you socially. You may be arranging a party for a loved one or for a child. It may at times feel as if entertaining friends is hard work, especially if your cooking is not turning out too well. Later in the day, you will be glad to slump in a chair and be alone. Some of you, however, may have a child in the hospital to visit.

Weekly Summary

Those of you Aries people who are on vacation will find the start of the week really blissful. You should be feeling at your best and looking it too. Being abroad can open up new horizons and interests for you. Now it can seem worth the effort to have learned that foreign language. You are sure to find doors open and lots of welcome and hospitality on your journey. Being with a loved one can make it all the better.

Those who are returning to work this week after a break ought to be in good spirits. This seems to be a favorable time to consider expanding a business. Your sense of optimism and positiveness may lead to a promotion. You can feel very pleased with the results of your recent hard work. There is still much more to be done, but you will be more inclined to tackle things with enthusiasm. Those of you who work in the theater may receive some good write-ups.

The rest of the week appears to be spent in a mad social whirl, entertaining various friends and loved ones. Although this can be good fun, it can also be quite exhausting. It may be wise to enlist the help of loved ones and not carry the burden all by yourself, financially or otherwise.

35th Week/August 27–September 2

Friday the 27th. You are really happy and contented to be by yourself at the present. You should be able to get a good deal of thinking and contemplating done. You do not often give yourself this kind of time. Conversations or correspondence with a lover can be heartening. Children can be very sweet and gladden your heart. You may enjoy reading or writing love stories; the latter can come out of your own experience.

Saturday the 28th. A secret meeting can lay the groundwork for a business deal. You can really convince a boss that you have the know-how and the extra cash to finance a new venture. You should be doing well with any new promotion or position that gives some authority. Co-workers and employees are likely to be impressed by your knowledge, especially of machinery or computer equipment.

Sunday the 29th. A charming friend may inspire you with his or her far-reaching ideas. You may have a lot of personal plans to put into operation. Seeing a good movie or show can be most enjoyable. A sermon may set you thinking deeply about a controversial subject. Those involved with political or revolutionary groups can hold successful gatherings and gain recruits.

Monday the 30th. A lover can be very passionate and exciting. You will be in the mood for love and ready to take advantage of it. Your warmth and kindness make you attractive and good to be with. You may find that you throw yourself with energy and eagerness into a creative project. You aren't likely to rest until it's done. You may write an angry letter to a government bureau or newspaper about a child's welfare.

Tuesday the 31st. It can be easy to express your feelings and ideas to a loved one. This will be a very good morning for any kind of computing, telephoning, and letter writing activity. You have lots of creative ideas pouring in these days. Make sure you use them to the full. Don't expect too much from a spiritual group to which you belong. You may feel somewhat critical and negative about it tonight.

Wednesday September 1st. You may find that a child needs new clothes to start a new term at school. The cost of this will be higher than anticipated. Unexpected expenses for a social occasion can also set you back a bit. You are likely to feel a bit frustrated creatively and may wonder whether you will ever make your dreams come true, or will ever find the time for a favorite hobby.

Thursday the 2nd. Don't get too irate or impatient about a financial matter this morning. You may need to give a donation to a charity or help a friend in need. A car, computer, or piece of domestic equipment can break down and need repair. The cost of this will just add to the bills you already seem to be running up. If you are not feeling well, you should make an appointment to see a doctor. It can be something very minor.

Weekly Summary

Taking time to get down to some private study or work can help finances a lot. You may be in the mood to dig a hole and crawl into it. On the whole, you Aries people tend to be loners and prefer to manage things by yourselves without others fussing about you. This can be a good time for you to deal with your spiritual needs; you may desire to meditate or contemplate for hours with no interference. Put aside your worries for a while.

You will feel a need for company again by Sunday. Many of you are likely to be attending some sort of spiritual service or ceremony. Reuniting with others of a like mind can be comforting to you personally, especially if you have been feeling under the weather of late. A mate or spouse may be in a warm, loving mood, but there can still be some cross words about certain financial matters.

You still seem to be in the doldrums when it comes to getting to grips with a money matter. This can be caused by official interference or simply carelessness on someone's part. Waiting is not your favorite game, but you are just going to have to be patient now and hope people will pay their bills. If you do not watch your temper on Thursday, you will end up the loser.

36th Week/September 3–9

Friday the 3rd. This ought to be a really splendid day for social affairs. A party can prove to be a wonderful event. You will enjoy some delightful conversations with some scholarly people. Colleagues can also have a good deal to say. Their sense of humor will make things more lighthearted than usual. However, practical issues are sure to claim your attention for a part of the time.

Saturday the 4th. This holiday weekend is a favorable time to visit relatives and have a family get-together. Although you will be delighted with some new appliance or a new car, there still may be some major repairs or alterations to be made. On the whole, you should feel a bit happier about spending your hard-earned cash and also more discriminating in what you purchase.

Sunday the 5th. A sense of balance and discipline can make this a very steady and calm day. You should be able to get a good many household tasks and duties seen to. It can be nice to sit with the family and plan some trips to far-off places or even just to the seashore. Students can be getting started on their work again with a great deal of enthusiasm and energy. An unexpected visitor may appear.

Monday the 6th. Children seem to be spreading chaos in your life this holiday. However, your attitude seems to be philosophical and good-humored rather than irate. This can be a trying time for students who are arriving at new schools. You may find yourself getting lost in a complex of buildings you are not familiar with. However, this can be a good day for creative people, as your imagination should be fired.

Tuesday the 7th. This is a favorable day for anyone dealing with disabled or problem children. Although they may not be easy to handle, you seem to have matters under control. You can find that creative ideas are hard to whip into shape. But you do seem to have plenty of insights and new ideas at this particular time. You may find that a lover has something unusual in store for you. It is sure to be a pleasant surprise.

Wednesday the 8th. You can deal with some intricate problems or situations just now. However, be sure to use as much discrimination and tact as you can when at a meeting. An interview for a new job should be quite successful. But you may find yourself rushing around all over the place to try to fit in all your routine chores and tasks. The day can be good for those involved in craft work or anything requiring a delicate touch.

Thursday the 9th. You should be able to make a fair bit of cash through crafts or piecework. You may find that it is necessary to travel some distance in order to see an important individual. If this is about a new job, it should be worth the effort. A car or other machinery will be reliable and helpful. You may need to go over a lot of details when signing an agreement.

Weekly Summary

This week can find you quite busy around the home. You seem to have a lot of little, detailed tasks to see to; they require patience and thought. Relatives can be a good deal more helpful than you expect, but it can take a lot of persuading to get some of them to lend a hand with any jobs about the home and yard. This seems to be a time for practical domestic matters.

You will enjoy meeting a lover over the weekend. However, you may be a trifle disillusioned about some situation that has recently arisen. You may need to take a more forgiving or compassionate view. This can apply to your dealings with children also. They still seem to be making demands for goodies, demands that you simply cannot or will not meet. You are likely to have a somewhat changeable attitude toward them, which may be confusing all around. Try to be more consistent when dealing with youngsters.

It isn't easy for you impatient Aries people to concentrate on fine details and tiny, delicate things, but this seems to be what you have to learn just now. From working with small animals in need of care, to doing dainty craft work, you are going to need lots of patience and a good eye.

37th Week/September 10–16

Friday the 10th. You can find a meeting at work very interesting. Try not to spend too much time gossiping with colleagues. A boss seems to be very pleased with your recent efforts and hard work. You will be feeling calmer and more disciplined than you have for a long while. A doctor may have some good news about a recent test. This is likely to be a constructive working day. Try to take the evening off to relax.

Saturday the 11th. A partner seems to have some very imaginative ideas for a social event. You will enjoy going to a film or theatrical production that has a fantasy quality. It can really energize you to be sharing a group activity with a mate or spouse. You may be involved in spiritual and philosophical activities on Rosh Hashanah. Others may share sports enthusiasms and support a team together.

Sunday the 12th. This can be a very happy day for you and a loved one. You should find that a lot of old grievances can now be left behind. Children are sure to be sweet-natured and good company. You are in a charming and loving mood, which will go a long way toward making others around you feel good. Creativity shared can produce some good results, especially in art and music. A concert can round off the day.

Monday the 13th. Things may get a bit out of hand when dealing with certain business or financial matters. You may have to seek some advice when presented with too many tempting possibilities for expansion. Take care when purchasing goods lest you be hoodwinked by a crafty salesperson. So keep your wits about you, and don't be gullible. Examine merchandise carefully before paying for it.

Tuesday the 14th. A sudden and unexpected turn of events may set back all your hopes and objectives. This may be due to a large bill or some other debt coming up that needs payment at once. An official can be interfering and leave you feeling annoyed and frustrated. Be patient with an older person who may be having trouble keeping track of his or her money. This will not be a good day for creative work.

Wednesday the 15th. Pay attention to the details of a contract or agreement this morning. It can be a good time to call a meeting of shareholders or family members. You may be able to smooth out a good many minor problems and petty anxieties. A talk with a therapist can become quite deep and should be fruitful. Travel later in the day can be exciting. You will tend to feel very deeply about political and philosophical issues.

Thursday the 16th. This can be a good day for you students, especially if you are working as a team or group. You can make a lot of useful discoveries and dig deeply into your particular subject or interest. This can be a very good time to study psychology or the occult. Police and legal activities will also be of considerable interest. You may have some surprising results in all aspects of your life.

Weekly Summary

Being with a partner or a mate seems to be very satisfying and enjoyable over the weekend. You will enjoy sharing time with others and doing things together. There should be less inclination to go off on your own. Tact, charm, and diplomacy are all high on your list now and can make a splendid impression on someone you would like to attract. Some of you may find a new romance at a party or social activity; a group meeting place can also be a rendezvous for others in love.

Business matters can get extremely complicated this week. You may wonder just how much you can expand and open up new horizons, or whether it may be better to cut back and hold your fire. It would be best to wait before making any decisions. Friends or cooperative ventures can be proving unreliable. Officials also seem to be tying everything up in red tape and causing problems.

If you are a student, you may be into some very deep and absorbing subjects. This is time when you want to explore much more deeply the meaning of life and your place in it all. You can be doing this along with a few other people. Among you, you may unearth some very interesting answers.

38th Week/September 17–23

Friday the 17th. This is a fine day for those interested in the theater. Musical shows or concerts can give you and a loved one a good deal of pleasure. You may have to placate a boss. Take no notice of nitpickers. Maybe their health is causing problems. You can do far more good by being sympathetic and ready to listen to another's tale of woe. A shoulder to cry on may be just what someone needs.

Saturday the 18th. A legal matter may need discussing. You can be asked for advice on alimony or some other financial claim. You are likely to be in a generous and expansive mood. This can make you a little too indulgent to a loved one. The day is good for professional matters. This can be a good time to consider making a move to larger premises. A long-distance phone call can cost a lot, so keep an eye on the clock.

Sunday the 19th. This Sunday ought to be an auspicious day for a career matter. You can be in the mood to get down to organizing and getting finances straightened out. You may feel a desire to get rid of a lot of possessions such as equipment and knickknacks that are just taking up room. You really feel you can do with far less around you, and your needs have become relatively few in recent years.

Monday the 20th. You seem to be on the right side of an employer this morning and are likely to feel very confident about a work matter. Practicality seems to dominate the day. Later on, you may hesitate to keep a social engagement or go to group meeting. Try not to dream too much about a future meeting with a lover. You could be disillusioned with the reality. Religious observances can occupy evening hours.

Tuesday the 21st. You may be making too many plans and have far too many expectations. If you have a lot of social engagements for the day, it may be a good idea to give some careful thought to cutting down a bit on all this manic activity. The day is favorable for wide-ranging and in-depth conversations with a mate or spouse. You aren't likely to be in the mood for trivia and will have no patience with idle chitchat.

Wednesday the 22nd. A friend may be somewhat cool and frosty to you now. You may wonder what on earth you have done. But it may not be anything personal at all. Try to remain detached. A group meeting tonight can be canceled, and this can be a real disappointment. You may have hoped to meet a loved one there. A theatrical outing can turn out to be very boring and costly.

Thursday the 23rd. You may decide that you enjoy your own company best after all the letdowns of yesterday. A visit to an in-law in the hospital is sure to be cheering for the patient. Students can find that a debate can turn quite electric. You can certainly thrash out a few new ideas and go a long way toward putting the world to rights. A team game is sure to be lively and produce one or two surprise results.

Weekly Summary

Your professional interests seem to be working out very well nowadays. You can find that you are getting in more work if you are self-employed and are expanding your business rapidly. You seem to be in a dedicated and serious mood about what you do and willing to work long hours. This certainly will help to bring in a steadier income. An employer is ready to commend you for your efforts this week.

You may begin to feel as if your attachment to a certain group of people is cooling off this week. At times, their pragmatic and mundane attitude can be quite dreary. A long-standing friendship may now be getting more and more distant. Perhaps you are in need of a change of some sort, as your boredom threshold tends to be a bit low. You might view everything and everyone with a happier eye if you can get away for a while.

If you take a little time off from your usual activities and have a day to yourself, you can recharge your psychic batteries. Thursday can be a good day for finding yourself some freedom. You can curl up and read some exciting and electrifying books or take a trip somewhere different all by yourself.

39th Week/September 24–30

Friday the 24th. You certainly put your all into your social engagements at present. You can have some really exciting conversations with a crowd of friends. Talks about science or astrology should be very revealing. Try not to overdo things, as you tend to be accident-prone. A fall could prevent you from going on a journey, so take great care not to rush about and watch your step.

Saturday the 25th. You can be very glamorous and highly magnetic to someone. If you want to make a good impression, keep that person intrigued and mystified. A partner will be very understanding of your needs right now. You may find that you share many philosophies and political convictions about life with someone special. Take the lead at a group gathering, and others will gladly follow you.

Sunday the 26th. There is no doubt that people find your conversation, or a talk you give, very interesting and forceful. You may be involved in some sort of political debate. Take care, though, to be as diplomatic as you can with a loved one. It is possible that your blunt and honest expression can be misunderstood and cause problems. This may be a good time for an art exhibit or concert.

Monday the 27th. You appear to be living in some sort of cloud-cuckoo-land where money is concerned. You certainly seem to be spending as if there were no tomorrow. Still, a good friend may deserve being honored and treated. This is not an auspicious day for shopping. Your judgment may not be at its best. You could end up with something you really will regret in a more sober moment. It may be hard to exchange it later.

Tuesday the 28th. A sudden request for money can pop up out of the blue. This can throw your neat plans out of whack and really upset you. You may be setting for yourself a lot of goals and have a lot of ambitions just now. But be prepared for the unexpected, and don't set up too many rigid barriers and limits. Take care if you are making a property purchase; don't rush in impatiently.

Wednesday the 29th. You still can have a lot of problems getting a creative or artistic project off the ground. It may be that you are running out of resources. Use all your tact and charm to get someone influential to help you out. You can find that a partner is willing to be helpful and self-sacrificing. You can rope in the neighbors too if you are involved in a local event. They will enjoy it with you.

Thursday the 30th. Neighbors are likely to annoy you at times. You can feel that they are being too noisy or boisterous with a party or other gathering. However, you will be wise to keep as quiet as you can if you don't want trouble. The more friendly you can be with local folks, the better for you. You may find travel difficult with road repairs, heavy traffic, and other annoying delays.

Weekly Summary

Your own need to shine and show others what you are made of can really come across this week. In fact, you are likely to find yourself in the right places at the right times. You will impress someone who can be influential in your life. You can make some time available this week to groom and glamorize yourself. You may find that a new dress, haircut, or suit can truly transform your image. Generally this will be a good week for personal interests.

Be even more careful than usual when out on any shopping sprees this week. Your judgment will not be at its best on Monday. In fact, you can at times appear to be in a dream or else very absentminded. This can lead to having your pocket picked or being conned by some get-rich-quick scheme. Say no rather than yes until you have thought things through coolly. Real estate deals also need to be entered into with some caution.

A neighbor's party may be more than you can bear. But you will need to keep your feelings to yourself just now. You appear to have a vested interest in getting on with local folks, and it would be foolish to upset the apple cart now. It certainly doesn't seem too peaceful in your neighborhood all around.

40th Week/October 1–7

Friday October 1st. This can be an ideal day for letter writing, or creative writing work. You can do particularly well with romantic subjects. Those of you who are into art and music may have a local exhibit or performance. Teachers can find children particularly good-tempered and easy to deal with. A powerful individual may enter your life now and be of enormous influence for good.

Saturday the 2nd. You may find that a parent is proving a bit of a problem with advancing age. Or you may have to be a little more strict with an older child. This can be a useful day when family matters can be discussed and solved. A relative may entrust an old and valuable heirloom to your care. You can enjoy looking over old letters and possessions, reviving old memories and sharing them with offspring.

Sunday the 3rd. A conversation with a mate or spouse may not be very satisfactory. The morning can be spent chattering and wasting time with family members instead of going to religious services. Later you can feel a yearning to get away from the petty annoyance of financial matters. However, a phone call to the right person may produce some extra cash. Creative writing or teaching can bring pleasure and satisfaction.

Monday the 4th. Students may want to get ahead with some project. But unexpected social events seem to interfere with any plans. Children are likely to act in unpredictable or disruptive ways. You may not find it easy to keep the situation under control and may as well give up trying. Just flow with events, and look on it all as a bit of a drama that does not require an expensive ticket to the theater.

Tuesday the 5th. This can prove to be a far more energetic and efficient day. You can enjoy a warm and caring lover's company. This can serve to restore your faith and cheer you up. The day promises to be good for those working with children or students. They can be a lot more enthusiastic than usual as well as more cooperative. Naturally this will help to put the subject across far better.

Wednesday the 6th. Although traveling can be a bit of a trial, you may find that meeting someone unusual makes it all worth the effort. This is a good day for making progress with your daily tasks. It may be a good time to catch up on correspondence or to send out bills to clients. Some of you may be using the phone or computer a lot more in your normal workaday lives. You may consider working more out of your homes.

Thursday the 7th. This is likely to be a plodding, slow, but useful day at work. You can get on conscientiously with what has to be done. Try not to rush the pace; let it go its own way. Be especially careful when driving long distances, as accidents caused by someone else's impatience can occur. You may end the day feeling a little headachy, perhaps the result of long periods of concentration.

Weekly Summary

A special person seems to be joining the family this week. This may be a new bride or a new baby. One way or another, you can be really excited by some cheering family occasion and get-together. If this takes place at your home and you are host, you arc likely to be hospitable, happy, and good company. Conversations, gossip, trips down memory lane, can all make this a nostalgic but happy weekend.

You may have a lot of dealings with children and adolescents this week. It may be part of your work if you are a teacher. However, a noticeable improvement in relations seems to occur now. Youngsters do appear to be a lot calmer and more inclined to be harmonious and helpful. This can be a good time to start off some sort of artistic or creative activity either for yourself or with young people.

Although there is a lot to do in your daily work, you may have to break off to deal with some unusual people. Those of you who have pets may feel worried about them and take them to see a specialist. Although this may require a journey, you pet lovers aren't likely to let that put you off.

41st Week/October 8–14

Friday the 8th. A business partner may want to straighten out a company or group situation, so you may need to unearth all sorts of facts and figures. A healing group can make a real transformation in you. You should be in a very charitable and compassionate mood now. This can lead to a deeper involvement in some sort of politically motivated group that has humanitarian aims or concerns the environment.

Saturday the 9th. This is a very good day for making a new start in a relationship. Therefore those of you who are considering an engagement or marriage will do well. You and a mate or spouse can enjoy being out with a group of friends tonight. You can really shine, and you will be the soul of diplomacy for once. Any legal matters that have been hanging fire can now be settled satisfactorily.

Sunday the 10th. Cheerful encounters with others makes this a pleasing and happy day. The morning can be a good time to discuss your more philosophical or spiritual views with another. Students should find debates and discussions worthwhile. You may find that a person you know from work is a more romantic figure than you supposed. Doing everyday tasks can be very peaceful and soothing.

Monday the 11th. You may feel a need to call a meeting of shareholders or business partners as a result of some sudden crisis. This may affect your personal financial position as well. Those of you who are connected with banks, the stock markets, and so on should be prepared for a few shocks and surprises. However, don't let anyone involve you in a get-rich-quick scheme. This is not a time to gamble.

Tuesday the 12th. Make good use of a fairly laid-back and quiet day to get a few neglected tasks done. For some of you, this can be a humdrum, even boring, day with little of note occurring. But it is good to get off the treadmill now and then. You may find time to work on some accounts, pay bills, and see to insurance or income tax matters. You can find the time to set up a new filing system.

Wednesday the 13th. In some ways you can feel a bit victimized by someone. A co-worker may be critical about your work, and this can really infuriate your sense of pride. Meetings with a variety of interesting people can enliven your day. Long and deep discussions can help to sort out the world's problems, or at least you may think they do. You may get a bit worked up about some issues nearer home.

Thursday the 14th. A new curriculum can make a study program more interesting again. You will enjoy scientific subjects or astrology, especially if meeting with groups of like-minded people. Conversations can get very deep but still remain detached. You may tend to feel that you will never come to a particular business agreement because people keep changing their minds.

Weekly Summary

Dealings with other people can give you a lot of insight into yourself and your own motives. You seem to be meeting a good many interesting and communicative people these days. This is always stimulating for you Aries people. There is nothing you enjoy more than a good debate with intelligent opponents. Some of you Aries lovers will find this a good time to propose or maybe even tie the knot.

If you have a lot of money matters to discuss, it may be a good thing to get partners and shareholders to a meeting. This way you can consider any recent changes and proposals with some detachment. This is not too good a time to begin any new financial commitments or to take any risks expanding an existing business. Some things are best kept under wraps, so don't be too open about everything.

You seem to be getting into some pretty deep waters when it comes to political matters or student debates and policies. You will be wise to keep as calm as you can, even when you feel that you are being criticized or someone is undercutting you. You should try to be philosophical and detached about it all.

42nd Week/October 15–21

Friday the 15th. This is likely to be a brisk and energetic time. You may enjoy going for long walks this morning to keep yourself fit. The day is favorable also for those who enjoy mountaineering or other such active and adventurous athletic activities. In fact, you will do best to use up surplus energy physically rather than in having a big row with someone. Later in the day you may get a good career break.

Saturday the 16th. This can be a delightful day for professional interests and activities. You may feel magnetically drawn to someone attractive if you are at work. However, it may be hard for you to think of anything to say to break the ice. You can feel a bit depressed over a bill, letter, or call about a financial matter. Driving anywhere can tend to be a slow affair with many delays.

Sunday the 17th. You are likely to feel that you are being underestimated by a boss. This can lead to some sort of confrontation in the coming week. Your partner or spouse may be at odds with you at present. If you have to make a public appearance, you may find that you feel a bit out of sorts. However, you will just have to stand alone and not rely on any one else for help. Remember that the buck stops with you.

Monday the 18th. Don't play into the hands of some unscrupulous acquaintance. Be a little wary and not too trusting, especially if money is involved. You can certainly enjoy a good professional reputation. In fact, you can also earn a good sum of money, which is sure to cheer you up. This can be a good time for sorting out old clothes and ornaments and clearing your cupboards and closets. Much can be given or thrown away.

Tuesday the 19th. A solemn social function can be depressing. You may meet a good many old friends. Maybe you will have to say goodbye to someone. This is not an easy day for dealing with officials or unsnarling red tape. Income tax matters, wills, insurance, and other problems can become burdensome and irritating. However, you will just have to forge ahead with it all and bring it to some sort of order.

Wednesday the 20th. You seem to be back on top of things again. A special person in your life may invite you to a little gathering this morning. The afternoon should see you feeling very jolly and happy but in a calm and gentle kind of way. You are likely to be very busy with your professional or public interests. However, you always find active days invigorating, so you will enjoy this one.

Thursday the 21st. This is likely to be a secluded and quiet day. You may need to work in private and thus get out of the rat race for a bit. The day is good for research work that requires a lot of detailed investigation. It is good also for surgery or medical matters of all kinds. You may find that you get emotional over someone's unnecessary critical comments about your work.

Weekly Summary

Although your career prospects have been looking up for a while now, you may still feel that certain things are dragging along too slowly. However, everything is sent to teach us a lesson, and yours this week is patience. Try not to feel too put down by the critical attitudes of colleagues. If you can learn from what they say, you will be the winner, not they. This is not an easy time for those of you who deal with the public in some way.

You seem to have so many plans and goals for the future right now. But you are not alone, as a partner or other special individual seems ready to go along with your hopes and wishes. For some of you, these may be plans for retirement; for others, more creative ventures. But all in all, you need to stick to your ideas and not let petty officials or negative people put you off.

You will spend the latter part of the week in a cheerful and happy mood. You seem very pleased to be left alone by others for a change. Spend some time alone, in seclusion, or just go away to a religious retreat for a while. This can put you in touch with yourself again. It doesn't mean that you will sit about doing nothing, though. You still will be keeping busy and on the go.

43rd Week/October 22–28

Friday the 22nd. A meeting can take place in a furtive or quiet way early in the day. This can turn out to be beneficial for you from a financial viewpoint. A therapy session will unearth some interesting hidden fact. You can find a healing session important to you personally later on. Generally this will be a time for attending to your own needs and health matters. Now is a good time for scheduling a medical appointment.

Saturday the 23rd. You will work very hard, but it may seem that little is being achieved. In fact, you may feel personally responsible for things going wrong. This is probably just an idea, and friends may try to reassure you. However, for a little while, a partner may seem to lose faith in you and tell you so. This can really hurt you. You too can feel let down by a special person.

Sunday the 24th. Some work you have done recently can bring in some cash returns. You may be involved in craft work, dressmaking, cooking, and other detailed work. However, as soon as your pocket is filled, it may have to be emptied again. Among your papers, you can find overlooked bills for some hefty amounts. A lover, older than yourself, may become more important. You may study religions together.

Monday the 25th. This is likely to be a brisk and lively day for shopping expeditions. But take care not to be deluded into buying faulty goods. You can carry on with your recent rush of activity at work, confident that you are now earning steadily and well. Overtime, extra bonuses, and other little perks can really help your bank balance now. Get some advice and make sure you invest your funds wisely.

Tuesday the 26th. This seems to be a good time to take a course to develop mechanical or engineering skills. You may find that repairs to a car are very costly and set you back financially. You can enjoy a meeting with a crowd of neighbors later in the day. You may all be interested in charitable matters. Or you will just enjoy watching movies together. The afternoon can be the best time for travel.

Wednesday the 27th. This seems to be an unusual day for those traveling on the highways. You may keep coming up against various road repairs and other interruptions. Still, you seem to take all ups and downs in your stride and keep your cool very nicely. However, others may not be so philosophical and can act like infants at times. You may find that a neighbor is being difficult about a property issue.

Thursday the 28th. This is a day on which to feel self-confident and show it. This can be very attractive to others. It may get you more attention than you want from the opposite sex. You should be pleased with a bonus or a promotion at work. Although you have a lot of detailed artwork or other fine work to do, your attention may tend to wander. An occasional coffee break can keep you on your toes.

Weekly Summary

You are likely to put a great deal of energy and push into your personal ambitions and interests at the start of this week. Take care not to ride roughshod over everyone in your eagerness to get ahead. Doing this is sure to cause a few conflagrations. Others may accuse you of being selfish just now. But the point it that you are bursting with energy and long for some sort of change in your activities.

Take things a little more slowly if you can this weekend. You may have to apply your mind and interest to various personal financial matters that need resolving. On the whole, things seem to be looking up for you. You ought to feel that you are being valued and paid in the way you deserve. You may take up a new course of some sort now that can eventually help augment your earnings or else make you better at what you do.

Neighbors don't seem to be that easy to get along with at present. Of course, they may be saying that it is your own critical or pushy attitude that is the problem. But your sense of humor is definitely a saving grace and can help smooth over any tricky moments.

44th Week/October 29–November 4

Friday the 29th. You can exude an air of quiet confidence in yourself. You may decide to go ahead with some money matter such as a mortgage or loan. This may be needed for various important repairs or improvements on the home. After a busy day at work, many of you Aries people will be very glad to be home. Someone special can help soothe your spirits.

Saturday the 30th. A relaxed and happy day puttering around the house or garden should put you in good spirits. You may have a few errands to do this afternoon, errands that cannot be left for another day. A lot of plans may be afoot concerning a child's education. These may involve sorting out books, buying new uniforms, and other important needs. Comedies at the theater can be very entertaining and also give food for thought.

Sunday the 31st. You may be a little confused about your priorities. There can be a problem with a youngster. Take care not to drink too much when out on the town with friends tonight. This can be a day of many surprises and letdowns, especially in connection with social engagements. You really need to keep your own counsel on a creative matter. Silence may be better than criticism.

Monday November 1st. Some of you Aries people will be in a creative mood. But it really does seem hard to get yourselves motivated or interested in anything in particular. What energy is available may as well be used to rest and just enjoy yourself for a change. You don't always have to be achieving something. Playing with children can be strenuous, but you will gain in understanding.

Tuesday the 2nd. This is more likely to be a happy, cheerful day for you personally. You can meet a lover this morning, and this can make you feel very good. However, some of the euphoria may dissipate by the afternoon. You may find that a journey is beset with problems. Some of these are likely to be mechanical, so be sure to have your car checked before you make that important trip to vote at your polling place.

Wednesday the 3rd. Your eagerness and enthusiasm for certain tasks can make light work of them. You can be dedicated to finishing off certain important jobs even though it may mean putting in overtime. Physically and mentally, you should be feeling calm, cheerful, and stable. It can be a good day for anyone dealing with pets. This should also be a favorable day for anyone having surgery or performing such operations.

Thursday the 4th. You can be really relaxed with workmates this morning. In fact, it may be a good time to have some sort of office party or social event. You may be busy with cooking, craft work, or needlework early in the day. However, later on you and a mate or spouse may have a journey in mind. You can also enjoy a pleasant social event together later tonight.

Weekly Summary

There seem to be a good many little tasks to see to at home this week. You will be relaxed and content to be in your own environment. However, a certain restlessness may come over you again after a few days of domestic bliss. Many of you Aries people can enjoy making the home look attractive. This may mean getting down to the nitty-gritty of decorating, do-it-yourself activities, and even tidying up the yard.

The weekend will be a good time for those of you who are in a creative mood. You may not be at all in the mood for socializing and more inclined to work on a favorite hobby. Many of you seem to be interested in writing or reading about travel just now. Perhaps ideas about this can be incorporated into your creativity. The theater can also give many of you a lot of pleasure and inspiration.

There seems to be a good deal of work to catch up on, and you are definitely in the mood to get it all done. You should be feeling very disciplined and remarkably orderly and practical. What is more, you really want to complete your tasks instead of leaving a trail of half-finished jobs. You can find workmates far more pleasant to be with these days.

45th Week/November 5–11

Friday the 5th. A superior seems to be ready to make some sweeping changes. This can make you feel very unsettled and apprehensive. You may be upset by a powerful individual's attitude toward a business scheme. Some of you may be working out terms of a divorce settlement. Or you may have to be in court about other matters. Students need to be sure they are well prepared for any exams.

Saturday the 6th. A partner may take advantage of your good nature and generosity. Naturally, this can make you feel a bit upset and annoyed. You may feel that you are being hurtfully rejected by someone who is quite influential. This is not an easy day for those in therapy. You can come across all sorts of blocks and inhibitions. You may feel a loss of faith in someone you have always thought special.

Sunday the 7th. Friends may be acting from odd, ulterior motives. You may feel quite unsure about whom to trust regarding a joint financial move. It can be a difficult day for social or group activities. Maybe you are not in the mood for sentimental and silly people. You can find this a good day for buying stock in bulk or finding unusual Christmas gift items at church fairs.

Monday the 8th. Trying to sort out a family financial matter can be hard work. But you really do need to make a fresh start in this area. You may have to work hard, perhaps put in a lot of overtime. But you will feel a sense of satisfaction in augmenting your paycheck. You may feel somewhat heavy and dejected at times, but work can provide a good antidote to the blues.

Tuesday the 9th. If you and a loved one intend to take a trip abroad, this should be a favorable time for it. You can enjoy meeting pleasant and interesting new people. The day is good for parties, going to the theater, and films. Generally this can turn out to be a relaxed and delightful day. You may enjoy reading travel books or romances, depending on your taste. Or you can enjoy long telephone conversations.

Wednesday the 10th. If you are enjoying an exotic late vacation now, this should be a particularly wonderful day. Friends and social activities will all help to make this an exciting time for many of you. Even those of you who are visiting in-laws will find things going well.

If you are on your honeymoon, this can be a very special day to remember. Both indoor and outdoor activities will be fun.

Thursday the 11th. You ought to be really relaxed, cheerful, and expansive by now. This is a day for enjoying yourself in your own way. You can have fun traveling around and seeing new sights, broadening the mind with new ideas. Students will find this an exceptionally good day. You can feel very confident about yourself; any tests or exams can be passed with flying colors.

Weekly Summary

For some of you Aries people, this can be a special week for partnership issues. You may find the start of the week a bit nerve-racking. Some of you may be getting married, some of you divorced. But your life pattern is likely to change through another person who is currently involved with you. For those of you who are taking the plunge, don't let wedding day nerves affect you too badly. This can be a difficult week for any Aries people involved in legal matters.

Take some advice; get your financial position straightened out this week. You may simply be collecting cash or seeing what you have to spare for a vacation, a trip someplace, or just for Christmas spending. Any new joint business ventures need to be carefully worked out this week before getting involved up to your neck. Some of you may be sorting out inheritance matters now and finding that dealing with officials can be frustratingly slow.

The week seems to end on a really splendid note for many of you. You may be taking a special vacation abroad in places you have always yearned to visit. For some, this may be a honeymoon. For others, it can be just a much-needed break.

46th Week/November 12–18

Friday the 12th. A meeting with a person of some influence in the financial world can really help you out with a career move. You need to be very honest about where you stand when dealing with others. This is a good time to lay your cards on the table when it comes to a professional matter. You may be inclined to make a thorough investigation or exposure of something important.

Saturday the 13th. This is likely to be a very good day for professional and career matters. You will work steadily and carefully at any projects at present in the pipeline. Your thoroughness can really impress an accountant or other official figure. Dealing with taxes, accounts, and so on will keep you busy. The day will be good for shopping, although you are most likely to look for practical items.

Sunday the 14th. A meeting of shareholders this morning, unusual on a weekend, may come up with some good ideas. But it will not yet be time to put them into operation. Later in the day you can find that something you bought recently is not quite up to your standard. This can make you feel quite upset, especially if it was an expensive item. A group meeting tonight can be frustrating.

Monday the 15th. Your friends can do a lot to help you now. You may be able to enlist the aid of a powerful group of people. This will help with any political activities. The day will be good for those of you in therapy; you can find it easier to talk about things that once were painful. Students can find that they are amazingly unconcerned about the results of an examination.

Tuesday the 16th. Your social life can be fun at the present, even though it is a bit noisy at times. You may meet a very important and influential individual at a group meeting or activity. Your confident and sunny approach should bring you positive results. You may be interested in machinery, especially cars. This can be a good day for those Aries who are in the automotive selling or repairing business.

Wednesday the 17th. You may find that you are not especially inclined to rush about now. Some of you may even be feeling a bit under the weather. You need to take care when traveling. This is likely to be a day when you will feel inclined just to stay in and be by yourself. Try not to get too depressed if things aren't working out as you planned. Try to avoid taking on tasks that require particular concentration.

Thursday the 18th. Now you should find your spirits lifted considerably. You can find that some important research or study into a professional matter is paying off. You really seem to have impressed a very clever or influential person with your efforts. This can be a good day for dealing with legal matters and publishing. A musical concert in which you participate can also go well tonight.

Weekly Summary

Those of you who deal with the public may find this a mixed blessing. You can be very charming and decidedly more inclined to be tactful than usual. This certainly will help when dealing with some pretty difficult customers or clients. On the whole, you are ready to get down to hard work. There is no slacking about you these days. You seem to be fired with ambition, especially to make plenty of money.

The weekend can find you socially busy and involved with various friends. This can be caused by the fact that someone important, perhaps a foreign visitor, needs to be entertained. You seem to have the main responsibility to see that all goes well. This can be a good time for group involvements of all kinds. Those of you who are involved in group therapy may find that you lead the others in some way or that you can help them understand themselves.

You will enjoy getting away from it all after the weekend and having some time alone. This may give you a little time for a meeting with a lover. Such encounters can have a transforming and magical effect. It will also offer an opportunity for some contemplation and quiet for those who prefer their own company.

47th Week/November 19–25

Friday the 19th. You may have a great desire to take a group of friends on a trip. Your studies in film and photography will be of interest to others. Perhaps a slide show of your travels may be on the cards. The day is good for students. A crowd of you may be inclined to celebrate tonight, especially if an important exam is finally over. You may be more sensitive to the needs of others at the present.

Saturday the 20th. Something that happens if you are at work may upset the apple cart. This can make you feel a bit irritable. But don't take your frustration out on a loved one. A group of people you know may disrupt your personal plans for a night out. It may mean having to give up your plans to help out with some other activity. However, a partner may not take too kindly to such changes.

Sunday the 21st. A benevolent and good-humored attitude can help soothe a mate or spouse this morning. You can get up feeling pretty good and ready for fun. It may be important to come to see that some of your hopes and wishes of late are a little impractical. However, don't give up on anything. A loved one may be able to help out with some detached advice or even lend some money. A religious service can inspire you.

Monday the 22nd. You do need to take a long, hard look at a financial situation. You may have been going a bit overboard with social activities and expenses.

Your mind may tend to dwell on morbid or involved matters. You can feel sometimes that you are working away and have little to show for it. News of a friend is likely to depress you further. Sharing your worries with someone else can help.

Tuesday the 23rd. Some lively goings-on at work can perk you up. You may find that dealing with the public keeps you on your toes this morning. The afternoon may be difficult for travelers. You may find that road repairs are needed, or you may come up against municipal works that halt or delay your journey. Be sure to listen carefully to the traffic news before setting off. Holiday travel may be getting an early start.

Wednesday the 24th. Unusual activities in your locality can make the day a lot of fun. You may be involved in various local or educational matters. Organizing social events for underprivileged people may be a part of your contribution forward making their lives more pleasant at Thanksgiving. You are in the mood to help out with charitable and community activities. Finding willing helpers should be easy.

Thursday the 25th. This can be a quite peaceful Thanksgiving Day for you Aries people. Instead of your usual action-packed activities, you may be doing a lot of planning, researching, and deep thinking. You may have a festive dinner with others who are interested in teaching or reading about psychology, the occult, and other hidden subjects. A discussion about some joint financial involvements can seem to move things forward now.

Weekly Summary

There will be a lot of special things that you plan to do early in the week. You may at last be in a position to achieve something that really interests you and that you can put your heart and soul into. Although you may be very friendly and inclined to be sensitive to the needs of others, the odd flare-up can still occur if you let someone at work push you around too much. However, you are more inclined toward compromise just now.

Your personal finances seem a little more stable this week, which is cheering. But you may feel that you have worked really hard to get very little in the end. However, there isn't a lot you can do to reverse the trend just now. So be patient, and things will change fairly soon. Shopping expeditions can be exhausting but necessary. At least you can save yourself some of that last-minute Christmas rush.

This should be a very good time to sit down and sort out your greeting cards, write your once-a-year letters of goodwill, and generally catch up on news from friends and relatives. You may receive some stimulating news about neighbors or local activities. It should also be a good time to catch up on some reading.

48th Week/November 26–December 2

Friday the 26th. A steady and practical attitude toward family matters can help a lot. You may feel inclined to get rid of a lot of possessions and do with less of everything. This is a good time to catch up on a relative's news. You may have someone to stay with you for a while and enjoy some intriguing gossip. A partner can seem withdrawn and silent at times but will be interested anyway.

Saturday the 27th. You are likely to be in a quite inspired mood. This can be usefully channeled into creative matters or a favorite hobby. If you take a trip, it is likely to be for pleasure as well as learning. A film or theatrical production should win good reviews. However, a certain social engagement may tend to be a bit of a flop despite your efforts. People just do not seem to be in the mood for fun.

Sunday the 28th. You may feel as if you got out of the wrong side of the bed this morning. Things just look bleak and boring, and you may long for a change. A mate or spouse will be very loving and affectionate, which will help a good deal. You may feel despondent if you haven't enough money to enjoy yourself or take your loved ones out for a treat. A church dinner can provide an alternative.

Monday the 29th. The morning is likely to be a lot more optimistic and cheerful than yesterday. Your positive approach to a child can be beneficial to you both. A more gentle and conciliatory attitude of late is helping to keep a group of people from quarreling over trivialities. You seem to be the wise and sensible one among your friends at present. In fact, they may be grateful for your philosophical words.

Tuesday the 30th. It will call for some discipline to get through a pile of correspondence and other demanding matters at work. You can find this a day when accounts, taxes, and other financial matters need looking at in detail. An official letter may make a big difference to your daily life. You may find that matters beyond your personal control are taking over at work.

Wednesday December 1st. Lovers may have a romantic secret to share. You can feel very compassionate about someone's problems. This may be a very good time to help with healing or spiritual activities. Working in groups may be the best way. The day promises to be good for anything that requires sensitive and diplomatic handling. You are less likely to jump in with both feet.

Thursday the 2nd. Your energies seem to be poured into group matters at present. You may take a position of some leadership and power. Take care to use this wisely; resist trying to control others. If you do, you will find a rebellion on your hands. It may be necessary to play the hypocrite toward someone. Although this goes against the grain, it may be the most tactful thing to do under the circumstances.

Weekly Summary

If you can find some time to deal with your creative interests this week, you can make use of a sudden upsurge of inspiration. Sometimes it can be hard to get motivated. Often you would prefer to sit and dream the time away pleasantly. But you seem to feel some sort of obligation just now to get certain of your ideas into circulation and brought from dreams to reality. You may need to enlist the aid of loved ones to help you in this.

It can be a fairly tough time at midweek, especially at work. This may affect your health or your good spirits in some way. However, a sense of determination to overcome obstacles and difficulties is natural to you Aries people. Like the ram in the flock, you are in the mood to tackle problems head-on and straighten them out. However, things are not that straightforward this week and may need a different and more subtle approach.

You and a mate or spouse can enjoy feeling romantic and totally absorbed in one another this week. This may be due to a special anniversary or other occasion for celebration. Make the most of the sweet and sentimental mood you are both in just now. Wednesday is likely to be a particularly pleasant time to be together.

49th Week/December 3–9

Friday the 3rd. Your need to be sociable these days may run to excess. You can tend to pile it on too much with a loved one and maybe turn that person off. Keep some sort of rein on your exuberance and desire to show off. For some of you, this can be a very happy and loving day as long as you keep an eye on this extravagant streak. Your tendency can be to eat too many sweet things and make yourself ill.

Saturday the 4th. It may seem as if a group of people are being two weak and wishy-washy about a certain financial problem. You will be yearning for a more decisive attitude. Try not to let other people's opinions paralyze your actions. This can be a disappointing time for you socially unless you are celebrating Hanukkah. Things you looked forward to may turn out to be quite different.

Sunday the 5th. You may fear that an official such as an auditor or a tax inspector is going to come up with some unexpected demands and red tape. Naturally this will be a worry for you this weekend. Your interest in a therapy group seems to be diminishing. It may feel as if you are stuck and cannot move forward. This is not a very cheerful day. It seems hard to take a detached attitude toward a money matter.

Monday the 6th. A meeting can certainly get to the bottom of recent problems. You may have a deep and interesting conversation with someone this morning. A group of spiritual friends may be very delightful later in the day. You can feel quite uplifted by words you hear or books that are read aloud. If you are leading such a group, you may have some surprises in store for those present.

Tuesday the 7th. A short trip or longer journey can make you feel cheerful and lively. You will be delighted by any change of scenery. Some of you may be visiting relatives and in-laws for an extended Christmas vacation. This can be a very auspicious time for those making some sort of new start. Any sort of spiritual commitment will feel like a rebirth at this very special time of year.

Wednesday the 8th. You are likely to feel very chirpy and cheerful. Travel can be great fun and seem like an adventure. However, a loved one seems to be a little disappointed about an engagement tonight. You may feel hurt by a lover's lack of ardor. You are certainly not in the mood for platonic relationships just now. It may be time for a change of romantic partners.

Thursday the 9th. Things are definitely looking up for you Aries lovers now. A loved one may be reserved but still have deep feelings. You will enjoy appearing in public in some way. You may find that you are now benefiting from a will or insurance policy. Money may need to be spent on professional requirements. You may need to get new clothes for an interview or to spend a little on enhancing your workplace.

Weekly Summary

This is not likely to be an easy week for joint financial matters. You still seem to have a great many longings and hopes for financial improvement. It seems as if too many people are involved in your business arrangements or still owe you money. Now is the time to stop pussyfooting and being kindly and softhearted. You may have to shock others into paying their dues.

This can be a good time to take a trip to see relatives, especially if they live abroad. The break will be good for you. You should be in a very energetic mood, determined to overcome all sorts of obstacles now. Generally, a philosophical and broad-minded attitude toward life can raise you above any current worries and problems. You seem to be entering into the more spiritual significance of the time of year rather than the mundane distractions.

You can end this period feeling quite ambitious and ready to get on with career and professional matters. You now are also a little more relaxed about it all. Maybe the financial side of things is less of a problem than before. In fact, a recent loan can help you to develop your career in ways you might not have thought possible.

50th Week/December 10–16

Friday the 10th. You will find that an older person can give a lot of practical advice concerning a professional matter. Try not to be too controlling or pushy when with a friend. You may find that you have to hold in some quite hostile feelings about someone. A team sport can make you react explosively. However, you seem to have your feelings reasonably under control for the time being.

Saturday the 11th. This can be a morning for making some careless mistakes at work. Take care; pay attention as much as you can. You may find plans for an evening out misfiring later in the day. You have a tendency to fool yourself about some sentimental spiritual notion. You will do better to see life from a more realistic viewpoint. A friend may deceive you about something and thus cause you unhappiness.

Sunday the 12th. Your hopes and wishes about a lover may come to nothing. You do appear to be a little disappointed about a friend's disinterested or callous attitude. This Sunday is good for sharing knowledge and spiritual understanding with others. You may have a secret rendezvous later in the day, but you seem to feel a bit anxious about it. You are likely to wish that life could be more straighforward.

Monday the 13th. This will be a far more auspicious day, especially for personal hopes and aims. You can begin to feel more confident and positive about yourself again. This can be a good day for any kind of team sports and activities. You tend to have a good-humored, happy-go-lucky approach to others. A friend can make you laugh and keep you happy. You can spend a pleasant, relaxed evening at home.

Tuesday the 14th. Although you really long for some time alone and a quiet day, you are likely to find that nothing goes according to plan. A brother or sister may have some news for you from overseas. A letter you receive this morning can certainly put the cat among the pigeons. You may find that a group of people are acting in a quite disruptive and annoying manner, but you can do little about it.

Wednesday the 15th. This can be a good day for those who just want to curl up cozily in their private retreats and get away from it all. However, if you have to travel, you may find that road repairs and other annoying circumstances can really delay and frustrate you. You may find that certain financial problems resurface now and clamor for attention. You may also feel troubled about the health of a loved one.

Thursday the 16th. It may be necessary to hide your light under a bushel this morning. You will be wise to try to see a teacher or tutor privately about study matters. A priest may be the person to approach with an emotional problem that you are secretly experiencing. You can really relax and feel happy in a group of spiritually minded people. Or you may feel in the pensive mood to indulge in some very personal dreams and fantasies.

Weekly Summary

Although you may be as ambitious as ever about a professional matter, you can tend to lose faith on Saturday. Take a good look at what is going on. It may just be that you have expected too much from a certain situation or person. You may have to get others going in order to achieve certain important career goals. It isn't always easy to get others motivated, let alone yourself. However, a sense of responsibility can make this a disciplined and organized time for work matters.

Your social life may now start rolling again as Christmastime draws closer. You can have all sorts of involved plans for entertainment, dinner parties, and so on. However, lack of funds will still tend to curb your desires and hold you back, which can be frustrating at times. But your imagination seems to be working overtime, and you can often create wonderful things from a small budget

A need may arise to visit relatives or a loved one in the hospital. Sudden problems that arise after the weekend can disrupt your plans to snatch some time for spiritual activities such as meditation or contemplation. Your more compassionate side will rise to the occasion; you are likely to do your best to help others in distress.

51st Week/December 17–23

Friday the 17th. Personal needs may assume great importance. You can read books that really do transform your way of thinking. Some of you seem to be interested in the study of psychology, law or crime and may even be writing about these matters. An active time socially can keep you on your toes. You will find yourself working with a team of energetic and lively people, but they will elect you leader.

Saturday the 18th. This is a very good day for making progress with your own interests and needs. You ought to be feeling powerful, positive, and cheerful. The morning can be a very good time for dealing with influential people or for legal activities. A need to take a realistic rather than a hopeful look at finances can bring you down to earth with a bump later in the day. Holiday expenses seem to have lightened your purse.

Sunday the 19th. You may be able to get a friend to pay an old debt. You hate asking others to cough up what they owe you but need to be a bit more cynical and realistic about it. This is not an easy time for any sort of teamwork or friendly cooperation. You will feel very angry to hear that others have been gossiping about you and a lover. You will consider it an intrusion on your private life.

Monday the 20th. A neighbor can be very gentle and kindly toward you, and you will be glad of someone to talk to who is sympathetic. A surprise letter or phone call from overseas can wake you up and energize you. The day is good for any local shopping. You are likely to find yourself busy dashing about on all sorts of little errands. It will be a good day for travel of all kinds.

Tuesday the 21st. You may be very much annoyed to hear some local gossip. It will not be an easy day for local travel, as you may run into road repairs and various other disruptions. At times, you may wonder when things will ever settle again in your vicinity. Take care to have a car checked over if you plan a longer journey. Computers and telephone equipment may also cause problems now.

Wednesday the 22nd. This day can be good for social interaction with friends and neighbors. You are in a really lively mood and ready for fun and jollity. It can be hard work entertaining a gathering of people in your home later on. But you will soldier on and make everyone feel as comfortable as possible. A parent may prove to be quite cold and strict or become a burden on you.

Thursday the 23rd. This can be a good time for those working with other people. You can find that relatives whom you haven't seen for a while turn up to a family gathering. Now is a good time for organizing your Christmas festivities so that all runs smoothly. You tend to be somewhat serious and calm and controlled. A family member can prove to be a great support and will keep youngsters out from underfoot.

Weekly Summary

This year may see some of you Aries people taking a deeper and more personal interest in the spiritual side of the Christmas festivities. It can be important to you to get involved and lend a helping hand wherever you can. People seem to be finding your personality attractive, unusual, and kindly. This can explain why you are getting so many invitations to social events. On the whole, you will be in a happy and cheerful mood.

Although money matters will assume importance again over the weekend, you refuse to dwell too much on any problems. Not that things are necessarily any less muddled or confusing. But you can be determined to enjoy yourself and find the presents you want for yourself and others. However, you may have to cut back just a little on some of your social activities that may be more expensive than others.

This seems to be a time for meetings with neighbors and other local folks. You may find that a good deal is happening right on your own doorstep. It will not be an easy time for those of you who have to make a journey for Christmas. Take care to check your vehicle. Find the easiest routes, and listen to the traffic reports before setting off anywhere.

52nd Week/December 24–31

Friday the 24th. You are likely to spend the morning at home. Things may get busy and even manic at times. You probably will spend time wrapping presents and making sure they're hidden from prying eyes. A child may discover that there is no Santa Claus after all. You can have a tough time explaining things in this case. You can feel tired and a bit frazzled by the time the rush is over and you are free to rest.

Saturday the 25th. Merry Christmas! This may be a fairly quiet holiday. Some of you may find that you have overexcited or sick children to cope with. For some reason, you just don't seem to enjoy yourself quite as much as usual. Perhaps this is because you haven't very much money to spend and need to be less generous. But you must remember the real spirit of Christmas Day and forget the tinsel and wrappings.

Sunday the 26th. Children can be a lot more cheerful and perky now. In fact you may have a hard time containing their energies and high spirits. A good time can be had by all, and you can enjoy the company of lively friends, Your sense of humor is sure to be restored, and you can be very happy and jolly. Lots of chatter and laughter should fill the day. A child may be in a pageant at church.

Monday the 27th. Your boss may have some good news for you at work. You can enjoy getting back to a daily routine and your usual activities. Sitting about doing nothing just doesn't agree with you Aries people. Some of you may have to undertake a journey of some sort. This can result in some lively and amusing experiences. You ought to be feeling a lot healthier now that you have time for yourself.

Tuesday the 28th. This can be another pleasant day for those of you who are at work. You can find colleagues in a very jovial and merry frame of mind. Take time out for dealing with thank-you letters and other correspondence or phone calls. In-laws, aunts, and uncles may come visiting, so be prepared. You may enjoy sorting out old clothes for a bazaar or thrift shop run by a local charity.

Wednesday the 29th. A partner will be in a relaxed and peaceful mood. You can enjoy sharing your New Year resolutions together. Making secret plans and dreams and sharing your yearnings and hopes can be very special. You may feel a good deal less ambitious about your career and professional interests. In fact, you probably will be more interested in helping others in some way.

Thursday the 30th. It may seem as if you and a mate or spouse are becoming good friends as well as lovers. There can be a detachment in your approach to others at present. But this is not likely to be cool or unfriendly. A social occasion spent in the company of a group of people can turn out to be very enjoyable. Some of you may find a future partner at such a gathering tonight.

Friday the 31st. The day begins in a fast-paced and energetic manner. You will enjoy lively moments with a partner. You probably are expansive, cheerful, and ready for fun. However, some complicated situation at work can arise and claim your attention before the day is through. This may mean having to be late or even forgoing a social engagement. But if you have no choice, you might as well put up with it.

Weekly Summary

This is supposed to be the week for you to enjoy yourself and have a good time. Alas, things don't always work out this way. For some reason, you seem to find Christmastime a bit of a drag and a bore this year. Maybe you need to do something totally different for once. However, circumstances may decree otherwise. Dealing with excitable young children seems to be a harder proposition than you thought. Thankfully, things seem to pick up again after the rush of Christmas Day is over.

Just getting on with your usual routine tasks or going to work as normal seems to make you feel a lot happier than all the festivities ever did. You may find that you are given a special job by a boss or other authority figure. It may involve some sort of traveling.

You and a mate or spouse will feel very happy in each other's company this week. You seem to be inclined to get close to each other and exchange your hopes and feelings for the coming year. Sharing spiritual interests can mean that you are making your aims more humanitarian and that you may want to work together as a team in the future.

DAILY FORECASTS: JULY–DECEMBER 1998

Wednesday July 1st. This will be a propitious day for bringing together friends, partners, and relatives in a social situation. Encourage everyone to go out for dinner rather than arrange things so that you have to cook. You may resent being stuck in the kitchen.

Thursday the 2nd. Partners are likely to play a significant role in your life now, both in and out of work. If you want to make progress on a current project, get someone with a lot of knowledge in on the act. Activities revolving around children can be expensive.

Friday the 3rd. It may be difficult to ascertain where you stand in a romantic relationship at this time. Someone who has been passionate about you may be cooling off. Friends can be deceptive about their true intentions. Be on your guard and trust your intuition.

Saturday the 4th. Someone you are negotiating with in business may be trying to pull the wool over your eyes. If you sense that something is wrong, plan to have it out with the person. Avoid most business this holiday. Hold back from signing legal or binding documents.

Sunday the 5th. You are likely to feel the need to have more privacy in your life. You may not want even close partners to know what you are up to. Escaping to a spot where no one can find you will be the ideal option. An old friend can be trusted to keep a secret.

Monday the 6th. If you are beginning any kind of educational course, the work can be very intense and demanding. Try to provide more time to concentrate on your studies. A summer athletic program or sports connection can be stimulating.

Tuesday the 7th. You may have problems in trying pin down key people in order to sort out an administrative problem. If you are able to leave a message with anybody, do so. It is likely to be your only point of contact. Your energy may be too scattered for you to be able to concentrate hard on any one matter.

Wednesday the 8th. You may feel restless and irritable. You will be tempted to try to push along a work situation that really is not your responsibility. This will be inadvisable. Do not go over people's heads, as you will probably cause a lot of aggravation if you do. Play by the rules, pointless as they may seem.

Thursday the 9th. Conflict can arise on the home front when you decide to make your career a top priority. If you negotiate directly with partners or family members rather than dictate, you get a much better response. In fact they may end up being quite supportive. A development in a property move will be reassuring.

Friday the 10th. You may be asked to organize a charity function. If you have time, accept the offer. You will probably get a lot of fulfillment from your efforts. If friends try to persuade you to lend them some money, do not do so unless you can afford not to have it repaid for a long time.

Saturday the 11th. Trying to get a new project off the ground single-handedly will not work well for you. But friends may not have the time to help out. Turn to neighbors or relatives instead; they may be only too willing to lend a hand. A favor you did for someone else not so long ago is likely to be repaid.

Sunday the 12th. You Aries people are not secretive by nature. But if someone asks you to keep a confidence, make a point of doing so. Shutting yourself away at home to relax and wind down from a busy week can be a good idea. Although you may feel restless, you probably need to recharge your batteries.

Monday the 13th. Do not put heavy demands upon yourself if you can help it. Your usually ambitious streak is likely to give way to a desire to take life easy for a while. If you have time on your hands, you can still fill it productively by tidying up small tasks which do not necessarily require much effort.

Tuesday the 14th. Too much time spent running around can make you feel exhausted before too long. Although you probably have been taking life quite easy lately, you may need more rest than you think. The evening will be better than the daytime to work on new objectives. Friends are good company.

Wednesday the 15th. You will now be able to push ahead personal goals. However, you need the cooperation of your family to achieve one particular end, and this may not be forthcoming. Work on your own as much as possible, although friends may be able to help with problems that family cannot fathom.

Thursday the 16th. This will not be an ideal day for attempting to slog your way through long, major tasks. Try to focus on a number of different projects, allocating a little time to each. You will be able to maintain higher energy levels by varying the types of work. Communicate from the heart with a loved one.

Friday the 17th. Financial difficulties can arise when you notice that there has been an oversight in your budgeting. Recent, heavy credit card purchases can worry you in light of this. Call up the company and explain the situation. You may be able to have your limit raised before overpayments go through.

Saturday the 18th. It is inadvisable to lend to other people material things that have sentimental value to you. Something given as a wedding gift may end up being broken, albeit inadvertently, and you will feel very upset. If you have become involved in a new romance, this is a day for testing your true feelings.

Sunday the 19th. Long-distance travel is not advised if you are worried about the condition of your vehicle. Perhaps you can borrow a car from a relative or friend or you can beg a ride from someone else. Try to vary your activities to ease your restlessness.

Monday the 20th. You may want to tackle several projects, but may actually find it hard to settle down to any one task at all. The trick will be to avoid scattering your energy. You can lose your focus quickly through paying too much attention to fleeting thoughts.

Tuesday the 21st. Be wary of jumping to the wrong conclusions. If you are introduced to somebody new, you may form an opinion that turns out to be an inaccurate judgment of character. A connection with the past is guiding you more than you are aware.

Wednesday the 22nd. Home and family life may hold more appeal than the business world just now. The past can seem more enticing to think about than the future. Tried and tested methods will suit you more than being the pioneer you usually are.

Thursday the 23rd. The main emphasis will be on warm and loving relationships. You are entering a new phase when romance and creativity will be strongly highlighted. Single Aries will have many chances to meet someone special. Efforts to reach out to other people will meet with a positive response.

Friday the 24th. You may be raring to go but find that the right people are not around to test out your plans and ideas on. Keep working on your ideas. Time spent looking after a child can be surprisingly quiet.

Saturday the 25th. You may be invited to an exciting fun event. Be sure to go. You are bound to enjoy yourself. It may also inspire you to do something similar soon, such as throwing a party. Do not forget to invite neighbors who you feel have been good to you.

Sunday the 26th. Memories of someone from your past can be useful in helping to solve a practical problem. You may recall what this person would have done given the same situation. Or there may be a technique that he or she showed you which can save you time. Watch your spending if you go out this evening.

Monday the 27th. If work seems like one long struggle to you at the moment, you may need to offer yourself extra incentives to keep going. Do not omit considering the future and what you want to achieve in the long run. Focus on how your current endeavors will help you to reach those all-important objectives.

Tuesday the 28th. Travels and ventures undertaken with a partner or close friend prove extremely stimulating. You may feel drawn to visiting a place that has strong memories for you from a very long time ago. Your mate can be everything to you at the moment: lover, friend, and spiritual adviser too.

Wednesday the 29th. Do not rely too much on people today. They just may not come through for you. You and your loved one may argue about items to buy for the home or the decorating scheme. You may not like to admit it, but secretly you will think that your partner scores higher points in the taste stakes.

Thursday the 30th. You now are likely to feel the need to show your love and appreciation of someone who means a lot to you. This will be especially true if you feel you have been a bit unreasonable toward this person lately. Romantic prospects are high for single Aries people wishing to meet new partners.

Friday the 31st. Emotional ups and downs can use up your energy. Try to avoid full-scale arguments with children who will not leave the matter alone. Getting on with something else may seem dismissive, but you know when enough is enough. Your home life will settle into a harmonious sanctuary later.

Saturday August 1st. Buying on impulse can be tempting when you are out shopping and confronted with a persuasive salesperson. You can be talked into purchasing something you neither want nor need really. Outbursts from children should not be ignored, but little ones are perhaps being a mite manipulative.

Sunday the 2nd. You may want to get away from your usual surroundings and explore new pastures. Unfortunately, you may not get around to it because of interruptions from other people. However, if you start out early you may avoid all that. A friend with a very different lifestyle is stimulating company.

Monday the 3rd. This will be another day when you may feel a very strong need to get away from routine. However, an erratic day at work can be more demanding than you expect. It can keep you quite preoccupied, and you probably will not have time for daydreaming about exotic destinations.

Tuesday the 4th. That restless urge you have had for some days now to go somewhere new and do something just a little bit different can be fulfilled at long last. It may actually be through your work that you manage to make a trip away. Be sure you know the route you are intending to take before you set out.

Wednesday the 5th. Your career, reputation, and status are strongly highlighted. It will be a day for thinking and planning ahead in regard to your professional interests and desires. If you run your own business, this will be a key time for focusing on how to gain new business and increase profits.

Thursday the 6th. If you are out to impress somebody important, you will most likely do so by appealing to his or her charitable or secretive side. Speak openly about quite private matters, and you will probably win this person's confidence. Friends wishing to borrow money may not be reliable about paying it back.

Friday the 7th. If you fundamentally disagree with the way a friend or loved one has acted recently, you may feel the need to express your feelings to the person concerned. However, it may be that you are taking the situation either too seriously or too personally.

Saturday the 8th. A dispute may arise between you and a friend or acquaintance. Single Aries can find that romantic prospects are potentially cut short by one who gets in the way of the relationship developing. Do everything you can to shake this person off.

Sunday the 9th. A change of scene ought to refresh you. But choose a relaxing place rather than somewhere busy and noisy. Recent emotional trauma may have left you feeling quite tired. Try not to forget an important anniversary or birthday.

Monday the 10th. This will be a day when a whole host of secrets may be revealed, especially in the workplace. Socializing with colleagues can lead to somebody letting the cat out of the bag. Keep what you hear to yourself, even if other people have overheard.

Tuesday the 11th. If there is something you really want to get done, you probably will have the most success by isolating yourself in order to do it. Other people can be quite distracting. You do not have time for idle chitchat. Work on fulfilling a long-range objective.

Wednesday the 12th. You can make a lot of progress with creative efforts now. The only thing that is likely to get in your way is a domestic problem of a practical nature. If you act quickly to remedy the situation, it may not throw you too far off-course.

Thursday the 13th. You may find it difficult to get on with a loved one now because you do not see eye-to-eye on basic issues. Time spent with a special child is stimulating up to a point. Then you may need a break from that relentless activity.

Friday the 14th. You may lose something important to you if you do not keep your wits about you. Stop rushing around so much, and you will be better able to keep track of everything. Social endeavors are very enjoyable this evening, so much so that you will not know when to stop and can easily overspend.

Saturday the 15th. You are now in the fortunate position of being able to fulfill a very important goal. It is likely that you will have to get other people involved in your plans in order to succeed. You probably will not get very far if you try to go it alone. The people closest to you are the ones to call on for help.

Sunday the 16th. You are likely to be content enough simply to get together with friends or neighbors for cordial discussions. If money is a worry at the moment, you will find it helpful to discuss ways of making more with your various associates. It is possible that they recognize more of your talents than you do.

Monday the 17th. A love relationship is very exciting now. If you have recently become involved with someone new, you do not want to be away from that person for too long. While you should not allow responsibilities to fall by the wayside, this will be a good time to indulge in fun together.

Tuesday the 18th. This will be a day for conserving your resources, including your energy. Make easier your working day by falling back on traditional methods and taking shortcuts wherever you can. Time spent with your family this evening is likely to be relaxing and enjoyable, even in front of the television.

Wednesday the 19th. You are likely to be in the mood to stay at home and take care of routine tasks. If you do not need to go into the office, you would benefit from working from home, as this seems to be the environment you are most productive in now. Privacy is all important for you, so make sure you get some.

Thursday the 20th. While you are very much a loner, you are never cold toward people. There will be a strong emphasis on the open and affectionate side of your nature now. Your ability to be candid and forthright will attract a new friend to you. You can also make a deeper connection with someone special.

Friday the 21st. It will be easy to get on with anyone and everyone at the moment. You also are likely to get your way with ease, no matter what it is that you desire. Your personal charm will be your key to success. A new, creative opportunity can open up on the work scene, and it can be just right for you.

Saturday the 22nd. Work duties and responsibilities around the home are likely to absorb much of your time and energy. You probably will feel happier once the place around you is tidier and everything is in order. Aries who are out-and-out workaholics may find it difficult to resist a tempting job offer.

Sunday the 23rd. Get your house in order now if you did not manage to do so yesterday. This is true of the proverbial house too. Focus on organizing your life so that everything runs like clockwork. You are often commended for your efficiency in the workplace. Carry this over into other areas of life.

Monday the 24th. If you experienced disputes with colleagues at work before the weekend, you now will be able to sort them out and smooth the situation over. Greater responsibility with promotion is likely to be on offer for those of you who want it. A romantic evening with a love partner will be totally blissful.

Tuesday the 25th. Friendships and group activities can give you the chance to explore more of your personal ideas and interests. You desire to spend time with someone you love. There is likely to be an opportunity to deepen the bond between you. This will be a key time for single Aries people to find partners.

Wednesday the 26th. A close personal relationship will continue to be a source of great pleasure. One little fly in the ointment may be that you argue over money matters with your lover. It will be important that you tell your partner if you do not feel he or she expresses feelings of love to you often enough.

Thursday the 27th. You may have to handle a joint partnership situation with kid gloves now if you want to get your own way. Large amounts of money or the lion's share of a property may be at stake. Temper a desire to speak your mind, even though it will be extremely tempting to do so.

Friday the 28th. While yesterday you had something to lose by speaking your mind, now there will not be much point in keeping quiet about issues that are really important to you. A romantic partner may be very passionate, but you may not be in the same mood. Say so rather than try to pretend otherwise.

Saturday the 29th. A social affair where you are the center of attention is likely to be the source of great joy. You can spend much of your time talking your socks off, and it will be quite an intense time for you. But the memories of today are likely to be ones that you will treasure for a long time to come.

Sunday the 30th. A day spent traveling around with a partner or good companion is likely to bring you a lot of pleasure. Perhaps visit a place you have not been to before, or make a point of visiting relatives who live a long distance away. If you can, share the driving.

Monday the 31st. New romantic involvements are possible for single Aries people, particularly if you are involved in the academic world at all at the moment. A trip that takes you across boundary lines can also bring you into contact with a prospective new partner. You married Aries people are likely to receive romantic gestures and overtures from your beloved.

Tuesday September 1st. A colleague at work may seem to want to steal the limelight from you. It is more likely, however, that you will be sharing it together when a boss acknowledges you both for work well done. Make an effort to discipline staff who are not toeing the line or pulling their weight.

Wednesday the 2nd. Somebody in a position of authority or influence seems to have a soft spot for you at the moment. If you need a favor from this person, go ahead and ask. It is also likely that the individual in question will reveal to you a confidence that you must, without question, keep to yourself.

Thursday the 3rd. A friend may introduce you to someone you take an instant dislike to. Although this can create an awkward situation, it is not really your problem. You will not necessarily have the same taste in people as your other friends and associates. Voice your feelings diplomatically to your friend.

Friday the 4th. You may sense that friends or another social circle of people with whom you mix are opposed to your ideals and the things that really matter to you at the moment. If you feel that you are going in different directions, it may be the right time to decrease your contacts with these particular people.

Saturday the 5th. You need time to yourself in order to sort out your priorities. New money-making schemes that you are thinking about can be developed into something truly lucrative. Work on realizing them. Try to avoid making a long-distance trip if you feel at all tired. It really will not be a good idea.

Sunday the 6th. Somebody important to you wants your support in a special way now. This person may need a shoulder to cry on or may just need an understanding attitude so that he or she can unburden a problem that involves a lot of guilt or hurt. You may have other plans, but people come first now.

Monday the 7th. Once again you are tending to put other people before yourself. If you are working this holiday, a boss may need extra support from you in order to get a job done on time. Aries usually enjoy stepping in to save the day when a crisis is occurring. Take time to relax and unwind this evening.

Tuesday the 8th. After a very giving couple of days, it is time for you to be utterly selfish, or at least self-centered. If you still have the energy to pursue personal schemes, get your ideas in order and begin to act on them. If you need rest more than you need results, make your life comfortable and easygoing.

Wednesday the 9th. Be careful with material possessions, especially objects of value. Something can disappear because you do not keep an eye on it. Avoid lending items of sentimental significance to other people. You will probably regret it if you do lend in an effort to be charitable.

Thursday the 10th. This will be a day when you may worry that your financial budget will not stretch to meet the expenses that a social occasion will create. If it would not be very bad form to miss the event, why not do so? If you must go, try to think of ways in which you can compensate for the overspending.

Friday the 11th. Try to avoid getting into a panic about your financial situation. If you can calm down for a while, you will see some positive solutions ahead of you. A discussion with your bank or credit account manager can bring an immediate answer to light. In the long term, more work may be the remedy.

Saturday the 12th. Do be wary of jumping to conclusions about new people whom you meet now. There is a tendency for you to be too critical of one particular person. You can actually misjudge this person's character because you are going only by appearances. A romantic meeting with a stranger is possible.

Sunday the 13th. Time spent working on the home will be very productive. If you began a decorating project a while ago, it can be brought to completion if you make an extra effort. New plans to smarten up your home are likely to put more value on it.

Monday the 14th. Strong memories of the past are likely to be on your mind. Sights, sounds, and fragrances all can trigger very vivid recollections. As you think about times of old, you may feel prompted to get in touch with someone you have not seen for years. An opportunity to travel or get involved in interesting work can grow out of the renewed contact.

Tuesday the 15th. Domestic difficulties can be solved if you employ the services of a qualified expert. The cause of a problem that has bothered you for some time can finally be located. You need to focus your thoughts carefully now if you are to achieve much on a personal or professional level.

Wednesday the 16th. There are all sorts of ways in which you can enjoy yourself and have fun now. You are likely to be in a more hedonistic and frivolous mood than usual. However, do not cast important responsibilities to one side. An unexpected visit from a friend may take up a lot of time. Be strict.

Thursday the 17th. Whether or not you believe in spiritual guidance from within or without, you appear to be being guided by some special force at the moment. Contact with an old friend arising from your thoughts and insights can be very productive. A whole range of new opportunities may open up for you.

Friday the 18th. It will be easy this week to lose track of professional objectives, simply because other concerns take over. A domestic crisis can be handled by taking quick action and contacting the right person for the job. If you are worried about a backlog of work, try to catch up as soon as you have more time.

Saturday the 19th. This will be a favorable day for going on a shopping expedition for an item of practical use. There may be good deals available on major appliances for the kitchen or bathroom. Social events that involve colleagues are likely to be fun. You will get to know those you work with much better.

Sunday the 20th. Be careful not to make this a weekend of all work and no play. The pattern that you are setting in place through what you decide to focus your energy on is likely to stay with you for a whole month ahead. Avoid going to the extremes of absolute boredom and complete overactivity.

Monday the 21st. A suggestion made by a friend or partner is likely to be so enticing that you drop other plans. For single Aries this will be a good day for getting to know better someone you feel romantically attracted to. If the opportunity to do so does not present itself, create one. This Rosh Hashanah holiday celebrates a new year filled with hope.

Tuesday the 22nd. You will enjoy this day the most when you are teaming up with people, whether at work or in your social and romantic life. Competitive sports activities involving a partner ought to be stimulating. An opportunity for work or promotion may come up. Grab it as soon as you learn of it.

Wednesday the 23rd. A romance can become a little awkward because one of you is not being totally honest about your priorities. If you do not feel on top of things in this relationship, it is time to talk, perhaps even to issue an ultimatum. Better cut through any pretense at total mutual admiration.

Thursday the 24th. One of the people you have to deal with at work will be likely to irritate you quite a lot. He or she may be a rather needy type of person who is intent on sapping your energy. You will probably spot this early on and run a mile.

Friday the 25th. This will be a good day for making an investment in a work of art if there is a piece that particularly takes your fancy. It also will be a useful time for selling items that you no longer wish to keep. Plan a garage sale this weekend if there are many bits and pieces that you wish to dispose of lucratively.

Saturday the 26th. A good friend may get you interested in matters that are out of the ordinary. If you do not usually go to church, you may decide to do so this weekend, based on your friend's enthusiasm. A trip to a place you have never seen before is likely to be exciting and prevent you from feeling bored.

Sunday the 27th. You Aries seldom allow yourselves to sit and be bored if you have even the vaguest sniff of something stimulating to do. The opportunity to be a part of a group going on a trip for the day may appeal to you. Check the time schedule though, as this may involve a late finish.

Monday the 28th. A very good career opportunity is likely to come your way now. The money and status will most probably suit your needs and tastes. However, a partner may object to your taking this up if it would mean relocation. Consider carefully your own and your mate's priorities before making a decision.

Tuesday the 29th. Taking on too much responsibility at work can be your undoing at present. While you may be seeking to make a good impression on a boss or other authority figure, you will be doing yourself no favors if you push yourself far beyond your natural limits. Bear in mind that if you set a particular standard, you may have to keep living up to it.

Wednesday the 30th. Your patience is tried by a friend who refuses to pay his or her share of a bill. Do not waste energy arguing. Conserve your resources in order to keep up with a hectic work schedule. Colleagues will be quite supportive.

Thursday October 1st. If you can gain other people's backing for your various endeavors, you will have every chance of making plenty of progress. It is surprising what a difference moral support can make when you are going through a difficult or stressful time. Practical help is also likely to be desirable.

Friday the 2nd. This will not be as good a day for team efforts as yesterday was. If you get together with friends socially, you may not have the chance to discuss what is really important to you. Independent enterprises are your most productive.

Saturday the 3rd. This will be a day for relaxing and really taking life easy. If you feel restless and have the need to keep yourself busy, your best bet will be to concentrate on tasks that are nearing completion. Or else just sort out odds and ends. Then wind down.

Sunday the 4th. Someone who has wanted to help you out in the past may reappear in your life now, as though by magic. It may be just a coincidence that the right person appears on the scene. Or you may feel something special and spiritual is happening.

Monday the 5th. Someone who you think is criticizing you may actually be paying you a backhanded compliment. Other people are being playful on the whole, rather than hurtful. You are on the edge of personal change, and it may make you very sensitive.

Tuesday the 6th. This can be a totally self-indulgent day for you if you are able to let go of a couple of responsibilities and do as you wish. A pleasant invitation is likely to come your way. For single Aries this can even lead to a romantic interest.

Wednesday the 7th. You are likely to have to put time aside to attend to sudden changes in your financial situation. An unexpected bill will arrive, and you may feel the need to investigate the matter in depth.

Thursday the 8th. This is likely to be a much better day than yesterday where money matters are concerned. An error on someone else's part can be located and admitted to. You may be the recipient of apologies or some kind of compensation for the worry you have been caused. Nevertheless, avoid a spending spree.

Friday the 9th. You can deal with people's problems as long as you have time on your hands. Certain individuals in your life seem to have a hard time taking care of themselves, and you may be able to help either in practical or emotional terms. Someone who had disturbed your peace may apologize for it.

Saturday the 10th. This will be a helpful day for catching up on correspondence and phone calls to people you feel you have neglected somewhat. Your own telephone may be ringing almost nonstop all day. So it is doubtful that you will get around to calling everyone you need to call. It is best to prioritize.

Sunday the 11th. Some say that familiarity breeds contempt. There is more than a grain of truth to this saying when you find yourself at loggerheads with either a love partner or family member. However, do not take other people too much for granted, no matter how much they may irritate you on occasion.

Monday the 12th. There is likely to be a wonderful opportunity open to you now to realize a long-held dream. However, a partner may stand in your way insofar as he or she feels jealous or left out of the situation. It will be worth explaining why you want to do what you want to do, so justify your choice.

Tuesday the 13th. A date arranged with a new love can end up with an argument when it comes to paying the restaurant bill. This will be the point at which you can establish very quickly just how much you are likely to get along in the long term. You may not mind sharing on a day-to-day basis, but not on the first date.

Wednesday the 14th. This will be a better day for romantic developments and love relationships. If you are a single Aries wishing to meet a new partner, accept an invitation to a party. This can lead to such a meeting. Married Aries people are likely to feel the spark of romance igniting once again.

Thursday the 15th. There is probably a tendency for you to contain your feelings more than usual. If you have a lot going on at work, you may feel that you need to conserve your energy and avoid getting too emotional over anything that happens. Watch a tendency to overdo the work thing. You need rest.

Friday the 16th. The main accent now will fall on work and health matters. If you have been overdoing it lately, the signs are likely to start to show. A slight cough and a lot of sneezing need not mean that you are coming down with influenza. These are probably signs of stress and a signal to slow down.

Saturday the 17th. While you may have a strong desire to help out and be supportive toward another, you should perhaps be careful to make sure that you do not leave yourself without a chance to rest and relax. Your tendency to ignore your own needs just now will turn out to be detrimental in the long run.

Sunday the 18th. You may be the recipient of an offer that you feel you just cannot refuse. A loved one seems eager to please and may invite you out on a very exciting date. This will be an excellent day for bringing together friends and their partners for a social gathering. If the weather is supportive, plan a picnic.

Monday the 19th. This will be a day for doing nice things for your partner or someone else who is important to you. Indulge your loved one with a special gift. If you both have a cause to celebrate, it may be fun to buy some champagne. Better still, suggest an evening out where there will be plenty of champagne.

Tuesday the 20th. This will be an excellent time for bridging any gap in communication in your key relationships. Bosses at work can be difficult to deal with, however. It is likely that they will not be able to give you straight answers to questions due to lack of information from the top. Try to be patient.

Wednesday the 21st. One of the important relationships in your life may be especially intense now. You will want to spend more time with a loved one in order to share a special experience together. If you need time off from work, explain the situation to your boss, who is likely to understand.

Thursday the 22nd. Resolve to cut some of the deadwood out of your life, including a bad habit. If you continually take on too much in your professional life, start saying no. Careful planning and thorough organization are key. You may also be able to let go of a responsibility you have had a long time.

Friday the 23rd. Your ideas about life and people are likely to verge on the deeply philosophical just now. Meeting someone unusual, perhaps someone with a different lifestyle, can get you thinking about ways of improving your own. A trip back to a place you once knew well can bring its fair share of surprises.

Saturday the 24th. An individual convinced that he or she knows better than you do may rattle you. It will not be so much this person's view on life that is likely to irritate you as the way in which it is expressed. Any note of condescension can make you fly into a rage. Others probably do not mean to be patronizing.

Sunday the 25th. This will be a favorable day for socializing with folks you work with. You can learn something interesting or useful by doing so. Be careful how you handle your budget now. It can be easy to part with money on impulse in order to help someone. You may regret it later on when you are in need.

Monday the 26th. It looks as though a boss or another influential figure in your career life will be able to pull a few strings on your behalf. Make the most of an opportunity for an introduction which might not come your way again. Besides, what develops after that phase will depend entirely on your own merits.

Tuesday the 27th. If you are having problems getting on with a person in a position of authority, this will probably have to do more with what has been left unsaid than what has actually been expressed. If you have been hiding information, purposely or not, it will be a good idea to come forth with it now.

Wednesday the 28th. Your relationships with friends can be quite rewarding now. But you have worked for what you get, since you have needed to delve down into resources of patience you usually dip into only in order to save your own sanity. Clearly, certain people are worth that extra effort, and others are not.

Thursday the 29th. The relationships that you feel you have worked hard to maintain can seem to go a little haywire. This is unlikely to be through any fault of your own. Given that you have made a real effort to meet a friend halfway, it will be up to him or her to do the same and pay you some respect.

Friday the 30th. You can often be a bit of a loner, needing to cut yourself off from other people and do your own thing. Today this side of your nature is being emphasized in more ways than one. Make sure you have some privacy at home if you cannot have the same at work. You Aries who want to get something off your chest should not hold back.

Saturday the 31st. Maintain a low profile and keep yourself to yourself, at least during the earlier part of the day. Later on, you may feel more like getting out and about. Try to avoid the temptation to call up your boss if you are worried about work issues.

Sunday November 1st. One of the main accents now is on completing matters that have been left unfinished for quite some time. Once this has happened, you will feel free to begin a new project. Somebody important to you may need your help in working out a tricky problem. Lend a listening ear.

Monday the 2nd. This will be a day for focusing on private interests primarily. Other people will have to do without your help while you get to grips with matters that have been neglected in your personal life. There will be fewer demands than usual at work, giving you the opportunity to do pretty well as you please.

Tuesday the 3rd. You need to take a firm stand on your financial situation now in order to prevent yourself from getting into the red, or deeper into the red. Unexpected expenses may have thrown you temporarily off-course. But if this is a more serious situation, you may need to make long-term plans and resolutions. Your vote is important; choose wisely.

Wednesday the 4th. This will be a day when you will be lucky enough to untangle any sort of mess that you have gotten yourself into lately, including a tricky financial situation. At the moment, you are probably putting out fires and picking up pieces. Before too long, you should be right back on form.

Thursday the 5th. If there has been a matter left outstanding between you and a neighbor, relative, or colleague, do not allow the situation to worsen or be prolonged. Take the initiative to do something about it. However, be diplomatic in your approach, or he or she may misunderstand your intentions.

Friday the 6th. The people in your neighborhood may be annoying because they are so noisy. The slamming of car doors late at night and the barking of dogs may prevent you from getting to sleep for a long while. Assertive action can ease the problem.

Saturday the 7th. You will be wise this weekend to find a balance between the time you spend at home and the time you spend away from it. You may have personal pursuits to carry through outside of the home. But try not to neglect family members who may need your help, or who just like your company.

Sunday the 8th. Your home life ought to be much more peaceful now. This will be a favorable time for getting on with household chores and completing decorating projects. Aries who want to invest in real estate can find a bargain if you hunt around. Take a friend or partner with you for a second opinion.

Monday the 9th. You may be reminded of the past in ways you would rather not be. If there is something you still need to sort out, something that perhaps is blocking you personally, take positive steps in this direction. Once this problem has been confronted head-on, it is likely never to bother you again.

Tuesday the 10th. A sense of lightness will fill your day as long as you avoid taking pointless risks. It may be one of those days when you will make a mistake and purchase something that is entirely unsuitable for the purpose you intend. If you can wait until another day to do your shopping, it will be a good idea to do so.

Wednesday the 11th. The day goes smoothly and turns out to be quite a lot of fun at the same time, especially at work. A boss is likely to be in a very happy-go-lucky frame of mind. If you happen to need a favor from him or her, take advantage of this happy mood and ask, before everything changes again.

Thursday the 12th. If you have too much to do and are expected to do more, you have only yourself to blame. This is no consolation when you are under extreme pressure. If ever there is a time for learning a lesson once and for all, it is now. You probably will not repeat the same mistake again.

Friday the 13th. This is generally held to be an unlucky date. However, there is no real reason for you to expect a particularly tough time of it. In fact, if you put your mind to it, you may be able to complete a work project that has been hanging around your neck like a very heavy weight for a long period of time.

Saturday the 14th. Partners will be your best company if you are intending to go on a long trip. A part of you is longing to be loved. If you are single, it is possible you will meet through academic interests someone who can love you the way you want. Aries in a fairly new relationship may consider settling down.

Sunday the 15th. Make the most of an opportunity to discuss long-term plans with your partner. Time spent together on a long trip can provide that opportunity. It will be a good idea to keep going with a work project that you know will require sustained effort on your part. Put in a few hours this weekend.

Monday the 16th. This will not be as fortunate a day for love relationships as yesterday. Work may have to take priority over personal interests. Responsibilities that have been somewhat neglected may start to worry you, and you can end up blaming your partner for having wanted so much of your time lately.

Tuesday the 17th. You may try to avoid a close encounter with a friend because you smell trouble lurking ahead for you. You are probably right about the trouble. However, avoiding the situation is likely to solve nothing. It will be better to have an out-and-out confrontation and have done with the matter.

Wednesday the 18th. You may feel on edge for no real reason. It is likely, however, that there is a very good reason behind your irrational feelings. Worries that the worst will come to pass where work responsibilities are concerned can be sending you into a blind panic. Calm down, and put things in perspective.

Thursday the 19th. An excellent opportunity to broaden your horizons through foreign travel or academic course work is likely to come your way. Aside from the obvious benefits to you, you can end up meeting a lot of interesting people and widening your long-term social circle through taking this up.

Friday the 20th. You are advised not to travel too far away from home if your car cannot be relied upon one hundred percent. There are certain places along known and unknown routes where it would be perilous to be stranded if you are not properly equipped to cope with situations you might face.

Saturday the 21st. Positive steps can be taken now to put certain future plans on a more definite footing. If you have been weighing the pros and cons of accepting an unusual offer, after much mental struggle you will now feel able to make a firm decision. You were right to take your time and think it through.

Sunday the 22nd. An older person will be the one to turn to if you are seeking advice on making a financial investment. This will also be true if you feel you need some kind of emotional support or an opportunity to express some pent-up feelings. Those with more experience in life can advise you well.

Monday the 23rd. It seems that you may be worrying too much about career matters at the moment. Much will develop in its own good time. Try to take a backseat when it is obvious you do not have the ability to control the situation. Talking to someone with a lot of experience in the same area as you can be helpful.

Tuesday the 24th. An authority figure connected with your career seems to be right behind you while you try to make a key decision. Someone who is backing you all the way to aim for what you really want is very reassuring. Just the same, you should not allow this person's view to influence your decision.

Wednesday the 25th. Friends can be a help to you and you can probably be a help to them in return. Group efforts are likely to save the day at work, where everyone seems to be struggling to meet deadlines. It will be a much better move to share worries and responsibilities than to struggle through on your own.

Thursday the 26th. This Thanksgiving Day will be a good time for you to take the first step in clearing up a disagreement with a friend. Nothing major may have taken place between you, but one small quarrel can have had the effect of making you feel estranged. It probably will not take much to bridge the gap.

Friday the 27th. Somebody you trust a great deal may offer you help with an old problem you have been wishing you could resolve on your own. There is little point in being proud when you have such a valuable offer and ally. There is every chance you will be able to resolve the situation once and for all.

Saturday the 28th. Consider calling a spur-of-the-moment meeting with someone you know who has the ability to help you reach a personal aim or objective. This person may have not only practical skills for you to call upon but also a piece of good advice and plenty of encouragement, both of which may benefit you.

Sunday the 29th. Vacillating between what you want to do and what you think you ought to be doing will solve very little this weekend. It is important that you make a stand for what you truly believe in if you are to make any kind of progress. Be brave. Come down on one side or the other, and stick to your stance.

Monday the 30th. It may be quite difficult for you to change your mind about an important decision you made recently, even though it makes sense to change it. Talking to someone about your predicament can help to solve the problem. Be wary of lending money to friends so near the holidays.

Tuesday December 1st. A friend who is desperately trying to raise some cash may come to you again for a loan. You will be wise still to stand your ground on your decision to conserve your resources. Unexpected costs related to a group or society that you belong to could suddenly swallow up your extra reserves.

Wednesday the 2nd. Relationships with friends and neighbors will be more amicable than they have been of late. Perhaps the Christmas spirit is starting to rub off on everyone already. Be wise; avoid making a long-distance trip that is not absolutely necessary. You will get yourself into a difficult situation otherwise.

Thursday the 3rd. If your true needs are not being taken into account by other people, you may have every reason to feel resentful. But ask yourself how much you have and have not been openly admitting lately, both to yourself and others. If you have taken on too much, you have only yourself to blame.

Friday the 4th. This is likely to be a good day for doing some Christmas shopping as long as you have time to ponder what you want to purchase and for whom. Try to be absolutely crystal clear with staff or colleagues about the kind of information they need to track if you are away from your workplace for long.

Saturday the 5th. Someone from your dim and distant past may come back into your life unexpectedly now. But this is likely to be a nice surprise, not something to dread. Plain curiosity will make you wish to meet this individual just to find out what has changed in the years during which you have not seen each other.

Sunday the 6th. Nostalgic memories may make you feel very happy or very sad. It will be easy to think that the past has been a lot better than your present situation. However, you may be seeing things from an idealistic perspective. You experienced some rough times, too, back then. Keep reality in view.

Monday the 7th. A romantic affair may no longer interest you, yet you will have a hard time letting the other person know your true feelings. This is likely to be to due to the fact that while you may not want the romance, you do not want to lose a friendship either. Only time will tell if you can have the latter.

Tuesday the 8th. This will be an excellent day for social meetings, especially if you are having a reunion with old friends or with relatives whom you have not seen for a long while. Single Aries people may already start to be kissed under the mistletoe.

Wednesday the 9th. You may be torn between wanting to spend time with someone you love and putting career matters first because, at least for now, these probably do have to take precedence. Tempted as you may be to throw caution to the wind and forget your responsibilities, it will not be a good idea. A romantic phone call can save the day for single Aries.

Thursday the 10th. Your working life seems to be a central focus, even though your mind is clearly on other things. While you want to make long-range plans, you will have time only to deal with more immediate concerns. Use your spare time this evening to do what you cannot do during the daytime.

Friday the 11th. Keep an eye on your health now. There is a tendency to overwork yourself and try to concentrate on too many things at once. This is likely to take its toll on your well-being. A slight temperature is a sign that you ought to be slowing down and focusing on one task at a time.

Saturday the 12th. Time spent with a love partner this weekend is likely to be idyllic. If you have had to be apart, it will be hard to tear yourselves away from one another once again when you both have to head off for work. But you will have time yet this weekend to cover a lot of ground.

Sunday the 13th. A partnership is a great source of joy. However, some element of conflict may arise between you when you decide that you need to pursue some of your own personal plans. It will be a good idea to give your partner advance warning of your intentions so that he or she can work around you.

Monday the 14th. This will be a favorable day for seeking advice on joint financial matters and real estate issues, particularly if you are not sure which parts of a complicated form you need to fill in. A friend seems to be taking liberties. If you are celebrating Hanukkah, family gatherings will be especially meaningful.

Tuesday the 15th. There is likely to be an obvious opportunity now to end an unsatisfactory situation or relationship. You may promise to be in touch with someone without any intention of doing so. While it may seem a little underhanded, you probably will realize that it is the only way to end all contact.

Wednesday the 16th. Those itchy feet of yours are back again. This will be a favorable day for making a trip away from home with a loved one, especially if you will be on vacation from now until the start of the year. Even if this is not so, an escape from your usual surroundings will be very pleasurable.

Thursday the 17th. Just when you thought that life was becoming much too dull to bear, along comes an opportunity to make some very exciting changes. If you accept an enticing offer that is being made to you, you must also accept that you will probably be creating a lot of upheaval in your life.

Friday the 18th. Trying to be in the right place at the right time will seem like a real art to you. It is likely that there will be much to do and little time to do it in. But persevere. You may be surprised at how much you manage to achieve in the end. You seem to be on the edge of making some major changes.

Saturday the 19th. You will be able to take life quite easy this weekend, particularly if you have managed to tie up most of your major work responsibilities. Some Aries will be on vacation. Put the flags out, as you deserve a salute for your outstanding efforts.

Sunday the 20th. A partner may be slightly envious of you because of a glowing compliment or other acknowledgment you receive. This can explain his or her irritable mood. You are not being callous, but you can see the funny side of it. A charitable gesture on your part will smooth the situation over.

Monday the 21st. The opportunity to take on new responsibilities is almost always just around the corner in your life. What comes your way now is to be said no to, calmly and firmly. If family members want you to organize large components of the festivities involving you all, remember that you have a choice.

Tuesday the 22nd. A good time is likely to be had by all when you get together with friends to socialize this evening. However, one particular person may have a bit too much to drink and end up being an embarrassment or burden to everyone else. Unless you are this person's closest friend present, try not to be the one who has to pick up all the pieces.

Wednesday the 23rd. This will be an excellent day for a long-distance trip if you have had one planned for some time. Friends really come through for you now when you need them to help out in a hurry. Reliability is the name of the game at times like these. All in all though, your day will go quite smoothly.

Thursday the 24th. Do not ask of yourself more than you are willing to give this Christmas Eve. Other people may be up for a wild social scene, but you are more likely to want to stay in and relax. An evening totally pampering yourself is probably going to do you more good than a lot of drinking at a noisy gathering.

Friday the 25th. Merry Christmas! It is likely to be a fairly quiet one this year. Other people may need your help with small jobs. But this is hardly likely to tax you to the hilt. Increased closeness among you and your family will be an extra bonus.

Saturday the 26th. Paying too much attention to the authority of someone else in your life at the moment can throw you somewhat off the track. If you are with parents in their own home, it probably has to do with old patterns being reestablished.

Sunday the 27th. It will be paramount that you take care of your own needs at this time. Partners can be challenging and may even want to be looked after. But ask yourself if this is really your job. You may already be thinking about new career possibilities.

Monday the 28th. It may be tempting to go shopping, but it probably will not be a very good idea. You may think you can pick up bargains. Most likely you will get sale fever instead and end up buying something you do not want. Stay at home or work.

Tuesday the 29th. This will be a better day for going shopping. Genuine bargains can be had. You may be able to pick up something beautiful that you will treasure forever. A boss at work is likely to be full of praise for the efforts you made before the holiday.

Wednesday the 30th. Nothing really gets in the way of Aries when you have your mind set on a course of action. Whatever you plan to do, you are likely to end up achieving in spite of any obstacles. This will be a good day for planning your social life.

Thursday the 31st. So much seems to have been promised to you in the year that is ending. Yet you may feel that the real changes are still to come. Focus on achievable objectives. As usual, you must guard against trying to cram too much into a busy schedule.

AMERICA'S MOST TRUSTED PSYCHIC NETWORKS

IVANA, ADVICE for the MILLENNIUM

ROMANCE MONEY HAPPINESS

MONEY BACK GUARANTEE

LIVE 24 HOURS

1-900-378-5959 $3.99 PER MIN.

USE YOUR CREDIT CARD & SAVE 50¢ PER MINUTE

1-800-449-7679 $3.49 PER MIN.

your Guardian ANGEL

Knows ∩ Protects ∩ Guides

10 MINUTES FREE!

CALL NOW TO HEAR WHAT SHE NEEDS TO TELL YOU!

1-900-378-6277 $3.99 per min.

Use Your Credit Card & Save 50¢ Per Min.

1-800-781-7865 $3.49 per min.

SERVING YOU 24 HOURS A DAY!

10 MIN FREE

Is it... TRUE LOVE? OR IS YOUR LOVER USING YOU?

Our PSYCHICS have ANSWERS to MARRIAGE & ROMANCE problems

1-900-378-6661 $3.99 PER MIN.

1-800-277-6661 $3.49 PER MIN.

USE YOUR CREDIT CARD & SAVE 50¢ PER MINUTE

Call NOW!

PSYCHIC ANSWERS

Love
Health
Money

12 FREE MIN

1-900-378-6464 $3.99 PER MIN.

1-800-781-7836 $3.49 PER MIN.

Use Your Credit Card & Save 50¢ Per Min.

TALK TO YOUR PETS

through our animal loving psychics

Call for the LOVE of Your PET

1-900-378-6468 $3.99 PER MIN.

Use Your Credit Card & Save 50¢ Per Min.

1-800-781-7865 $3.49 PER MIN.

NOSTRADAMUS has FORECAST the FUTURE for more than SIX CENTURIES!

NINA NOSTRADAMUS PREDICTED THE 1989 SAN FRANCISCO QUAKE WITHIN 11 MINUTES!

6 FREE MIN

1-900-378-6386 $3.99 PER MIN.

1-800-781-7896 $3.49 PER MIN.

Use Your Credit Card & Save 50¢ Per Min.

Make The Most Important Call Of YOUR LIFE!

ISABEL "WEEZY" SANFORD Star of "The Jeffersons"

RUSSEL TODD Known as "Dr. Jamie Frame" Another World

SUSAN BROWN Known as "Dr. Gail Baldwin" General Hospital

AS SEEN ON TV

MASTER PSYCHIC READINGS

1-900-378-6225 $3.99 PER MINUTE

USE YOUR CREDIT CARD & SAVE 50¢ PER MIN.

1-800-988-6785 $3.49 PER MIN.

Affection Connection

SINGLES LINE

CONNECT NOW!

Call Now To Meet Someone Interesting & Exciting In Your Area

1-800-993-2722

connie francis

"Where the Love is..." FOR YOU!

9 minutes FREE

MY AUTHENTIC *Love Psychics* WILL HELP YOU FIND THE *Love of Your Life* AND MAKE YOUR *Dreams Come True*

1-900-378-5858 $3.99 PER MIN.

1-800-781-7865 $3.49 PER MIN.

Use Your Credit Card & Save 50¢ Per Min.

PAST LIFE READINGS

YOU MUST LEARN ABOUT THE PAST IN ORDER TO SAVE YOUR FUTURE

1-900-378-6161 $3.99 PER MIN.

Use Your Credit Card & Save 50¢ Per Minute

1-800-781-7836 $3.49 PER MIN.

ANCIENT ACCURATE ANSWERS

from Authentic Psychics

LUCK - LOVE

10 MINUTES FREE

TRUE CHANGE

24 HRS LIVE! Incredible Readings

1-900-378-6262 $3.99 PER MIN.

1-800-781-7865 $3.49 PER MIN.

Use Your Credit Card & Save 50¢ Per Min.

Does he really love me?

Will I ever get married?

Is he being faithful?

Call To Find Out How To Get Your

FREE Sample
Psychic Reading!

1-800-686-5261

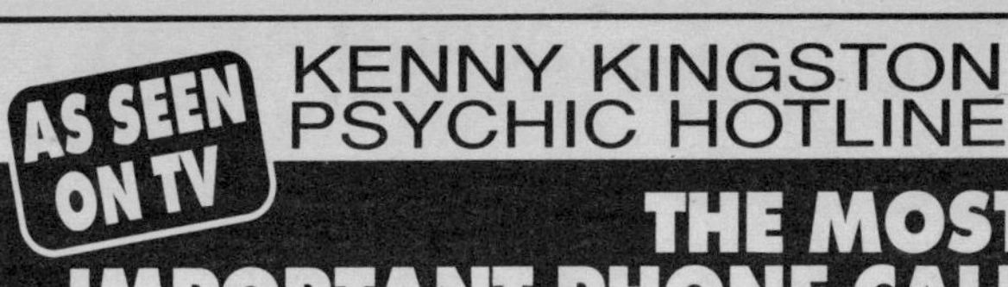

Stephanie Williams

William Katt

Sharron Farrel

CURIOUS? TRY A PSYCHIC FREE

You've heard how psychics have changed the lives of others, and you want to try a psychic reading. Call the Psychic Readings Line first - **1-800-549-4736** - try it free. If you have personal questions about romance, love or relationships, sample the Master Psychics on **1-800-282-6711** for free advice and more. And, if you want to hear our most gifted psychics speak and interpret before you choose, call for Free Samples on **1-800-709-2224**. Adults over 18; optional paid services available. Entertainment only. 24 hours a day, 7 days a week.

FREE SAMPLES ON EVERY CALL

Sample the power of a gifted live psychic. Dial **1-800-569-6902** - listen free, then decide. Call to sample and choose from a hand-picked panel of renowned readers, seers, and advisors. And, for urgent matters of fortune or fate, dial and sample **1-800-803-5477** - FREE! Curious about what Cupid has in store for you? Dial **1-800-295-3012**, you'll find a psychic who may change your romantic future - plus, now you can try it free. Entertainment only. Optional paid services offered for use by adults over 18 only.

TROUBLE WITH LOVE, MONEY OR LUCK?

Dial **1-800-820-7215** for free samples with amazing psychics who speak what they see and feel. Or, sample the Psychic Power Line **1-800-955-8677**, where gifted psychics share visions and dreams to help you open your future and change your fate. And, if you want to find a top psychic for confidential readings, try **1-800-695-7364**, our special private line for free samples and more. No credit card required. Samples for entertainment only. All paid service optional. Adults over 18 only.

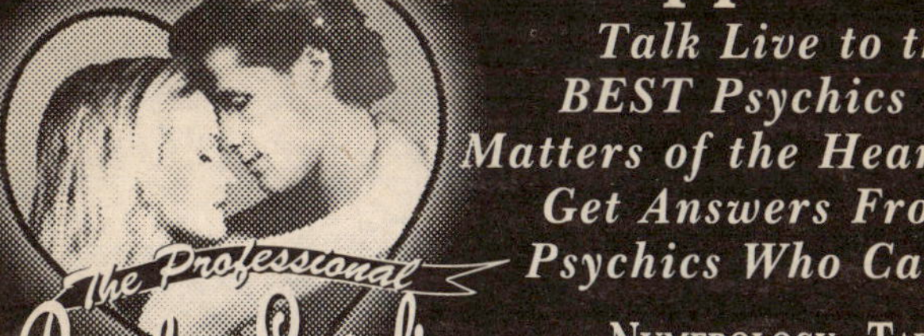

Find Love & Happiness
Talk Live to the BEST Psychics in Matters of the Heart. Get Answers From Psychics Who Care
The Professional
Psychic Loveline®
NUMEROLOGY · TAROT
ASTROLOGY · CLAIRVOYANT
AS LOW AS $1.93/MIN
1-800-472-9015
CREDIT CARD OR CHECK
1-900-860-6500
FIRST 2 MIN FREE $3.99/min. after
1st 2 min. Always FREE
*900 calls only
24 HOURS. 18+. ENTERTAINMENT PURPOSES ONLY.

AMERICA'S BEST PSYCHIC SOURCE
Astrology · Clairvoyants · Tarot
Have the life you always dreamed of with amazing insights from gifted psychics
1ST 2 MIN FREE EVERY TIME YOU CALL
*900 CALLS ONLY
FIRST 2 MIN. FREE! $3.99/MIN AFTER
1-900-420-0033
CREDIT CARD OR CHECK.
1-800-472-4966
AS LOW AS $1.93/MIN!
24 HOURS. 18+. ENTERTAINMENT PURPOSES ONLY.